ROMAN ESSAYS

AND

INTERPRETATIONS

By

W. WARDE FOWLER M.A.

HON. LL.D. EDINBURGH, &c.

Author of *The Roman Festivals of the Republic, Social Life at Rome
in the Age of Cicero, The Religious Experience of the Roman
People, Roman Ideas of Deity in the Last Century of
the Republic*, &c.

OXFORD
AT THE CLARENDON PRESS
1920

OXFORD UNIVERSITY PRESS

LONDON   EDINBURGH   GLASGOW   NEW YORK

TORONTO MELBOURNE CAPE TOWN BOMBAY

HUMPHREY MILFORD

PUBLISHER TO THE UNIVERSITY

PREFATORY NOTE

I HAVE included in this selection of papers none that were simply critical of the work of others : only those in which I seemed to myself, rightly or wrongly, to be moving towards some fairly definite conclusion on points of permanent interest. Should I be criticized for including some short and apparently trifling papers which I have called ' parallela quaedam ', I should reply that I like to show that the apparently marvellous may be sometimes wholly or in part authenticated by modern parallels. At the end I have placed character sketches of two great Roman historians, Niebuhr and Mommsen, and an essay on the Julius Caesar of Shakespeare.

Whether I am right in reprinting and revising papers, many of which were written long ago, the critics will decide. I can only say that they are fragments of work into which I have put my best abilities, and in the writing of which I have found much pleasure, whether in the hurry of a busy tutorial life at Oxford, or in the leisure of old age in the country.

I have to acknowledge gratefully the permission of the Council of the Society for the Promotion of Roman Studies, and of the Council of the Classical Association, to reprint papers originally published in their Journals. A considerable part of the material of the volume has not been published before.

I am greatly indebted to my old friend Mr. P. E. Matheson for kind help in reading the proofs.

W. W. F.

KINGHAM, *June* 19, 1919.

A 2

CONTENTS

PART I

PART II

PART III

PART IV

THE LATIN HISTORY OF THE WORD
RELIGIO

THIS word, which in its modern form is in use all over Europe, had a remarkable history in its own Latin speech and literature. That history seems to me to have more than a mere linguistic interest, and I propose in this paper to indicate in outline where that interest lies. Of the much disputed etymology of the word I will only say this : that the question stands now very much as it did in the time of Cicero and Lucretius, who took conflicting views of it. Professor Conway, whose authority is great, tells me that apart from the evidence of usage and the feeling of the Romans themselves, there is nothing to decide whether it is to be connected with *ligare*, to bind, as Lucretius thought, or with *legere*, to string together, arrange, as Cicero believed. His feeling is in favour of Cicero's view, as less prejudiced than that of Lucretius ; so is mine. But our feelings are not of much account in such questions, and I may pass on at once to the *history* of the word.

In Latin literature down to Christian times, *religio* is used in a great variety of senses, and often in most curious and unexpected ones ; but all these uses can, I think, be reduced to two main types of meaning, one of which is probably the older, the other derivative. The one reflects the natural feeling of the Latin when face to face with the supernormal or supernatural, before the State with its priesthoods and religious law had intervened to quiet that feeling. The other expresses the attitude of the citizen of a State towards the supernatural, now realizable without fear or doubt in the shape of the recognized deities of his State. I must explain these two uses to begin with.

I. *Religio* is the feeling of awe, anxiety, doubt, or fear, which is aroused in the mind by something that cannot be explained by a man's experience or by the natural course of cause and effect, and which is therefore referred to the supernatural. This I take to be the original meaning of the word, for the following reasons :

1. *Religio* is not a word which has grown out of any State usage, or been rendered 'technical by priestly law or ritual. It has no part in the *ius divinum*, like the word *sacrum* : we search for it in vain in the indices to the *Corpus Inscriptionum*, where it would inevitably be found if it were used in a technical or legal sense. In its adjectival form, as applied to times and places, we may also see the results of this non-technical meaning. *Dies religiosi, loca religiosa*, are *not* days and places which are proclaimed as such by the official administrators of the *ius divinum* : they are rather such days and places as man's own feeling, independently of the State and its officials, has made the object of *religio*. ' *Religiosum* stands in contrast with *sacrum* as indicating something about which there is awe, fear, scruple, and which has not been definitely brought within the province of State law, nor handed over to a deity by ritualistic formulae.' [1] If this be so, then we may safely refer the origin of the word to a period when powerful State priesthoods had not as yet, by ritual and routine, soothed down the natural awe which in less perfect social forms man feels when obstructed, astonished, embarrassed, by that which he cannot explain or overcome.

2. That this is the true and the oldest meaning of the word seems also proved by the fact that it survived in this sense throughout Latin literature, and was indeed so used by the ordinary Roman layman. It is familiar to us in a thousand passages. *Religio* may stand for a doubt or scruple of any kind, or for anything uncanny which creates such doubt or scruple. To illustrate this I may select a single passage from Caesar, as a writer who would be sure to use a word in a sense obvious to every one. In describing the alarm of the soldiers of Q. Cicero when besieged at Aduatuca, he says :

Alius castra iam capta pronuntiat, alius deleto exercitu atque imperatore victores barbaros venisse contendit ; pleri-

[1] See a paper by the writer in the *Hibbert Journal* for 1907, p. 847.

que novas sibi ex loco *religiones* fingunt, Cottaeque et Titurii calamitatem, qui in eodem occiderint castello, ante oculos ponunt.[1]

Here Caesar might almost as well have simply written *metus* instead of *religiones* ; but he wishes to express not only natural fear and alarm as to what may happen, but that fear accentuated by the sense of something wrong or uncanny, for which the soldiers or their leaders may be responsible— in this case the pitching of a camp in a place which they believed to have been the scene of a former disaster. Let us note that these soldiers were out of reach of the protecting arm of their own *ius divinum* : they were on foreign soil, ignorant of what supernatural powers might be present there. Their commander-in-chief, it is true, was the chief adminis-trator of that *ius*. Caesar was pontifex maximus : but Caesar was not there, and if he had been, his presence would in those days and in such a place have made little difference. They are in the same position towards the supernatural as their ancestors had been before the State arose, and in describ-ing their alarm Caesar uses the word *religio* in the same sense in which it had come into use in those primitive ages.

Livy, writing of a pestilence and its moral effects, says that ' nec corpora modo affecta tabo, sed animos quoque multiplex religio et pleraque externa invasit ' :[2] where by *religio* he means the feeling of anxiety which took practical shape in the performance of various rites, foreign for the most part Such examples could be multiplied a hundredfold : and the word came at last to be used for anything that produces a feeling of wonder or even of curiosity, seeing that we do not understand it. Thus Pliny says that there is a *religio* in men's knees, because we kneel on them to supplicate, and clasp the knees of those from whom we ask mercy ;[3] there is something uncanny about that part of the body—something we cannot explain. In the same way he says that no animal is ' religionis capacius ' than the mole, because its heart and its teeth are supposed to have some mysterious medicinal powers.[4]

---

[1] *B. G.* vi. 37.   [2] iv. 30.   [3] *H. N.* xi. 250.   [4] Ibid. xxx. 19.

In this way the adjective *religiosus* came to be applied to human beings in a sense not far removed from that of *superstitiosus*, which is, so far as I know, always used of persons addicted to rites or fancies outside the pale of the Roman State-religion. This sense seems to be an early one : it occurs in the fragment of an 'antiquum carmen' quoted by Aulus Gellius : [1] 'Religentem (attentive) esse oportet, religiosus (over-anxious) ne seis.' Lucretius' use of the substantive may also be mentioned in this context : for him *all* that we call religion was superstitious and degrading, and could therefore be properly called by that word which the Romans invariably used to express their doubts, fears, and scruples.

Lastly, before I go on to the second chief meaning of the word, I may mention the significant fact that *religio* is never personified as a deity, as were Pietas, Sanctitas and almost all the virtues at one time or another. It is not a virtue : it does not necessarily lead to a definite course of action, and embodies no sense of duty or moral value : it is primarily and essentially a *feeling* to which human nature is liable under certain circumstances.

II. I now come to the second chief sense in which the word is used, and which brings it a step nearer to our own use of it. This sense was mainly due, I think, in Roman literature to Cicero, though it may be far older in common use : and is perhaps the result of the Greek originals, e. g. Posidonius, whom he was following when writing the *de Legibus* and the *de Natura Deorum*, &c. ; but this is a point which I must here pass over. From Cicero in any case I can best illustrate this new turn of meaning which the word acquires.

When Cicero was a young man, not yet too learned or philosophical, he defined the word clearly according to its common usage, with an addition of some importance. 'Religio est quae superioris cuiusdam naturae, quam divinam vocant, curam caerimoniamque affert ;' [2] i. e. a *feeling* of awe that inevitably suggests the discovery of the proper rites by which the object of that feeling may be propitiated. But later on

---

[1] iv. 9. 1 ; cf. Baehrens, *Fr. Poet. Rom.*, p. 36.   [2] *De Invent.* ii. 161.

in his life, in the second book of the *de Legibus*, which deals with the State religion, he uses the word with much freedom *of the particular cults*, or all of them together, which are the result of the feeling.   Thus in x. 25 ' suos deos aut novos aut alienigenas coli confusionem habet religionum ', i. e. private persons may not introduce new cults ; for there would in that case be a confusion both of religious feeling and duty. In x. 23 he calls his own imaginary ius divinum a *constitutio religionum*, a system of religious duties.   Thus the word is passing into the sense of the *forms of cult*, as ordered and organized by the State, the feeling, the *religio* proper, being only aroused when scruple is felt as to the accurate performance of these rites.   In vii. 15 we read ' qua mente, qua pietate colat religiones ', where it answers almost exactly to religious duties. In xvi. 40 he tells how the Athenians consulted the Delphic oracle ' quas potissimum religiones tenerent ', and the answer was, ' eas quae essent in more maiorum '.   Again in xi. 27 we find ' religio Larium ', the cult of the Lares.   But the feeling which prompts the cult, and which is aroused afresh if it be neglected, is seldom entirely absent.   The phrase *religio sepulcrorum* (xxii. 55) suggests quite as much the feeling as the ritual : and a little further down we are told that the pontifical law of burials ' magnam religionem caerimoniamque declarat '—the word *caerimonia* being necessary to express the ritual following on the feeling.   And lastly this word may be used to gather up and express in totality a number of acts of cult, because the same feeling is at the root of them all. Thus in xix. 47 the question is raised whether a pontifex should know the civil law.   The answer is, ' quod cum religione coniunctum est : de sacris, de votis, de feriis, de sepulcris ', the pontifex has to do with these matters, which can all be expressed together by the word *religio*.

These examples seem to show how the word might pass into the sense in which we still use it ; the feeling which prompts us to worship, and also the forms under which we perform that worship.   The feeling is common to human nature, civilized or not : that is the original meaning of the

word : the worship, organized by a priesthood, is the work of the State—that is the second, or as we may call it, the Ciceronic meaning. And in the same age it is also so used by Lucretius, who includes under it all that was for him the world's evil and folly, i. e. both the feeling and the cult—delusion, myth, superstition, as well as the organized but futile worship of the family and the State. 'Tantum religio potuit suadere malorum.' [1] In an age of cosmopolitanism, when the old local character of the cults was disappearing, and in an age of philosophic-religious syncretism when men like Posidonius, Cicero, Varro, and others were thinking and writing about the nature of the gods and kindred questions, a word was wanted to gather up and express all this religious side of human life and experience : it must be a word without a definite technical meaning, and such a word was *religio*. To take a single example, besides those already quoted from Cicero, there is the famous aphorism which St. Augustine [2] ascribes to Varro : ' expedit falli in religione civitates.'

Thus while *religio* continues to express the feeling only, or the cult only, if called on to do so by Latin writers, it gains in the Ciceronian age a more comprehensive connotation, as the result of the contemplation of religion by philosophy as a thing apart from itself ; and this, as we shall see directly, enabled the early Christian writers, who knew their Cicero well, and modelled their prose on his, to use it in much the same sense as that in which we use it to-day.

Time fails to trace the word in the pre-Christian literature of the early Empire, and to see how it is affected by the finer quasi-religious Stoicism, or again by the Caesar-worship of the day,—the nearest approach in antiquity, as it has been called, to a cosmopolitan religion. So far as I can see, it did not take from either of these sources any new turn or type of meaning. Seneca, for example, has but little use for it ; though he was, as Professor Dill has said of him, one of the few heathen moralists who warm moral feeling with the emotion of modern religion, he had little real interest either

[1] Lucr. i. 101   [2] *Civ. Dei*, iv. 27.

in the feeling or the cult. If he made himself a religion out
of his Stoic principles, it was not one that he could have
described by the word *religio*. For him, though tinged by
emotion, it was still *sapientia* : he could hardly have assented
to the later teaching of Lactantius [1] that *sapientia* and *religio*
are inseparably connected. Nor did the worship of the Caesars
bring any new turn of meaning : here it could express the
cult ('caelestes religiones'[2]), but the feeling at the root of
a genuine religious cult was not there to be expressed. This
is perhaps significant both of the true meaning of the word,
and also of the weak point in Caesar-worship : but I must
not now dwell upon it. I will only mention one passage in
which Pliny the Younger uses it of the cult of Trajan, because
the kind of feeling which it there represents—loyalty and
devotion to an individual—is in some sense a new one, and
may be a foreshadowing of the Christian use. Pliny writes to
Trajan from Bithynia reporting celebrations on the Emperor's
birthday : 'Diem . . . debita religione celebravimus, com-
mendantes dis imperii tui auctoribus et vota publica et
gaudia.'[3] Here it means the feeling of devotion prompting
the 'vota et gaudia', as well as those acts themselves. There
is nothing in it of the old fear, scruple, anxiety : it is the
devotion and gratitude which expresses itself in religious
festivities.

But there was to be a real change in the meaning of the word,
the last but one in its history. The second century A. D. was
that in which the competition was keenest between various
religious creeds and forms, each with its own vitality, and each
clearly marked off from the others. It is no longer a question
of religion as a whole contemplated by a critical or a sympathetic philosophy : the question is, which creed and which
form is to be the true and the victorious religion. Our wonderful word again adapts itself to the situation. Each separate
religious system can now be called a *religio*.[4] The old poly-
theistic system can now be called *religio Deorum* by the

[1] *De Vera Sap.* iv. 3.   [2] Tac. *Ann.* i. 10.
[3] *Ep.* x. 102.   [4] 'e cohorte religionis unus,' Apul. xi. 14, of Isis.

Christian, while his own creed is *religio Dei*. In the Octavius of Minucius Felix, written probably in the first half of the second century A. D., the word is already used in this sense. His *nostra religio, vera religio*, distinguished from all other *religiones*, is the whole Christian faith and Christian practice as it stood then ; the depth of feeling and the acts which give it outward form. The one true religion can be expressed by this word, though it is quite different from anything the word has as yet been called on to mean. In Lactantius, Arnobius, Tertullian, this new sense of the word is to be found on almost every page : but a single noble passage of Lactantius must suffice to illustrate it. ' The heathen sacrifice,' he says, ' and leave all their *religio* in the temple ' : thus it is that such *religiones* cannot make men good, or firm in their faith. ' Nostra religio eo firma est et solida et immutabilis, quia mentem ipsam pro sacrificio habet, quia tota in animo colentis est.' [1] *Religio* here is not awe only or cult only, or scruple about details of cult, but a mental devotion capable of building up character. ' The kingdom of God is within you.' It is worth noting that it can now be explained by the word *pietas*, which was not possible in the old days, because *pietas* was a virtue and *religio* was not a virtue but a feeling. Lactantius says that philosophy, ' quae veram religionem, id est summam pietatem, non habet, non est vera sapientia '.[2]

Thus the word has meant successively (1) the natural fear and awe which semi-civilized man feels in the presence of what he cannot explain ; (2) the cult by which he strives to propitiate the unseen Powers, together with the scruple he feels if the propitiation is in the least degree imperfect ; (3) the whole sphere of worship, together with all belief in the supernatural, as viewed from the standpoint of the philosopher ; (4) the competing divisions of that sphere of worship and belief, each being now a *religio*, and the Christian faith being for the Christian the *vera religio*. There is one later stage in the history of the word, which I can only mention here. It suffered a degradation when it was made to

---

[1] *De Iustitia*, v. 19.   [2] *De Vera Sap.* iv. 3.

mean the monastic life : the life of men who withdrew themselves from a world in which true religion was not. But
even in this degraded form it reveals once more its wonderful
capacity to express the varying attitude of humanity towards
the supernatural. Outside the monasteries—the homes of
the *religiosi*—were a thousand fears, fancies, superstitions,
which the old Roman might have summed up by his word
religio, the anxious fear of the supernatural : inside them,
for many ages at least, was still something of the *vera religio*
of the early Fathers, the devotion and the ritual combined,
the pure life and training, *religio Dei*.[1]

THE ORIGINAL MEANING OF THE WORD
SACER

In Roman religious law the word *sacer* indicated that the
object to which it was applied was the property of a deity,
taken out of the region of the *profanum* by the action of the
State, and passed on into that of the *sacrum*. We have an
exact account of it which can be traced through Verrius
Flaccus to a scholar apparently of the age of Cicero, Aelius
Gallus. ' Gallus Aelius ait sacrum esse quodcunque more [2]
atque instituto civitatis consecratum sit, sive aedis sive ara
sive signum sive locus sive pecunia sive quid aliud quod dis
dedicatum atque consecratum sit : quod autem privati suae
religionis causa aliquid earum rerum deo dedicent, id pontifices Romanos non existimare sacrum.' [3] This very explicit
passage makes it plain that the state, through its religious
authorities, had appropriated the word, and fixed it to
a definite meaning, at some period when there were already
temples in which deities could dwell and enjoy the possession

---

[1] For further comments on the word, see index to my *Religious Experience*,
&c. ; and for a different view, W. Otto in *Archiv*, xii. 533 ff.

[2] This is Lachmann's correction for MS. ' quocunque modo '. See Marquardt, *Staatsverwaltung*, iii. 145.

[3] Festus, p. 424 (Lindsay). Cf. Gaius, ii. 5.

of their own property, made over to them by the State to do them honour and propitiate them.

But this highly developed idea of deities dwelling in fixed spots in the city, and holding property, is at Rome a comparatively late one. The earliest document of the *ius divinum*, the so-called calendar of Numa, can be placed with confidence in the regal period, between the inclusion of the Quirinal in the city of the four regions and the building of the temple of Diana on the Aventine ; [1] and this temple of Diana, and that of the Capitoline trias which belongs to the same age, are the first two temples in the proper sense of the word, and the earliest in which any kind of statue is known to have been placed. Before that the *fanum* was a small open enclosure with a rude *ara*, probably of turf, and nothing more.[2] The word *sacer* must have developed its later technical meaning in and after this period. Is it possible to discover with any approach to certainty what meaning it had in still earlier times ? We might naturally look for a meaning of the same general type, but less accurately defined, and so to speak, less theological. For until deities or spirits come to be localized in particular spots and to have special priests attached to them, the vocabulary of worship must be necessarily less clearly cut than in an age when that worship was becoming the most important part of the State's ' cura '.

Perhaps this earlier meaning of *sacer* is indicated in a curious passage of Macrobius, who wrote it with a book before him *De religionibus*, by Trebatius Testa, the friend of Cicero. ' Hoc loco non alienum videtur de condicione eorum hominum referre quos leges sacros esse certis dis iubent, quia non ignoro quibusdam mirum videri quod, cum cetera sacra violari nefas sit, hominem sacrum ius fuerit occidi.' [3] The explanation that follows is of no value to us ; but the fact

---

[1] See *Rel. Exp.*, p. 94.

[2] Marquardt, op. cit., p. 161 ff ; Wissowa, *Rel. und Kult. der Römer* (2) 468.

[3] Macrob. *Sat.* iii. 7, 5. The explanation is a curious example of the semi-mystical tendency of Trebatius' time. The souls of *homines sacrati* were *dis debitae*, and might therefore be sent *ad caelum* as soon as possible, i. e. by any one who had the chance.

that some Romans were puzzled by the impunity of the slayer of the *sacer homo* is one of the utmost interest. They were puzzled, because they had always understood the word *sacer* in the sense in which it was defined by Aelius Gallus. A thing that was *sacrum* was known by all to be the property of a deity, and to violate it was *nefas*, a deadly crime. Yet here was an object called by this solemn adjective, *homo sacer*, which might be violated without any *nefas* : a man whom any one might slay with impunity.

Evidently *sacer* was used here in an exceptional sense, and surely in a very ancient sense ; for no one will deny that the *homo sacer* is a survival from a primitive age into one of highly developed civil and religious law. *Sacer esto* is in fact a curse ; and the *homo sacer* on whom this curse falls is an outcast, a banned man, tabooed, dangerous. We may compare him with the primitive Semitic outcast described by Robertson Smith in an appendix to his *Religion of the Semites*.[1] He has been showing that the ' holy ' thing is not originally something made the property of a god, but something simply tabooed for whatever reason, without reference to gods or spirits. Then he goes on : ' Closely allied to this curse is the ban by which impious sinners or enemies . . . were devoted. The ban is a form of devotion to the deity, and to ban is in the O. T. sometimes rendered " consecrate ".' So too the *homo sacer*, we may suppose, was cursed and consecrated at

---

[1] p. 434. Dr. Marett, *Threshold of Religion*, p. 126, compares *sacer* and taboo, but is thinking of *sacer* in all its senses. Of course that which is the property of a god can be called taboo as much as the accursed man ; but in that sense it is a survival from an older age into the religious law of a theological one. Dr. Marett tells me, what is very interesting in this connexion, that taboo tends in the Pacific to connote ' prohibited by religious law '. He also sends me an illuminating note on the magico-religious aspect of the feeling about the man who has shed blood, &c.—the sinner, in fact (rather than the criminal). ' If you have anything to do with him, something awful will happen. What follows then from a social point of view ? From the first, he 's an outlaw : which means that no one will stand up for his rights. But he is also a leper, a plague-spot in society. The practical moral is, " Get rid of him ". That was the simple duty of savage society. The *devotio* to a deity is a further elaboration along the magico-religious line of thought.'

the same moment. He is therefore *sacer*, not in the sense appropriated by the framers of the *ius divinum*, of things made over to a deity in order to please and glorify him, but in the more primitive sense of ' accursed and left to a deity to avenge himself on if he be so pleased '. And as he was not in any true sense the property of the god, or valued by him as such, like objects called *sacra* under the religious law, any one putting him to death would not be committing what was *nefas*. In no sense whatever could he be thought of as a sacrificial victim ; if he had been such, it would certainly have been *nefas* for any one but a magistrate or priest, or the authorized assistant of such officials, to lay hands on him. Let us pursue this point a little further.

In the ritual of sacrifice at the altar under the *ius divinum*, the victim must be wholly acceptable to the deity ; it must be pure and perfect, and its passage out of the region of the *profanum* into that of the *sacrum* is only consummated when it has been slain, and its entrails examined to see whether they show any flaw that might make it an undesirable gift to the god.[1] The *sacer homo*, on the other hand, was made or declared *sacer* by the community or its authorities,[2] and his slaughter, in whatever way it might ensue, would not seem to have anything to do with its passage from the *profanum* to the *sacrum*. Again, all sacrifice at the altar was accompanied with prayer, as Pliny expressly tells us (*N. H.* xxviii. 10), and the language of the oldest prayers makes it clear that the deity was believed to be glorified or strengthened by the process (e. g. macte his suovetaurilibus esto) ;[3] but in the case of the *homo sacer* such an idea is unthinkable. Whoever in short will go carefully through the altar ritual will see that

---

[1] This is, I think, the right way to look on the process of *sacrificium*. The preliminary steps, e. g. the pouring on the victim of *mola salsa* and libations of wine, are only consummated by the actual slaughter, and that again might fail to put the victim into the region of the *sacrum*, if its *exta* were not found perfect.

[2] See below at the end of this paper.

[3] Cf. the prayers in Cato, *De Agric.* 132, 134, 139, 141. Cf. *Rel. Exp.* pp. 183 ff.

it is in every point wholly inapplicable to the *homo sacer*. This will explain a passage of Festus which seems to have puzzled the lawyers. 'Homo sacer is est quem populus iudicavit ob maleficium : *neque fas est eum immolari*, sed qui occidit parricidii non damnatur.' Here Festus, or rather Verrius Flaccus, seems to me simply to mean, 'in this case there is no question of altar sacrifice, though the word *sacer* might lead one to fancy so : any one may kill the *sacer homo* '. So Lactantius, with Varro before him, writing of the Argei, who were supposed to have been at one time human victims, says, 'non quidem ut homo ad aram immolaretur, sed uti in Tiberim de ponte Milvio mitteretur '. [1]

And indeed there is no record of a *homo sacer* being slain at the altar, or slain with the axe at all. The shedding of his blood, for whatever reason, seems to be carefully avoided. The harvest thief is hung ; the man who had suffered *sacratio capitis et bonorum* in historical times might be thrown from the Tarpeian rock ; the parricide, who must have been *sacer*, though we are not expressly told that he was, suffered the horrible penalty of the sack and was thrown into the sea. [2] So too the guilty vestal was buried alive. The only case of a human victim being slaughtered at an altar is that of the two mutinous soldiers, if such they were, who were beheaded at the Ara Martis in the Campus Martius by order of Julius Caesar, and their heads fixed up on the Regia : [3] a strange ritual which is so closely analogous to that of the yearly sacrifice of the October horse that we must suppose it to have been a somewhat wanton imitation of that rite. Lastly, in

[1] Festus, s.v. *sacer homo*. Lactantius, *Inst.* i. 21. Wissowa (op. cit., p. 388, note 11) has seen that the *homo sacer* cannot be the subject of a *sacrificium* : ' der mit Strafschuld beladene Verbrecher konnte ebensowenig als eine Ehrung den Göttern dargebracht werden, wie die Missgeburt, die man stillschweigend beseitigt.' I am glad to find A. Rosenberg of the same opinion as that expressed in the text (*Hermes*, 1913, p. 363).

[2] Cic. *Pro Rosc. Amer.* 26. 72. See an interesting parallel, both in feeling and practice, in *The Pagan Tribes of Borneo*, ii. 196.

[3] Dio Cassius, xliii. 24. Mommsen, *Strafrecht*, p. 913 ; Wissowa, op. cit., p. 421, note 2, considers it an undoubted case of imitation of an ancient rite. See also my *Roman Festivals*, p. 249, note 2.

the case of the *ver sacrum*, though the animals were believed to have been sacrificed at the altar, the human beings were kept till they were grown up and then driven beyond the frontier.

So far then the distinction between the *homo sacer* and a sacrificial victim seems clear. But here we meet with a difficulty in our argument. When we examine the records of the ancient rules of law relating to the *homo sacer*, we find that in most instances he is placed in connexion with a deity or deities to whom he might seem to be 'sacrificed'. Not indeed in every case : Festus, s. v. Terminus, tells us that Numa Pompilius 'statuit eum, qui terminum exarasset, et ipsum et boves sacros esse' without any clear reference to a deity Terminus. So too in the XII tables : 'Patronus si clienti fraudem fecerit sacer esto ;' where it is only from a Greek writer that we learn that the man was to be *sacer* 'to' Jupiter, i. e. apparently Ζεὺς ὅριος.[1] But of the harvest thief it is said that 'suspensum Cereri necari iubebant :'[2] though it is to be noticed that the word *sacer* is not here used. The husband who sold his wife was to be sacrificed (if we may so translate Plutarch's θύεσθαι) to the infernal deities :[3] and of the son who struck his father it was written, 'divis parentum sacer estod'.[4]

Here let us notice that with the exception of Ceres, it is the *di inferi* who are mentioned ; and even Ceres may reasonably be supposed to have been in this context originally Tellus Mater, whose place she frequently usurped in historical times.[5] Now these are the deities of the *devotio* : Decius for example, after having been made *sacer* under the directions of the pontifex [6] (so the process may be explained) and having invoked all the gods of Rome to help the State, finished with the words 'ita pro re publica Quiritium, exercitu legionibus auxiliis populi Romani Quiritium legiones auxiliaque hostium

[1] Serv. *Aen.* vi. 609 : cf. Dion. Hal. ii. 74.　　　　[2] Plin. xviii. 8, 12.
[3] Plut. *Rom.* 22.　　　　[4] Festus (p. 260, Lindsay).
[5] Wissowa, op. cit., p. 192 ff.
[6] Livy viii. 9. 6–8 : and cf. the explanations of the ritual by Professor Deubner in *Archiv für Religionswissenschaft*, 1905, p. 69 ff.

mecum dis Manibus Tellurique devoveo '.[1] Evidently there
is some analogy or close connexion between the *devotio* and
the *consecratio* of the *sacer homo* : and as the self-immolating
victim of the *devotio* was a kind of vicarious sacrifice for the
whole host, so we may perhaps infer that the *sacer homo* was
in some sense made over to the infernal deities in expiation for
the mischief he had brought on the community. If this be
so, the word *sacer* must here be translated not ' sacred to ' but
' accursed and devoted to ' ; and this is why he is an outcast
and ' holy ' or dangerous. These infernal deities had no
regular ordered altar sacrifices : [2] if one wished to appease
them with a victim one must curse him and make him *sacer*
in the old sense of ' taboo ', and then leave him to his fate,
as Decius rushed into the middle of the enemy.

If this is the right meaning of the word *sacer* in *sacer esto*, we
may, I think, trace it back to the older stage in which it meant
simply ' taboo ' without reference to a deity ; and we have
seen that it seems to be so used in one or two of the ancient
laws. But with the growth of the State and its religious
law the attachment to a deity expressed in the dative case
became more usual, though this deity could not as yet be
one of those to whom altar sacrifice was regularly made,
nor could the word *sacer* be used here of the criminal in the
same sense in which it was used of the true sacrificial victim.
Later on again, however, we come upon cases in which a man
who violated a *lex sacrata*, particularly that which made the
tribunus plebis sacrosanct, was declared *sacer Iovi*, and his
familia was to be sold at the (plebeian) temple of Ceres

---

[1] In a later formula quoted by Macrobius (iii. 9, 10) as used at the siege
of Carthage, the deities are Dis Pater, Vediovis, Manes. Dis Pater is the
Greek name for Orcus.

[2] This was so until the Graeco-Roman period and the introduction of
Greek deities of the underworld (e. g. at the *ludi saeculares*, when black
victims were sacrificed at night). For animal sacrifice at the Parentalia
the only evidence is that of Virg. *Aen.* iii. 67, which need by no means
be taken as proving a Roman practice. Vediovis and the Manes had no
temples or altars, so far as we know, till towards the end of the republican
period. By the *devotio* a man's life was put into their power : and so with
the *sacratio*. (See article Inferi in the *Mythological Lexicon,* p. 256.)

Liber Libera.[1] I take this to be still the old sense of the word : the man is, so to speak, taboo and any one may kill him, e. g. by throwing from the Tarpeian rock ;[2] and the same was probably the case of the man ' qui regni occupandi consilia iniisset' (Liv. ii. 8. 2). But the mention of the heavenly deity in the dative is a novelty, and strictly speaking, an anomaly. The Jupiter in this case was probably the great deity of the Capitol, whose cult was specially connected with the idea of good faith and covenant. But even here I think it would be safer not to speak of the victim as being ' sacrificed to Jupiter '.

If we now ask how the *homo sacer* came to be declared *sacer*, since he did not become so by any sacrificial act, we may perhaps see three stages of the process, answering to the three main periods of the development of Roman society. (1) In the age of taboo proper, before the appearance of the State and its *ius divinum*, we have of course no Roman evidence to help us ; and perhaps we cannot well go further than to call it a collective or sociological declaration. Dr. Marett, to whom an Oxford man naturally goes for help in such matters, seems to make it the result of public opinion among savages, and the penalty by no means always a measurable quantity.[3] *Sacer esto* could be the verdict of the group most immediately affected by the crime, either by what the Australians call ' growling ', or by the voice of an authority : but what the group or the authority was in Latium we cannot be sure. (2) In the age of the early city-state and its *ius divinum*, we may assume that the declaring authority was the *rex*, aided no doubt by the *pontifices* : for in historical times it was the pontifical college that declared an act *nefas*, or a man *impius*,[4] and the inference is a safe

---

[1] Livy, iii. 55. 7.   [2] Mommsen, *Strafrecht*, p. 933.
[3] *The Threshold of Religion*, pp. 90–2.
[4] This is the view of Marquardt, *Staatsverwaltung*, iii. 277 ff. I cannot find a definite proof of the statement that the pontifex maximus declared a man *impius*, but the assumption seems a safe one. In the case of Clodius and the Bona Dea mysteries the pontifical college declared the act *nefas* before further steps could be taken. Cic. *Att.* i. 13. 3.

one that in this matter of religious law they also were the possessors of the final formula of *sacratio*. From the pontifex of the republican age we naturally argue back to the Rex of the earlier period. (3) Under the republic, though the pontifices may have possessed the necessary formula, there is strong evidence that this was preceded by a judicial trial. The passage of Festus referred to at the beginning of this paper runs 'homo sacer is est quem populus iudicavit ob maleficium', and under the *sacratae leges* some form of trial might certainly be expected. Mommsen therefore assumes that a trial and magisterial pronouncement were always necessary.[1]

To sum up what has been said : the relation between a deity or *numen* and any object brought into connexion with him, can always be indicated by the word *sacer*, but that relation is not always of the same kind. Originally the word may have meant simply *taboo*, i. e. removed out of the region of the *profanum*, without any special reference to a deity, but ' holy ' or accursed, according to circumstances. Naturally this word was seized upon by the framers of a *ius divinum*, to express that which is consecrated or sacrificed to a deity, as the idea of benevolent *numina*, with dwellings within the city at particular spots, gradually developed itself : hence the prevailing idea of the word throughout Roman literature is not a sinister one, but rather one suggesting a happy relation (*pax*) between the Roman and his gods. Nevertheless the older meaning of taboo in the sense of accursed could not be forgotten or extinguished ; and it was retained in another department of the *ius divinum* for the criminal who was declared to be left to the infernal deities, or their agents, to be disposed of, and later again for the man whose *caput* and *bona* were ' consecrated ' in historical times.[2] But by

---

[1] I am indebted for this statement of Mommsen's view, which he says is maintained throughout the *Strafrecht*, to the late Master of Balliol, who kindly allowed me to read the proof of the first chapter of his book on Roman Criminal Law. This reading suggested to me the subject of this paper, and also supplied me conveniently with a few of the passages I have noticed.

[2] The compound *consecratio* retained this meaning throughout : e. g.

the end of the republican period such cases as these were rare, and the other and cleaner meaning of *sacer* had so entirely come to prevail, that, as Aelius Gallus said, it was puzzling to many Romans that an object called *sacer* could be violated with impunity.[1]

MUNDUS PATET

24TH AUGUST, 5TH OCTOBER, 8TH NOVEMBER

THE *mundus* of Rome was believed to be a hole or underground pit or vault on the Palatine.[2] It was said to be closed by a stone called the *lapis manalis*, which same name, oddly enough, is also given to an entirely different kind of stone, with which the *pontifices* occasionally worked some sort of magic in a drought.[3] Plutarch, in the chapter in which he

in Pliny's Panegyric on Trajan, 64, we read : ' ille iuravit expressit ex-planavitque verba quibus caput suum, domum suam, si sciens fefellisset, deorum irae consecraret.'

[1] I may add in a footnote the curious use of the word (apparently in an antique form) mentioned by Varro in two passages in book ii of his *De re rustica* i. 20 ; iv. 16). Sacrificial animals were not reckoned fit for sacrifice until a certain number of days after birth (e. g. ten in the case of pigs); after this they were called in Varro's time *puri*, but formerly *sacres*. In each case he quotes a line of Plautus in the *Menaechmi*, which, as we have it, stands thus (ed. Lindsay, Oxford, ii. 289): ' quibus hic pretieis porci veneunt sacres sinceri ? ' Cf. Festus, 318 (420 Lindsay). It may be that Plautus was here translating a Greek word (ὅσιος ?), and so misled Varro into fancying that *sacres* was here really used in a primitive sense. The word *sinceri* seems to be added to make the meaning clear to a Roman audience. The *ignis sacer* of medical writers (Plin. *N. H.* xxvi. 121 ; Virgil, *Georg.* iii. 566), i. e. an eruption on the skin, may also be mentioned : the word here may be supposed to mean ' uncanny' or ' dangerous'. Lastly, the use of the word in the term *sacra via* suggests that that path was originally reserved for religious purposes under the *ius divinum* of the city of the four regions ; but its early history, except so far as excavation has thrown light on it as a material object, is entirely lost to us.

[2] I leave its position to experts. See *Year's Work in Classical Studies*, 1915, pp. 12–13. O. L. Richmond in *J. R. S.*, 1914, p. 225 ff.

[3] See my *Roman Festivals*, p. 232.

describes the foundation of Rome,[1] says that the *mundus*,
like the process of marking out a city, was of Etruscan origin ;
that firstfruits of all kinds were thrown into the pit, and that
each new settler brought a bit of earth from his own country
and cast it into the pit ; he places the pit in the Comitium
instead of the Palatine, but notes the word *mundus* as applied
to it there, and the identity of this word with that for the
heaven or universe.

Plutarch says nothing of another notion, namely that on
three days in the year, those noted above, the *lapis* was
removed to give egress to the denizens of the underworld.
This we learn from Varro, quoted by Macrobius : ' mundus
cum patet, *deorum* tristium atque inferum quasi ianua patet.' [2]
So too Ateius Capito quoted by Festus [3] : ' Mundus ter in
anno patere solet, diebus his : postridie Volcanalia (et a.d.
III non. Oct.) et ante diem VI id. Nov. Qui quid ita dicatur
sic refert Cato in commentariis iuris civilis : *Mundo nomen
impositum est ab eo mundo qui supra nos est.* . . . Eius inferiorem
partem veluti consecratam dis manibus clausam omni tempore
nisi his diebus qui supra scripti sunt maiores (censuerunt
habendam), quos dies etiam religiosos iudicauerunt.' Here
it is necessary to note that the only words of Cato are those
in italics : [4] there are other words of his following these, to
which I shall refer directly, but Cato had nothing to say of
the *lapis manalis* and the ghosts, so far at least as we know :
for these ideas Varro is our oldest authority, followed by
Ateius Capito in the age of Augustus.

Since I wrote my book on the Roman Festivals I have often
wondered why these three days, August 24, October 5,
November 8, were selected as holidays, so to speak, for the

---

[1] Romulus, 11.

[2] Macrobius, i. 16. 18. He adds evidence that the days were *religiosi* :
an army might not give battle, nor any military operation of importance
be performed ; nor might a marriage take place.

[3] Festus, 144. Paulus, 145, gives the dates, which are mutilated in
Festus.

[4] See the fragment in H. Jordan's *Catonis Libri Deperditi*, p. 84, with his
note.

ghosts. If the old Romans really believed in their return to
the upper world on those days, the days must have had some
special importance in connexion with ghost-life ; but no one,
so far as I know, has ever yet discovered what this importance
is. The days fixed in the old Calendar of Numa as those on
which ghosts would be roaming about in apparent freedom,
and on which they might be expelled from the house by the
paterfamilias, were 9th, 11th, and 13th May (Lemuria), and
the more civilized festival of the dead was in February
(Parentalia). Why should three other days be allowed them
for freedom in late summer and autumn ?

In the book just referred to,[1] taking a hint from O. Müller's
Etrusker, I suggested that the ghostly function of the *mundus*
was an accretion, perhaps or probably of Graeco-Etruscan
origin, on a very simple original fact. The pit might be the
penus of the new city, i. e. the underground storing-place for
the grain ; and thus we can understand why it should be
open on a day (August 24) which follows the Consualia,
a festival which almost beyond doubt has reference to harvesting, and immediately precedes the Opiconsivia, which
almost as certainly represents the storage of the grain as
completed.[2] ' Nor is it difficult to understand why, when
the original use and meaning had vanished, the Graeco-
Etruscan doctrine of the underworld should be engrafted
on this simple Roman stem. Dis and Proserpina (Greek
deities) claim the *mundus* : it is *ianua Orci, faux Plutonis,*
fancies familiar to Romans who had come under the spell
of Greek and Etruscan religious beliefs.'

Quite lately I have been able to develop this suggestion
a little further. I think, unless I am under a delusion, that
I can explain not only August 24, but with some little probability, also October 5 and November 8 as days on which
we might expect the *mundus* to be open, not for the egress of
ghosts, but for a very practical purpose of the farmer. I
conjecture that it was the place in which was stored, not, or

---

[1] *Roman Festivals*, p. 211. Cf. Müller-Deecke, *Etrusker*, ii. 100.
[2] See Wissowa, *Relig. und Kultus der Römer*, p. 168 (ed. 2, p. 203).

not *only*, the grain of the last harvest which would be needed for food, and for which the storehouse (*penus*) would need to be frequently opened in the old farmhouse, but the place of safety in which the *seed-corn* was stored. This was a sacred treasure almost more precious than the grain destined immediately for food : and it must be housed securely and hidden most carefully from enemies of all kinds.

The *mundus* as Cato describes it, though on the Palatine in his day it would be only a symbolic survival from the original storing-place, seems to me strongly to suggest a use for human beings as well as ghosts. ' Mundo nomen impositum est ab eo mundo qui supra nos est : forma enim eius est, *ut ex his qui intravere cognoscere potui.*' [1] The *mundus* then was a place into which a man might descend : we may imagine it as a kind of cellar with an opening in the centre of its roof, which was closed, except on the three days, by a stone, after the fashion of a trap-door. On the top of this there was no doubt a covering of earth, for the sake of concealment, an obvious safeguard which seems to be reflected in the descriptions both of Plutarch and Ovid.[2] The poet wrote :

> Fossa fit ad solidum. Fruges iaciuntur in ima
> et de vicino terra petita solo.
> fossa repletur humo. . . .

But I must now go on to explain my justification for this very matter-of-fact conjecture.

In August the opening of the *mundus* took place the day before the Opiconsivia, i. e. the 24th ; and in the latter festival it is pretty well agreed that we should see a representation of the completed storage of the corn of the recent harvest. My conjecture is that on the previous day the seed-corn for the autumn sowing was separated from the rest of the grain, and deposited in an underground storing-place, for the security that was absolutely essential for the existence of the

---

[1] *Potui* is Scaliger's emendation for *potuit* of the codex. The pit discovered by Professor Boni in 1914 in the peristyle of the Flavian palace answers fairly well to Cato's description. See *Year's Work*, 1915, p. 12.

[2] *Fasti* iv. 821 : cf. Plutarch, *Rom.* 11.

community. Varro tells us that in his time the finest ears were separated on the threshing-floor from the rest of the corn, in order that the *semen* (seed-corn) might be as good as possible.[1] As a rule the corn seems to have been threshed as soon as it was brought home from the field ; Varro and Columella imply this,[2] though they do not state it in so many words ; and in primitive times, when your enemy might at any moment make a raid on you, this would be desirable in order to secure the precious treasure as quickly as possible. We know nothing from literary sources of the place of storage, but I venture to think that not only the curious underground altar of Consus, opened at the Consualia on the 21st, but also the opening of the *mundus* on the 24th, suggest the method that would obviously be the safest, that of concealing the treasure underground.[3]

It is of course possible that both the grain for food and the seed-corn were deposited in the same place. But apart from the extra security which two storing-places would give to the farmer, I think that the dates of the other two openings of the *mundus* may suggest that it was the receptacle of the seed-corn only.

The oldest kind of grain used for food in Italy was that rough kind of wheat called *far*, which in historical times was used in the city only for religious purposes. But in some districts it was still grown, and Pliny tells us that the sowing

[1] Varro, *R. R.* i. 52, *init.* ' Quae seges grandissima atque optima fuerit, seorsum in aream secerni oportet spicas, ut semen optimum habeat ' (i. e. the farmer). Cf. Pliny, xviii. 195 ; Columella, ii. 9, 11 ; and also Virgil, *Georg.* i. 197, who says that the farmer must pick out the largest by hand, or they will degenerate in the keeping.

[2] Varro, *R. R.* i. 50, 51 and the beginning of 52 already quoted. When the corn has been reaped, it must be brought to the area (threshing-floor), which Varro then describes in c. 51 ; then, returning to the crop, he urges the separation of the seed-corn from the rest. The same is clearly implied in Columella, ii. 21.

[3] See Mommsen's note in *C. I. L.* i, ed. 2, p. 326, followed by Wissowa, *Rel. und Kult.*, p. 167 (ed. 2, p. 201). As from 5 to 10 *modii* of various kinds of seed were needed for each *iugerum*, a fairly roomy receptacle would be necessary. There is a good account of modern ' silos ' in Tristram's *Land of Israel*, p. 108.

went on through the month of October.[1] A date as early as the fifth, in the practice of the later people of the city, would suit well enough for the opening of the storing-place for the purpose of taking out the necessary amount of grain for sowing. But the third of the days of opening, November 8, bears more remarkable testimony to their original meaning. All readers of Virgil will remember that in his first Georgic (219, ff.) he urges the postponement of the sowing of wheat (*triticum*) till after the setting of the Pleiades : and in this he is borne out by Columella.[2] No doubt Virgil represents the traditional practice of the Italian farmer. Now the apparent or cosmical setting of the Pleiades, i. e. that which alone can have been known to the husbandman throughout early Roman history, seems to have taken place on or about November 9 ; different ancient authorities give different days, but all at the beginning of November, and the writer of the article *Astronomia* in the *Dict. of Antiquities* fixes the actual day of apparent setting as the 9th.[3] That the opening of the *mundus* should have taken place on the 8th is thus

---

[1] Pliny, *H. N.* xviii. 205 : cf. Varro, i. 34. Cf. Cornford in *Essays and Studies presented to W. Ridgeway*, p. 155, for early autumn sowing in ancient times, quoting Plut. *Frag.* 23.

[2] ' Ante tibi Eoae Atlantides abscondantur, Gnosiaque ardentis decedat stella Coronae, Debita quam sulcis committas semina quamque Invitae properes anni spem credere terrae.' Varro, i. 34, rather vaguely describes sowing as extending from the equinox to the *bruma* ; but Columella, ii. 8, quotes and supports Virgil : only in this passage he seems to be thinking of the *true* morning setting of the Pleiades, i. e. October 24, though in other places he obviously alludes to the apparent setting. See *Dict. of Antiquities*, s. v. *Astronomia*, p. 227.

[3] *Dict. of Antiquities*, loc. cit. ' The true morning setting was at Rome at that epoch on 29th October, the apparent morning setting on 9th November.' This date has been confirmed for the time of the Roman kings by Dr. Fotheringham, who has most kindly made elaborate calculations for me. He sums them up thus in a letter : ' Anyhow, you will see that the date given in the *Dict. of Antiquities* (9th November) appears to apply excellently to the time of the kings. It does not seem to apply so well to the time of Julius Caesar, to which it was intended (in the dictionary) to refer.' In a later letter he wrote : ' As the Roman 8th November did not occupy a fixed place in the natural year before the time of Julius Caesar, I presume that a general and not an exact coincidence with the cosmical setting of the Pleiades is all that is required.'

a striking fact, and strongly suggests that the seed-corn of the better wheat crops, as distinct from the more ancient *far*, was at this time being taken out of the *mundus* for the November sowing.

Now supposing that our hypothesis is a reasonable one, and that the *mundus* was originally a receptacle for seed-corn, how are we to account for the accretion on this simple and useful practice of the doctrine of the *mundus* as *faux Plutonis*, *ostium Orci* and so on, and of the liberation of the ghosts when the stone trapdoor was removed ?

In the first place, there is no difficulty in attributing a religious character with taboos such as Varro mentions [1] to such receptacles of the means of man's subsistence : that is sufficiently well shown by the sacred character of the store-chamber of the house, which produced in time its own spirits or deities, the Penates : and the underground altar of Consus points in the same direction. Professor Deubner has lately shown [2] that there are two main periods in early Roman religious thought, and that undoubtedly the purely ritualistic one is the oldest, when deities and a theology are only in the making, if as far advanced as that. To this older stratum belongs the original use of the *mundus* as I explain it. No deity is here concerned, unless it be the Ops Consiva of the day following that of the opening of the *mundus* in August, and that deity is plainly no more than the store itself with its religious character beginning to take tangible shape in a worship.

Upon this older stratum of religious ideas there lies what we can only suppose to be a later stratum deposited by another race, in which the idea of existence after death in an underworld was more important than the practical ideas of the pure agriculturist. Such a race was the Etruscan. In a valuable summary of our present knowledge of Mediterranean burial, kindly sent me by the author, Professor von Duhn, he attributes a somewhat grossly material idea of the dead alike to the oldest population of Italy, and to the

[1] Macrobius, i. 16, 18.
[2] In *Neue Jahrbücher für das klassische Altertum*, 1911, p. 323.

Etruscans, both of which races *buried* their dead and supplied
them with such objects as they were supposed to need, in
contrast to the true Italic peoples (Sabines excepted) who
used cremation, and show signs of being the ancestors of those
who developed the orderly, sensible ritual of the Parentalia.
The conjecture in my recent volume [1] that the notion of an
underworld and its horrors was Etruscan, but resting on
a substructure of much more primitive belief, is not so wild
as I feared at one time that it might be.

Exactly how the new way of looking at the simple old
practice came about it is impossible to say ; but each of us
can make some kind of a guess for himself if he pleases. My
own guess is that the primitive storing pit was transferred
from the farm or the pagus to the newly-founded city, and the
three days of opening were retained and fixed ; that in due
time its original meaning was lost, owing to the city ceasing
to be a practical centre of agricultural operations : and that
as this cessation happened about the same time as the Etruscan dominion in Rome, the *mundus* took on a new meaning
connected with the Etruscan ideas of a nether world. [2] The
stone, of which we are told on a single authority that it was
called *lapis manalis*, the same name as that of the stone of
Jupiter Elicius, took on the name of that other stone through
a misinterpretation of the word *manalis*, which was wrongly
supposed to mean ' belonging to the Manes '. [3]

[1] *The Religious experience of the Roman people*, pp. 391 ff.

[2] The best account of the word *mundus* known to me is in Nettleship's
Contributions to Latin Lexicography, p. 528. I have abstained from invoking
the aid of etymology ; but if Nettleship is right, the word may be developed
from a root *mu*, meaning to enclose, or fence round. In regard to an Etruscan
origin of a similar word, see Müller-Deecke, *Die Etrusker*, ii. 100, n. 65a.

[3] Cf. Paulus, 128. In case the contrast between the original Latin
meaning of the *mundus* and that here assumed to have been superimposed,
should astonish any one, let me refer him to the remarks of Dr. J. B. Carter
in Hastings' *Dict. of Religion and Ethics*, i. 464. He points out that the
Romans do not seem to have been much interested in the lower world, and
that every bit of description of it comes from writers under Greek influence,
and all the details are identical with those of the Greeks. Hence it is probable
that the Roman lower world was not mythologically adorned till Greeks
(and Etruscans) did it for them. As we have seen, the idea of a stone

Now I may reasonably be asked why, if I make so much
of the seed-corn and its place of deposit, we do not find more
distinct traces of the importance of these among other peoples,
Mediterranean or other. My answer is that I do so find them,
though they seem to me to have lain unnoticed since Mannhardt developed his theory of the corn-spirit. For the animistic period that theory undoubtedly holds good, and has
been confirmed by the immense mass of additional evidence
brought together by Sir James Frazer in his *Golden Bough*, but
I have for some time felt that there is a yet more primitive
way of looking at the mystery of the renewal of vegetation ;
and in many of the examples of the familiar forms of the
corn-spirit I am inclined to see traces of the sacred character
of the seed-corn itself, and of the place in which it was stored.
My friend Sir James Frazer has most kindly pointed me out
a number of such unindexed examples in the second volume
of the *Golden Bough* (ed. 2), though without expressing definite approval of my views on this subject ; but in order
to weigh the matter thoroughly, it is advisable to read the
whole of chapter iii in that volume, as well as to let the mind
dwell on isolated instances.

I think I see signs that the last sheaf of the harvest, which
in innumerable instances is treated with reverence or made into
human form, may represent the precious seed-corn set aside
at the time of threshing. A good example is taken by Sir James

covering the abode of the dead, the removal of which gave egress to the
ghosts, is found only in Festus, 144, and nowhere alluded to in Roman
literature. It has been compared to the Dillestein of German mythology
(Preller-Jordan, ii. 67), but a perusal of the description of that mysterious
stone in Grimm's *Deutsche Mythologie*, iii. 806 (Engl. trans.) makes it clear
to me that there is nothing in common between the two. The Dillestein was
a ceiling or grating of the underworld, lying at the bottom of our earth.
I may add to this note a few words of Sir James Frazer's, contained in a letter
to me : ' The ancient explanation of the *mundus* is perhaps not wholly irreconcileable with your theory. For observe that the spirits of the dead are
often supposed to watch over or further the growth of the crops : that is
why the firstfruits are often presented to them. For examples see the
Golden Bough (ed. 2), ii. 459, seq.' On the connexion at Rome between
Tellus Mater, the dead, and the crops, see my *Religious experience of the
Roman people*, pp. 121, 138 ; cf. Dieterich, *Mutter Erde*, cap. iv.

Frazer from Mannhardt.[1] At Westerhüsen in Saxony the
last corn cut is made into the shape of a woman, brought to
the threshing-floor, and kept there till the threshing is done.[2]
Just below on the same page we have an example from
Tarnow, Galicia, in which the last corn cut is made into a
wreath and called the wheat-mother, &c., and kept till spring,
when some of the grain is mixed with the seed-corn. The
last sheaf is often larger and heavier than the rest, and this
Sir James Frazer explains (p. 176) as a charm, working by
sympathetic magic, to ensure a large and heavy crop in the
following harvest. Is it not rather a survival of the selection
of the finest ears to use as seed-corn ? For it seems that this
last sheaf is often taken from that part of the field where the
corn is finest : examples of this practice will be found on
p. 184 (from Kent), on p. 189 (Scotland), p. 193 (ancient
Peru), a passage to which I will return directly, and p. 195
(ancient Mexico) ; p. 200 (Malay peninsula) and in Sumatra
(p. 198), the best grains of rice are picked out to form the rice-
mother, and are sown in the middle of the bed, with the
common seed planted round them. When the time comes
to transplant the rice from the nursery to the field, the rice-
mother receives a special place either in the middle or in
a corner of the field, and is planted with a prayer or charm.

Further, this last sheaf of fine grain is sometimes deposited
in a special place, and even in an underground cavity or
cellar, like the firstfruits which Plutarch tells us were deposited
in the Roman *mundus*, a practice which I take to be the fore-
runner of those numberless instances in which the last sheaf
or some puppet representing it, is kept stuck up on the farmhouse during the winter. The great care taken of the maiden,
as this puppet, garland, or sheaf, is so often called, would be
a survival of the care originally taken of the precious seed-
corn.[3] A good example of storage in a special granary occurs

[1] *Golden Bough* (ed. 2), ii. 172.

[2] i. e. it is kept separate, as intended for seed-corn. Cf. Mannhardt,
Mythologische Forschungen, p. 334, translated in *G. B.*, p. 181.

[3] According to Festus (p. 125, Lindsay) the mundus was known as
'Cereris mundus'.

2252

C

on p. 193 (*G. B.* vol. ii); from ancient Peru, described by
the historian Acosta : a portion of the most fruitful of the
maize is thus deposited with religious ceremony. So in *G. B.*
ii. 459, a little hollow filled with grain is left on the threshing-
floor, according to Frazer (or his informant Casalis), as
a thankoffering to the gods. Is this explanation the right
one ? Again (p. 194), in Mexico the priests, with the nobles
and people, went in procession to the maize fields, where they
picked out the largest and finest sheaf, brought it home,
and laid it upon an altar. ' After sacrificing to the harvest-
god, the priests carefully wrapped it in fine linen and kept
it till seed-time. Then it was carried once more to the field
from which it had been taken, and deposited in a subterranean
chamber, which was closed and covered over with earth.
Then followed the sowing, after sacrifice had been made for
an abundant harvest ; and finally, when the time of harvest
drew near, the buried sheaf was solemnly disinterred by the
priests, who distributed the grain to all who asked for it.'
This I take to be an animistic and magical development
of the simple practice of storing the seed-corn. One more
example : in Java (pp. 201-2), two garlands are made of
ears of rice, and called the rice-bride and rice-bridegroom,
whose wedding is celebrated just before harvest. ' Later on,
when the rice is being got in, a bridal chamber is partitioned
off in the barn, furnished with a new mat, a lamp, and all
kinds of toilet articles. Sheaves of rice, to represent the
wedding guests, are placed beside the bride and bridegroom.
Not till this has been done may the whole harvest be housed
in the barn. And for the first *forty* days after the rice has been
housed, no one may enter the barn, for fear of disturbing
the newly-married pair.' [1] I read this to mean that the sheaves
here called wedding guests were really those reserved for

[1] Does this mean that the first use of the grain for sowing occurred forty
days after it was thus deposited ? It is curious that the time between
the Opiconsivia on August 25, and the opening of the *mundus* on
October 5, is exactly forty days, a coincidence which I do not in the
least wish to emphasize ; but the number forty has often a religious
significance.

seed-corn, only after which reservation the housing of the general harvest could begin.

Lastly, I will just allude to a feature analogous to some of those just noticed, in the ritual of Demeter and Persephone at the Thesmophoria. Miss Harrison has described this and commented on it in her *Prolegomena to the study of Greek Religion*, chapter iv, translating a valuable passage from the scholiast on Lucian, *Dial. Meretr.* ii. 1. ' At some time not specified ' (so she sums up our information), ' but during the Thesmophoria, women carefully purified for the purpose let down pigs into clefts or chasms called *megara* or chambers. At some other time not precisely specified they descended into the *megara*, brought up the rotten flesh and placed it on certain altars, whence it was taken *and mixed with seed* to serve as a fertility charm. As the first day of the festival was called Kathodos and Anodos it seems likely that the women went down and came up on the same day.' This account is curiously confirmed by a discovery of Sir Charles Newton at Cnidus, quoted by Miss Harrison on p. 125. There, in the sanctuary of Demeter, he found a crypt which had originally been circular, though later compressed by an earthquake, in which were bones of pigs and other animals, and the marble pigs which now stand near Demeter of Cnidos in the British Museum. This crypt seems to remind us of the *mundus*, and so perhaps do the *megara* described by the scholiast.[1] We do not know what the *mundus* contained, though the description of it given by Cato [2] strongly suggests that it contained something, or was originally meant to do so. But the crypt at Cnidus, and the *megara* of Demeter, contained pigs, which in Greece were the special victims of the deities of earth and fertility, and these were used as a charm, mixed with the seed-corn, to obtain good crops. All this belongs, however, to an age of religion and fully

[1] In his *Modern Greek Folklore and Ancient Greek Religion*, Mr. J. C. Lawson has some interesting remarks about the beehive structures at Mycenae, suggesting that they may possibly have been megara, ' temples of chthonian deities such as Demeter ' : see p. 94 ff.

[2] Apud Fest. (p. 144, Lindsay).

developed deities ; and I would here again suggest that
behind it there lies the simple custom of storing the seed-
corn for safety in a subterranean crypt. The seed and the crypt
are both holy, as we might expect, and as we gather from
the fact that women alone, and fully purified, were allowed to
descend into the crypt and bring up the necessary supply of
seed. It is not without interest to note that the Thesmophoria,
when this took place, is in autumn (11th Pyanepsion), and
presumably about the time of the autumn sowing.

Dr. Farnell's more elaborate account [1] of the Thesmophoria
and kindred festivals of Demeter and Persephone has also
many points of interest in connexion with my subject, and
I think it may be worth suggesting that experts in Greek
religious usages should see whether my theory has any bearing
on doubtful points. I note with interest his reference to
a fragment of Anacreon [2] in support of the possibility that
one early (and lost) meaning of θεσμός was θησαυρός. Is
it remotely possible that the objects carried at that festival,
as indicated by its name, were baskets of seed for sowing ?
Dr. Farnell tells us that Triptolemus was believed to have
distributed the seed for this purpose.[3] As so many strange
explanations of this mysterious word have been suggested,[4]
I need hardly fear to suggest yet another. Sir James Frazer [5]
has hazarded the conjecture that the *sacra* were called θεσμός
because they were the things *laid down*, or as I would add,
put into a thesauros. I only go a step further and suggest
that these *sacra* were originally portions of seed-corn : for
the Thesmophoria was a late autumn festival and clearly
connected with sowing.

In conclusion, all I have been doing in this paper is to turn
over a stone to see if there is by any chance anything there.
I am not at all sure that there is anything there really worth
picking up ; the explanation of the three days may lie some-

---

[1] *Cults*, iii. 105 ff. [2] Bergk, *Poet. Lyr.* iii. 271.
[3] *Cults*, iii. 184.
[4] See e. g. Miss Harrison's *Prolegomena*, pp. 137 and 143.
[5] See Miss Harrison, op. cit., p. 137.

where else, and I do not forget that the beginning of November is a great time for ghosts in many parts of the world, a fact which is reflected in the Christian calendar. Or there may be some mysterious connexion between firstfruits and seed-corn, and between both of them and the dead, which has not yet been entirely fathomed. I hope I may be allowed to hazard a hypothesis without doing any one any serious harm.[1]

THE OAK AND THE THUNDER-GOD

IN the third edition of *The Golden Bough* (1911), the distinguished author inserted a chapter on the worship of the oak, and the intimate connexion of that tree with the Aryan god of the sky and thunder.[2] The second part of the chapter sums up the evidence for that connexion ; evidence which has been collected, not only by Sir James Frazer himself, but by Dr. A. B. Cook, with great diligence and ingenuity in the *Classical Review* (vols. xvii and xviii), in *Folklore* (vols. xv and xvi), and in his great work on the Sky-god, of which the first volume has recently appeared. This evidence has made it certain that of all trees the oak [3] is the one most generally held in reverence by the peoples dwelling in the temperate zone which is its habitat ; this at least is proved for Greeks, Italians, Celts, Teutons, Slavs, and Lithuanians. It is equally certain that among all these races, except perhaps the Celts, the deity of (or in) the oak was also regarded as the deity of (or in) the sky, who descends to earth in the form of lightning, or in more anthropomorphic conception, hurls his bolts upon the earth. So far all is clear.

But then comes a serious difficulty. How are we to explain

---

[1] For further developments see Miss Harrison's paper, ' Ichneutae ', in *Essays and Studies presented to William Ridgeway* (1913), and Dr. Cornford's ' Ἀπαρχαί and the Eleusinian Mysteries ', in the same volume.

[2] ii. 349–75.

[3] I use the word in a generic sense, so as to include *Quercus ilex* as well as *Q. robur* and its varieties.

this intimate association between the religious character of the oak and that of the sky, between this particular species of tree and the mystery of thunder and lightning, in the mind of the primitive Aryan ? How are we to answer the question whether the tree or the lightning came first in his religious thought ?

At the end of his chapter Sir James Frazer attempted an explanation of these difficulties. When writing it he had come to the conclusion, but not without hesitation, that the oak is the primary object of religious awe in this connexion, and the thunder and lightning a secondary one. It is unlikely, he argued, that a god of thunder should come to be regarded as a god of the oak merely because thunder and rain come from the sky, and because the oak reaches skyward, and is often struck by lightning. He preferred to think that the oak was the primary object of worship, and that the worshippers may have connected it with lightning when they kindled fire with oaken sticks ; the appearance of the spark in the wood suggesting perhaps the idea that lightning was the result of a similar process worked by some great Being up in the sky.

In the summer of 1912 a different solution of the difficulty accidentally occurred to me, based on evidence which was not known to my friend Frazer when he published his chapter in the previous year. I straightway communicated it to him, and in his reply he told me that it looked to him as if it might turn out convincing. The following year, 1913, on p. ix of the preface to vol. vii of the new edition of *The Golden Bough* (*Balder the Beautiful*) he fully accepted my solution in two or three charming sentences, such as he alone knows how to write, and now believes that the oak was secondary, the lightning primary, in the order of Aryan worship. I published two very brief papers on the point, one in the *Archiv für Religionswissenschaft* (1912, p. 317), and another in *Folklore* for that year. It may be worth while to recapitulate once more the substance of these papers.

In June 1910, while I was in Edinburgh, there occurred in the south of England a period of constant electric storms,

culminating at my Oxfordshire home in a storm of the utmost
violence, of which I have given an account in *Kingham Old
and New*, ch. viii. So many trees were struck that on my
return I could make them the objects of my walks, and
became much interested in the different ways in which trees
of different species were treated by the lightning. And why
among the damaged trees was there not a single beech ? It is
a common belief, I found, that beeches are never struck; but
I could find no scientific book to tell me the truth or the
reason of this.

At last my friend Mr. Gadney, the Oxford bookseller, sent
me the fourth and last volume of Schlich's great work on
Forestry.[1] In this volume I found, in a remote corner (so to
speak) near the end, a few precious pages about the effects
of lightning on trees, which instantly struck me as likely
to throw light on the questions raised in *The Golden Bough*.
Here, in a tabulated form, I found the results of sixteen years
of patient observation carried on and recorded by the foresters
of Lippe-Detmold. Fortunately the stock of trees in the
forest was known, so that a perfectly accurate conclusion
could be drawn as to the comparative danger from lightning
to each species.

The forest was stocked as follows ; oak 11 per cent.,
beech 70, spruce 13, Scotch fir 6. Thus the beech is far the
most abundant tree in the forest, and the oak comparatively
rare. Yet in the sixteen years only 33 beeches were struck,
while the stricken oaks numbered 310, spruces 34, Scotch
firs 108. The danger to a beech being taken as 1, that to
a spruce was 6, to a Scotch fir 37, and to an oak no less than 60.
These results were borne out by other observations made in
France and Bavaria, and I believe that in Germany the
subject had been further investigated before the recent war
broke out. There is practically no doubt at all that the oak
is more frequently struck than any other species of tree.[2]

[1] This volume was the work of Dr. Hess, Professor of Forestry in the
University of Giessen.

[2] Why this is so need not concern us here, if we are confident as to the
fact. Various explanations have been given : see pp. 662 ff. of vol. iv.

To this I may add from my own observation, that the oak is more conspicuous when it has been struck than other species : the bark is stripped more completely, the tree begins to die at once, and in a year's time is little more than a naked skeleton, discernible by the eye at a great distance. An untrained eye would notice a stricken oak at once, but not a stricken elm or ash.

On reading this chapter of Dr. Hess's volume I became assured not only that there is a good deal of truth in the belief of our folks about the immunity of the beech, but also that we have here a natural explanation of the religious connexion between the oak and the thunder. For the oak must have been a very abundant tree both in Europe and Asia in the days of the migrations ; Sir James Frazer has convincingly shown that its timber was very largely used by man in remote ages, e.g. by the people of the European lake-dwellings,[1] who also seem to have used acorns largely to feed their pigs. Certainly the proportion of oaks to other trees must have been far larger than in the forests of Lippe-Detmold, and the damage done to them so much the more conspicuous. And if we may argue from the well-known fact that in Greece and Italy at least, and probably also in Northern Europe, any spot or object struck by lightning was made sacred, and became matter of religious awe, each stricken tree would be liable to become an object of worship,[2] and the number of oaks thus consecrated would greatly exceed that of all other trees.

But there remains the question whether this liability of the oak suggested the idea of a god in the sky who descended into a tree in the lightning-stroke, or whether on the other hand the Sky-god was a primary conception, and the worship

---

[1] *Golden Bough*, ed. 3, ii. 352 ff.

[2] See Usener, *Kleine Schriften*, iv. 477 ff. (Keraunos). For Greece, Frazer, op. cit., p. 361, note 4 : for Italy, Wissowa, *R. K.*, ed. 2, p. 122. Festus (p. 377, Lindsay) : 'Serufertarios dicebant, qui quaedam sacrificia ad arbores fulguritas faciebant, a ferto scilicet quodam sacrificii genere.' Cf. the gloss on Fulguritum (p. 82, Lindsay). The Zulu idea is that anything struck by lightning has in it the power of the lightning : Crawley, *Mystic Rose*, p. 232 (from Calloway).

of the oak a consequence of his activity and power. Here we are in the region, not of fact, but of conjecture ; and I do not suppose that the truth can ever be ascertained for certain. For myself, however, I am disposed to think (as Sir James Frazer now thinks) that the facts put together above point to an extension of the conception of a Sky-god and his powers under the influence of new experience, material and religious, in a land of forests. The benevolent heaven-god of the steppes, worshipped by a pastoral people, might become associated with the oak in the mind of that same people when he was found to strike that tree especially in the forest which they were labouring to clear for purposes of agriculture.

It may be that recent theories and discoveries about tree-spirits and vegetation deities have kept our attention too exclusively fixed on Man as a worshipper in the agricultural stage, or in the struggles with nature which eventually landed him in that stage. But in the earlier nomadic life which I suppose we may postulate for the settlers in the Greek and Italian peninsulas,[1] the Sky-god was, I believe, a real Sky-god, ' pure as the naked heaven, majestic, free '. If on the very threshold of Roman religious history we find him associated with the oak as Jupiter Feretrius, we have now an explanation which so far seems to cover the facts.[2]

---

[1] ' So far as I can see, all the existing political societies, in the ancient world round the Mediterranean, and the modern world of Europe, seem to have arisen ultimately out of a state of things in which peoples who began their existence on the great grasslands which lie to the east, in south Russia and beyond, and to the south in the deserts of Arabia beyond Jordan, have been forced or tempted to leave them and migrate into moister and more forest-clad regions, nearer the Mediterranean and Atlantic.' Professor J. L. Myres, *The Dawn of History*, p. 14.

[2] Liv. i. 10. 4 ; Dion. Hal. ii. 34 ; Aust, in Roscher's *Lexicon*, s. v. 'Iuppiter', p. 671 ; *Rel. Exp.*, pp. 129 ff.

THE *TOGA PRAETEXTA* OF ROMAN CHILDREN

ROMAN children of free birth, both boys and girls, from the time they could walk freely to the age of puberty, wore the *toga praetexta*, a robe with a purple border running along its straight edge,[1] which border could be made conspicuous when the toga was properly adjusted. When his parents thought a boy sufficiently developed they had him publicly invested with the manly toga (*toga virilis* or *pura*) which was entirely white and without a stripe ; and girls went through a somewhat similar ceremony. What was the meaning or object of this purple-edged toga when thus worn by children ? They wore of course another ornament, the *bulla*, an amulet hung round the neck ; but we can hardly call the *praetexta* an amulet in historical times, whatever it may have been in its origin.[2] Nor was it only a mark of tender years, like the jacket of a junior Eton boy, for it was worn also by grown men under certain special circumstances.

Let us glance at these other uses of the *toga praetexta*. In civil life it was worn only by curule magistrates, i. e. those whose authority descended constitutionally from that of the Rex. In the first volume of his *Staatsrecht* (p. 402) Mommsen was inclined to correlate this part of the magisterial insignia with the right of being accompanied by lictors and fasces, and thus to explain its eventual extension to magistrates of *municipia* ; but the censors are an awkward difficulty in this reasoning, seeing that they had the *toga praetexta* but not the lictors and fasces. I should be disposed to think that the privilege belonged to those only who had the right of performing sacrifice on behalf of the community, which belonged originally to curule magistrates only. In course

---

[1] For the exact nature of the toga and its stripe see *Companion to Latin Studies*, ed. 2, p. 191.

[2] The account given by Macrobius, *Sat.* i. 6. 7 ff., is obviously an impossible one.

of time there were naturally extensions of the privilege ; and from a passage in Cicero's speech against Piso, taken together with the comment of Asconius which is luckily preserved, we learn that even *magistri collegiorum*, as well as *magistri vicorum*, used to wear it at the Compitalia, a movable feast of great antiquity. Cicero expresses disgust that Sextus Clodius, *homo impurus*, had worn it in this capacity.[1]   No doubt sacrifice of some kind was offered by these magistrates when they wore the *praetexta*.

Next we note that this toga was worn by all the priests of the most ancient priesthoods during the performance of sacrificial duties, and that the Flamen Dialis, the most important and ancient of them, wore it always and everywhere.[2] The Fratres Arvales used it on the first two days of their great festival, and laid it aside on the third at the end of their sacrificial work.[3]   In the ceremony of *devotio* the person offering himself, who is at the same time priest and victim, puts it on for the act of self-sacrifice.[4]   The Vestals did not wear it ; but here again the connexion of the purple stripe with sacrifice is apparent, for we are told that the *suffibulum* or head-dress of the Vestals, worn when they sacrificed, was *praetextum*.[5]

It is clear, then, that the *praetexta* was a holy garment, worn by priests during the time of sacrifice, by the priest of Jupiter at all times, and by magistrates who had the right to sacrifice on behalf of the State. As worn by children too it must originally have been a holy garment, for the children of *ingenui*, both boys and girls, were regularly employed in the household as ministrants attending on daily sacrifice ; that a special name attached to them in this capacity (*camilli*

---

[1] Cic. *in Pisonem*, iv. 8 ; Asconius, p. 7 of Clark's edition. For the connexion of the Compitalia with the *vici* and the *collegia*, see *Roman Festivals*, p. 280. The *praetexta* was no doubt worn by these *magistri vicorum* or *collegiorum* for the sacrificial part of their duties : see below.

[2] Serv. *Aen.* viii. 552 ; xii. 169.

[3] Henzen, *Act. Fr. Arv.*, pp. 11, 14, 21, 28.

[4] Liv. viii. 9 ; x. 28 ; *Rel. Exp.*, pp. 207 ff.

[5] Festus (Lindsay, pp. 474, 475).

and *camillae*), shows at once the antiquity and the regularity of the practice.[1] In the religious service of the State the children of the priests themselves were thus employed originally, a privilege which later extended to other children born of parents married under *confarreatio* and still living.[2] These children must be *investes*, i. e. still unripe for the *toga virilis* ; they must not have gone out into the world, where they might meet with contaminating influences both material and spiritual, and so be made unfit for those home duties that called for perfect purity. They were ' holy ', and wore the holy garment which their fathers used only when performing religious duties ; but like the Flamen Dialis, they wore it at all times and places, for like him they were extremely precious both to family and State.[3]

There must have been a time when all children of *ingenui* assisted at the family *sacra*, attending on their father as priest. As the religion of the State outgrew that of the household, the idea of holiness and the corresponding dress survived in the State only for priests and magistrates having the right to sacrifice, i. e. capable of performing those priestly functions which were of supreme importance to the State. But the dress was retained for the children, not only because of the constant demand for them as ministrants, but because they were in reality unspotted from the world—an ethical idea here superimposing itself on the ceremonial one. And as a distinction began to assert itself between *ingenui* and *non-ingenui*, the *toga praetexta* came also to have the significance which used to be regarded as the chief one, i. e. it was looked on as a mark of free birth.[4]

But though these two ideas of ethical purity and free birth

[1] Wissowa, *R. K.*, ed. 2, p. 496 and note ; Marquardt, *Staatsverwaltung*, iii, p. 227 ff. ; Serv. *Aen.* i. 730.

[2] See J.R.S., 1916, p. 187.

[3] There are some suggestive remarks on holy garments in R. Smith's *Religion of the Semites*, p. 433. For the preciousness of children in the patriarchal family see Myres, *The Dawn of History*, p. 20.

[4] Macrob. i. 6. 12, says that it was never originally lawful for children of *libertini* or *peregrini* to wear this toga, though *libertini* eventually secured the privilege.

got the better of the older idea of the children's toga, there
are passages in Roman literature which seem to me to indicate
that the true meaning was never entirely lost to the conserva-
tive mind of the Roman of good family.

Horace, *Epode* v. 7. The boy victim of Canidia's sorcery
cries :

> Per liberos te, si vocata partubus
>   Lucina veris adfuit,
> *per hoc inane purpurae decus precor,*
>   per improbaturum haec Iovem,
> quid ut noverca me intueris aut uti
>   petita ferro belua ?

There is here surely the faint echo of a religious appeal
in the third line, for it is an appeal to Jupiter that immediately
follows it. The *toga praetexta* makes the boy in some sense
sacred.

Persius, *Sat.* v. 30, alludes thus to his first manhood :

> Cum primum pavido custos mihi purpura cessit
> bullaque succinctis laribus donata pependit . . .

The word *custos* is significant ; one may think of it as
expressing something more than an ethical guardianship
based on a respect for tender years. We could not apply
the word to any part of the modern boy's dress, however
characteristic of boyhood. Persius evidently reckons the
toga with the *bulla*, as having the power to keep off evil
influences.

Festus, s.v. *Praetextum sermonem* (pp. 282–3, Lindsay) :

Praetextatis nefas erat obsceno verbo uti, ideoque praetextum appellabant sermonem, qui nihil obscenitatis haberet.[1]

By *praetextati* here boys are evidently meant, for just
above he has been writing of the three *praetextati patrimi et
matrimi* (boys) who conduct a bride home after a wedding.
By *obsceno* is meant no doubt ill-omened. The *praetexta*

---

[1] I have given in the text the gloss as it stands in Paulus : in Festus
(p. 282) it runs : ' Praetextum sermonem quidam putant dici quod praetextatis nefas sit obsceno verbo uti : alii quod nubentibus, depositis prae-
textis, a multitudine puerorum obscena clamentur.' For the *obscena verba*,
or *fescennini versus*, see Marquardt, *Privatleben*, i. 52, note 4.

was a holy garment still, and when the bride's three boys
wanted *obscena clamare*, as was the practice on such occasions,
they took off the *praetexta* beforehand.

Quintilian, *Declam.* 340 (the most striking passage I have
found) :

Illud sacrum praetextarum *quo infirmitatem pueritiae
sacram facimus et venerabilem* (cf. Culex, pp. 25–6).

This makes an excellent comment on the passages given
above from Horace and Persius.

Pliny, *Nat. Hist.* ix. 127 (writing of the various uses of
purple dye) :

Fasces huic securesque Romanae viam faciunt, *idemque pro
maiestate pueritiae est.* Distinguit ab equite curiam, dis advo-
catur placandis, omnemque vestem inluminat, in triumphali
miscetur auro. Quapropter excusata et purpurae sit insania.

In the last words *purpura* is the purple-fish, which Pliny
in his quaint manner thinks of as having a mystical or uncanny
power (cf. the *religio* in men's knees, above, p. 9). In the
case of the boy the purple symbolizes his *maiestas*[1]—a word
which entirely bears out the idea of boyhood which our other
extracts have suggested, though expressing it still more
strongly. Perhaps what was in Pliny's mind was that the
serious awfulness of the Roman priest and magistrate, representing the State, is also present in the free-born boy when
he wears the *praetexta*.

To these passages I will just add one from Columella ; it
does not mention the toga, but gives a good idea of the germ
from which the idea of its sacredness originally sprang. He
quotes a number of authors, Greek, Carthaginian, and Roman,
as agreeing that the duties of the household should be undertaken only by those who are chaste and continent ; and that
for certain things the service of boys and girls is necessary,
e. g. for going into the *penus*, the storehouse and seat of the
Penates, in order to bring out provisions.[2] One of the Roman
authors mentioned here by Columella is C. Matius, the friend

---

[1] *Maiestas*, a strong word to use of boyhood, may be explained as combining the ideas of potency, dignity, and inviolability.   [2] Columella, xii. 4.

of Cicero and Caesar, who wrote on domestic economy. Thus
we may be sure that the idea of the ceremonial purity of the
boy, apart from his ethical innocence, was not wholly extinct
at the end of the republican period.

I have another word to say about the Roman children,
and especially the boys, before I leave them. What I have
already said will have shown how valuable they were in religious
ceremonial both in the family and the State ; but there are
other facts which prove that they were far indeed removed
from that savage condition of childhood which has been so
much brought forward of late to throw some dim light on
features of primitive Greek usage. It would seem that where
there are elaborate initiatory rites at the age of puberty,
lasting perhaps for months, and symbolizing some notion
of a death and re-birth, there also the boy is up to that time
regarded as a nonentity, and of no value to the tribe. As
Miss Harrison puts it, ' till he has utterly put away childish
things, he cannot be a full member of the tribe, he may not
know the tribal secrets or dances, he cannot perform any of
the functions of the full-grown man '.[1] Now all this might
be said of the Roman boy, but in a very different sense. From
his infancy until he takes his *toga virilis*, which is the sole
sign of anything in the nature of an initiatory ceremony,
he is growing in knowledge as well as stature, and not only
in ·knowledge of useful arts, but of the practice of public
life. In the good old days of the republic, though incapable
of ' performing the functions of a grown man ', he is learning
all about them from his father. ' The older lads were constantly with their father, and by seeing what he did and sharing
in it, they learned their future duties. They assisted in the
service of the gods ; they listened as their father gave advice
to his clients ; and from him they learnt the traditions of
the family and the national heroes.' [2]

The fact is that among the Latins, and probably among
their kindred in Italy, the rites of initiation at puberty, if

[1] *Themis*, p. 19.
[2] Mr. Murison, in *Companion to Roman Studies*, ed. 2, p. 227. Cf. my
' *Rome* ', in the University Library series, pp. 61 ff.

there had ever been any such as those of which Miss Harrison finds traces in Greece, had disappeared under the influence of that wonderful family life for which it seems impossible to find an adequate explanation ; and under the same benign influence the importance and value of children, especially the boys, had steadily increased, to the lasting advantage of the race. Among the Pagan tribes of Borneo, where I have found such an instructive commentary on primitive Roman usage, I note the same phenomenon less fully developed. Messrs. Hose and McDougall tell us that they have no initiatory rites at puberty ; [1] and as we might expect after what has been said above, the boys help their parents in the house at an early age and onwards, and are in this way educated in social duties.

The value, nay the *maiestas*, of Roman boyhood, is most beautifully pictured in the *Aeneid* ; for just as Aeneas is surely meant to represent the ideal Roman in manhood, so is Ascanius meant to represent him in boyhood. And the study of their characters is all the more interesting, because they are not what has been happily called ' static ' characters, but develop and grow in grace as the action of the poem proceeds. I have elsewhere written of the gradual strengthening of the father's character ; [2] let me conclude these remarks with a brief sketch of the development of the son. It will confirm what I have said already, and help us to understand better what Juvenal meant by his four famous words, ' Maxima debetur puero reverentia '.

When we first meet with Ascanius at the destruction of Troy, he is a mere child ;

> Ecce autem complexa pedes in limine coniunx
> haerebat, parvumque patri tendebat Iulum ; [3]

big enough indeed to walk, for he trotted beside his father as they left Troy :

> Dextrae se parvus Iulus
> implicuit sequiturque patrem non passibus aequis. [4]

---

[1] *Pagan Tribes of Borneo*, i. 164 ; cf. ii. 24 and 185. It is now known that rites of initiation are entirely absent in many primitive races.

[2] *Rel. Exp.*, pp. 422 ff.   [3] *Aen.* ii. 674 ff.   [4] *Aen.* ii. 723,

And it is most important to notice that he is chosen as the object of one of those fire-omens of which the Romans were fond, and of which we have another example in vii. 71 ff. ; an omen which prompted Aeneas to call aloud upon Jupiter, who ' subito fragore Intonuit laevum '.[1]

In the first stages of the wanderings he is still a small boy, and made much of by women, first by Andromache on the coast of Epirus, and then by Dido. But he is growing : Andromache, seeing him, is reminded that her boy would be growing too :

> Sic oculos, sic ille manus, sic ora ferebat :
> et nunc aequali tecum pubesceret aevo.[2]

Dido might take him on her knee, but he was big enough to learn to ride, and delighted in his pony. Virgil loved this boy fondly, as this picture proves :

> Gaudet equo iamque hos cursu, iam praeterit illos,
> spumantemque dari pecora inter inertia votis
> optat aprum, aut fulvum descendere monte leonem.[3]

On the arrival in Sicily we note a great advancement in his career ; he takes part with his father, doubtless as *camillus*, in the rites of the *Parentalia* at the grave of his grandfather.[4] In the games that follow his part is to lead the boy-riders in the *ludus Troiae* ; and here we discover that he has a tutor or guardian, Epytides, *custos et comes*, and also a boy-friend Atys,

> Genus unde Atii duxere Latini,
> parvus Atys, pueroque puer dilectus Iulo.[5]

Almost directly after this he suddenly takes on himself a man's part ; at the first news of the burning of the ships by the women he gallops off to the spot, and calls on them to stay the fatal crime.[6]

> Heu miserae cives ! non hostem inimicaque castra
> Argivum, vestras spes uritis. en ego vester
> Ascanius !

---

[1] *Aen.* ii. 681 ff.   [2] *Aen.* iii. 491 ff.   [3] *Aen.* iv. 157 ff.
[4] *Aen.* v. 74 ff.   [5] *Aen.* v. 568 ff.   [6] *Aen.* v. 667.

D

His frightened *magistri* [1] could not stop him (669). Clearly Virgil meant to show that he was old enough to act for himself, and not only to take a rapid resolution, but to speak with force and point. But he is not yet more than a boy, and he may not accompany his father, it need hardly be said, on his descent into Hades ; in the sixth book Ascanius is not even mentioned.

When we come to the last six books, the books of war and bloodshed, we find Virgil in a difficulty about the boy. He could not make him grow up of a sudden, and probably did not wish to do so ; yet if he remained a boy, he could not take part in the fighting—that was what no Roman boy did as *praetextatus*.[2] Ascanius was in fact in danger at this point of falling out of the story altogether. Virgil ingeniously saves him from this fate by introducing him just where there is no fighting at the moment ; he is on the very edge of it, but (except for an instant) is kept out of it.

In the seventh and eighth books we see little of him ; he is once more the medium of an omen, and soon after this he hunts on horseback while his father is on his mission to Etruria, unwittingly killing a favourite stag and helping to kindle the war.[3] In Book VIII he is only mentioned as the subject of a prophecy of the foundation of Alba Longa.[4] But in the ninth book we see more of him than in any other. Critics have often puzzled their heads to explain why the immortal episode of Nisus and Euryalus is inserted in this book, without any very obvious connexion with the story.[5] I am rather inclined to think that one reason—certainly not the only one,—was to bring Ascanius once more to the reader's mind as a boy just verging on his first manhood.

He cannot join the two young heroes in their attempt to reach Aeneas at Pallanteum, though he would gladly do so. They, so to speak, have taken the manly toga and are ripe

[1] Servius explains *magistri* by *custodes*, of whom Epytides was perhaps chief. Another was Butes, ix. 649.

[2] See Marquardt, *Privatleben*, p. 131, note 7, for a possible exception.

[3] *Aen.* vii. 116 and 478 ff.   [4] *Aen.* viii. 48 ff. ; cf. i. 267 ff.

[5] See e. g. Heinze, *Virgil's epische Technik*, p. 438.

for service, though Euryalus is really still a boy and addressed
as such by Ascanius. But Aeneas's son can take his father's
place without going into the battle, and does so. He is at
the council to which Nisus and Euryalus ask admittance in
their excitement (*trepidos*), and is the first to bid them enter
and speak. In the scene that follows, one of the most beautiful
in all poetry, the old counsellor Aletes gives the hint to
Ascanius, ' with all his life before him ',[1] to join with the gods
and his father in promising never to forget the heroic pair ;
and the boy catches at it, and in a speech that is almost
inspired, rises above his own boyhood, addressing Nisus with
an appeal to the Penates and Vesta such as his father himself
might have made, and then turning to the younger with the
language of fond boyish affection, he promises to care for his
widowed mother as if she were his own, should death overtake
Euryalus.[2] All accompany the youths to the gates of the
camp :

> Nec non et pulcher Iulus,
> *ante annos animumque gerens curamque virilem,*
> multa patri mandata dabat portanda ; sed aurae
> omnia discerpunt et nubibus inrita donant.[3]

This of itself would be enough to show what Virgil thought
a noble Roman boy might do when suddenly called on to act
in the absence of his father. But there is still more : in the
attack on the camp that followed the deaths of the two youths,
Ascanius is for the moment drawn into the fight by the
taunts of Remulus, and kills him with an arrow. But this
must not go further ; Apollo intervenes for the destiny of
Rome in the world :

> Macte nova virtute, puer, sic itur ad astra,
> dis genite et geniture deos.[4]

These famous words are not supposed to be heard by the boy
himself, but mark Apollo's secret delight ; then he descends
in the form of the guardian Butes, and bids him stay his
hand. Ascanius is withdrawn almost entirely from our
sight during the fighting of the next two books.

[1] This is Mr. Mackail's happy translation of ' integer aevi ' (ix. 255).
[2] *Aen.* ix. 295 ff.   [3] *Aen.* ix. 310 ff.   [4] *Aen.* ix. 641

He reappears in the twelfth book, but not to shed blood ;
he is still a boy. He assists his father at the sacrifice that
should seal the treaty with Latinus ;[1] he assists him too
when wounded by the spear of Turnus.[2] And he is still a boy,
but on the very verge of his first manhood, when his father
bids him farewell before going to his last fight :[3]

> Ascanium fusis circum complectitur armis
> summaque per galeam delibans oscula fatur :
> ' disce, puer, virtutem ex me verumque laborem,
> fortunam ex aliis. Nunc te mea dextera bello
> defensum dabit et magna inter praemia ducet.
> Tu facito, *mox cum matura adoleverit aetas,*
> sis memor et te animo repetentem exempla tuorum
> et pater Aeneas et avunculus excitet Hector.'

In such clear strong touches Virgil has left an enduring
picture of the growth, physical and mental, of a noble Roman
boy, whose *toga praetexta* suggested not only the weakness
of boyhood and its need of protection by a holy garment,
but kept daily before the eyes and mind of its wearer that
duty to family and State which was the foundation of all that
was best in the Roman character.[4]

WAS THE FLAMINICA DIALIS PRIESTESS OF JUNO ?

WE always used to believe that as the Flamen Dialis was
the priest of Jupiter, so his wife was the priestess of Juno.
I do not know who was originally responsible for the inference,
which was natural enough in the days when we used to believe
that the Italian Jupiter and Juno were man and wife. I do
not find it in Ambrosch, who is perhaps the surest-footed of
the earlier writers on the Roman religious system. But soon
afterwards the assertion was made by Preller, though not quite
so definitely as by later writers ; the Flaminica, he says, was

---

[1] *Aen.* xii. 168.　　　[2] *Aen.* xii. 385.　　　[3] *Aen.* xii. 433 ff.
[4] The substance of this account of Ascanius was inserted in *The Death of Turnus,* pp. 87 ff.

' eine priesterliche Dienerin der Juno '. On this statement
Jordan in his edition added no comment (i. 122). Marquardt
in his book on the Roman religious constitution says plainly
that she was the priestess of Juno, and here again Wissowa,
who edited the second edition, made no remark. Roscher
in his tract on Juno and Hera went a little further ; the
Flaminica Dialis 'hatte den Opferdienst der Juno zu versehen '.
Hence the same statement has found its way into the article
on Juno in the *Mythological Lexicon*, and is repeated still
more emphatically in Aust's excellent article on Jupiter in
the same work. I do not wish to say a word that might
seem to be scoffing at this succession of distinguished scholars,
to whom I owe so much ; but I confess that this is not the
only occasion on which I have found German professors
following each other like sheep through a hole in a hedge,
without inquiring whether they were going the right way.

But I must own that I might myself never have been led
to test the value of these assertions, if they had not been used
to support a much more important inference, and one of the
utmost interest for the student of early Italian religious ideas.
Preller allowed himself to assert that the Flamen and his wife
appeared before the people as in some sense the living images
of the deities of light whom they served. Roscher took the
hint, and after his manner, carried it out to its logical consequences. He saw in the Flamen and his wife and the rules
of life which governed them, a means of getting at the ideas
which lay at the root of the cult of Jupiter and Juno. In his
view these are husband and wife, as well as gods presiding
over marriage (*Myth. Lex.*, s. v. ' Juno ', p. 590 ; cf. ' Juno
and Hera ', p. 63). Or, as the author of the article on Jupiter
puts it, ' die alterthümliche Institution des Flamen und der
Flaminica beweist auch, dass die paarweise Götterverehrung
in Italien eine ursprüngliche war '.

This inference is to the explorer at first sight as water in
a thirsty land. He knows that the cult is the only absolutely
safe guide in the study of old Italian religion ; he knows that
the question—a vital one—whether the oldest Romans

thought of any of their deities as married couples, cannot be decided by literary evidence alone.[1] But if it can be proved that the priest of Jupiter was the husband of the priestess of Juno, he feels at once that he has hold of something definite and trustworthy. The peculiar sanctity of the marriage tie in this case, together with the strange restrictions under which the pair was placed, and the undoubted antiquity of the priesthoods, taken in comparison with evidence from other races as to the relation of gods and priests, prepare him to accept the inference as one of great interest. If the water so much desired by the explorer should *not* turn out to be a mirage, we may fairly believe that Jupiter and Juno were really a married couple, and that the oldest Italians had got at least as far as this on their way towards polytheism. But alas, the water is no water, and the mirage has deceived many.

We know that the Flamen Dialis was attached to the cult of Jupiter ; but what is the evidence that the Flaminica was priestess of Juno ? All the writers I have quoted, and some others of less importance, cite but a single passage, and that from an author whose authority on such a subject is far from weighty, and who in this particular instance expresses himself doubtfully. Plutarch in the 86th Roman Question writes of the Flaminica as ἱερὰν τῆς Ἥρας εἶναι δοκοῦσαν. In this 86th quaestio Plutarch may have been drawing, directly or indirectly, on a gloss of Verrius Flaccus (cf. Festus, s. v. *Maius mensis*, Lindsay, p. 120) ; but there is nothing in Festus to bear out his remark about the Flaminica, and the word δοκοῦσαν shows pretty clearly that what he says of her is simply his own suggestion, which of itself must be quite worthless. Apart from this passage I can find no ancient authority for the idea that the Flaminica had anything to do with the cult of Juno.[2] The truth is rather to be found in such glimpses as we find in good Latin authorities, who were interested in the actual facts of the cult.

[1] See my *Religious Experience of the Roman People*, pp. 114 ff.
[2] Nor have I ever seen one quoted since 1895, when this paper was first published.

In a Verrian gloss on *flammeum* I find the following (Paulus, p. 82, Lindsay) : ' flammeo vestimento flaminica utebatur, id est Dialis uxor et *Iovis sacerdos*, cui telum fulminis eodem erat colore.' This definite statement, coming from a good authority, that the Flaminica was *Iovis sacerdos*, is borne out by a passage of Macrobius. On the *nundinae*, he says, quoting Granius Licinianus, she offered a ram to Jupiter in the *regia* ; [1] on the other hand, on the Kalends of every month from March to December, which were specially sacred to Juno, it is not the Flaminica who sacrifices to Juno, but the *regina sacrorum* (Macrob. i. 15. 19). And so far as I know, none of the rites in which the Flaminica was concerned have any reference to Juno. Thus it is impossible to hold any longer to the old fancy that the Flaminica was Juno's priestess, or to build on this assumption important conclusions about the early Italian conceptions of the relations of Jupiter and Juno.[2]

It is as well also to remember that by the old Roman methods of marriage, which brought the bride under the *manus* of her husband, she thereby took upon her the duty of attending to the *sacra* of her husband's family, and abandoned for good and all those of her own father's. Especially was this so when a pair were married by *confarreatio*, from which there was practically no possibility of release (Festus, p. 79, Lindsay), and which was necessary to the marriage of the Flamen and Flaminica Dialis. Thus the Flaminica after marriage must have been devoted to the cult of Jupiter, unless it can be shown that the Flamen had any part in the worship of Juno ; and for this there seems to be no evidence at all.[3]

---

[1] *Sat.* i. 16. 30.

[2] See e. g. Sir James Frazer's *Adonis, Attis, Osiris*, p. 410.

[3] In the second edition of his *Relig. und Kultus der Römer*, p. 191, Wissowa has at last declared his adhesion to the view that before the introduction of the Capitoline worship from Etruria there was no relation between Jupiter and Juno such as to suggest that they were a married pair.

THE ORIGIN OF THE LAR FAMILIARIS

THERE is a pretty story, connecting the great family of the Valerii with the origin of the *ludi saeculares,* which has come down to us through one of the name, Valerius Maximus. It has an interest as being one of the many family legends which contributed to the semi-fictitious history of Rome in which Romans themselves delighted ; and incidentally it serves my purpose at the present moment by giving us a glimpse of what I believe to be the *wrong* idea of the *lar familiaris.*

Valerius, or Valesius as the writer calls him, was a rich Roman who had a villa near Eretum in the Sabine country. He had three children, two boys and a girl, and was a happy man. But a terrible pestilence fell upon the land, and all three children fell desperately ill ; the doctors could do nothing for them. The father went to the hearth to get warm water for them, and there it occurred to him to fall on his knees and pray the *Lares familiares* to transfer the plague from the children to himself. Then a voice was heard telling him to take boat down the Tiber ' to Tarentum ' and fetch warm water for them from the altar of Dis Pater and Persephone. Sore puzzled, he obeyed the voice, and eventually discovered that underground altar at a place called Tarentum in the Roman Campus Martius, the scene of the first festival of the name (ludi Tarentini), and of the nightly celebrations of the *ludi saeculares* in the year 17 B. C.[1]

The story cannot well be much earlier than the second century B. C.; the origin of the Greek (or Graecized) form of the *ludi* dates from the year 249 B. C., and it is this form which we see in the Valerian legend.[2] And in the very first sentence of the story, in the phrase *lares familiares,* we have additional proof of its lateness. Valerius in fact is simply using the language of his own time, when the plural Lares

---

[1] Valerius Maximus, ii. 4, 5.

[2] See *Rel. Exp.,* p. 440. Dis Pater and Persephone are Greek deities.

had come to be used vaguely for the household deities in general, and when the specially defined range of function of each of them was fast being forgotten. We all know of course that Vesta was the spirit of the hearth-fire, from which position she was never deposed ; so too with the Penates, the spirits of the *penus* or storeroom. But towards the end of the republican period the new arrangements of the house in the city, and more or less also in the villa rustica, seem to have rubbed off the individualities of these spirits. The house came to be divided for practical purposes into two parts, the Roman part and the Greek part, and of these the Roman part was retained for reception rooms, while the household spirits, Vesta, Penates, and Lar or Lares, retired into the Greek part, the peristylium and its belongings, which was reserved for the family and its intimate friends.[1] It is easy to see how such a change as this would affect the domestic spirits. They were all reckoned together henceforward as Lares or Penates, or Lares *and* Penates.[2] When you prayed to them, it was convenient to address them all by one collective name, and this is exactly what Valesius did when he knelt before the hearth. As his immediate object was to get hot water, and as the hearth was at all times ideally the religious centre of the house, he naturally addressed the Lares there ; but what he meant by Lares was the whole group of household deities, which, by the way, he might just as well have called *di penates*. And it does not in the least follow from this that the genuine original Lar had anything whatever to do with the hearth-fire.

One of the many valuable contributions of Professor Wissowa to our knowledge of the real Roman religion is his convincing proof (so at least I regard it) that the Lar of the primitive Roman family was not an inhabitant of the

---

[1] See *Social Life at Rome in the Age of Cicero*, p. 242.

[2] Wissowa, *R. K.*, ed. 2, p. 168 and note 9. In this way Lares came to be used for the home—a use for which I need not quote proofs. How this came about may be seen, among other passages, by Cic. *de Legibus*, ii. 42 ' vexati nostri Lares familiares ', &c. (of what happened to his house during his exile).

house, much less the spirit of an ancestor, as has so often been maintained since the early days of our knowledge of animism. Preller, who wrote before the appearance of Tylor's *Primitive Culture*, and also before that of Fustel de Coulanges' famous book *La Cité antique*, came very near the truth, for he was not using the comparative method, which needs very careful handling in Roman matters. These two books seem to have overwhelmed Preller and the early Roman evidence, but the authorities they go upon are nearly all of them writers of the Empire. I may quote here a few lines of de Coulanges : [1]

Ces âmes humaines divinisées par la mort étaient ce que les Grecs appelaient des démons ou des héros. Les Latins leur donnaient le nom de Lares, Mânes, Génies. ' Nos ancêtres ont cru, dit Apulée, que les Mânes, lorsqu'ils étaient malfaisants, devaient être appelés larves, et ils les appelaient Lares lorsqu'ils étaient bienveillants et propices.' On lit ailleurs ; ' Génie et Lare, c'est le même être ; ainsi l'ont cru nos ancêtres.' Et dans Cicéron : ' Ceux que les Grecs nomment démons, nous les appelons Lares.' (This last is from Cicero's *Timaeus*, 11 ; and the other passage is from Censorinus, *de die natali*, 3.) [2]

Forty years after the appearance of these two remarkable books, when we had been thoroughly inured to the belief that the Lares were dead ancestors, two others of considerable note reiterated it with a much larger knowledge of things Roman—the excellent *Familienfeste* of E. Samter, and the no less valuable work of the Italian De Marchi on *la Religione della vita domestica*.[3] I am not writing an article for one of those vast encyclopaedic collections of facts and theories, or facts manipulated to suit theories, which are now in fashion in the learned world ; and I may leave these two writers to the student, merely noting that after studying them again and again I remain unconvinced either that the Lares were

---

[1] *La Cité antique*, p. 19.

[2] In spite of what Cicero here says in his translation of Plato, we shall soon find him helping us in the right direction. Apuleius and Censorinus are simply using the language of their own time.

[3] Samter, pp. 105 ff. ; De Marchi, i. 28 ff.

originally inhabitants of the house, or that they were the dead ancestors of families. When I wrote my *Roman Festivals* I was still to some extent in doubt, and allowed myself to write of the Lares that ' they *may* have been the spirits of dead ancestors duly buried '.[1] But since then the appearance of Wissowa's *Religion und Kultus*, and his controversy with Dr. Samter on this point,[2] has left no further doubt in my mind. I am only here intending to fill up what was a gap in Wissowa's original argument ; but I may note that he has made use of my fencing in the second edition of his great book.

Wissowa's main arguments are the following ;

1. There is no place for the Lares in the primitive house. Its centre point, the hearth, was occupied by Vesta ; the *penus* by the *di penates* ; and these two represent the essentials of human life, together with the spirit of the spring (whatever that was, it was certainly never known as a Lar).

2. There is no association of the Lares with the cult of the dead ; the spirits of the ancestors are *di parentes* (a sufficient appellation), and their cult, if it can be so called, went on at the grave of the family. Ingenious attempts have been made to prove that the dead were originally buried in the house ; but the archaeological evidence is entirely against this.[3] ' If the Lares worshipped in historical times at the hearth (as in the story of Valesius) were really the spirits of dead ancestors, then those ancestors must have been buried under the hearth ' ; and this neither Samter nor De Marchi is bold enough to maintain.

3. Our oldest sources of information connect the Lares not with the house but with the land. These are (*a*) the hymn of the Arval Brethren,[4] whose special duty it was to look after

---

[1] p. 337.   [2] *Archiv* for 1904, pp. 42 ff.

[3] The terremare of North Italy, from the inhabitants of which the Romans were almost certainly descended, had their cemeteries outside the settlement : Peet, *Stone and Bronze Ages in Italy*, pp. 364 ff. This principle held good with their descendants.

[4] Henzen, *Acta*, p. 26 ' Enos Lases iuvate neue luerve Marmor sins incurrere in pleores, satur fu fere Mars ', &c. The *semunes* are the only other

the religious protection of the ager Romanus : here they are associated with *Mars* in the invocation during the sacred dance—a deity whom no one has ever yet tried to connect with the cult of the dead ; (*b*) the Lares are the chief object of worship at the Compitalia, a very ancient festival of the farm ; and their seats were not in the house but at the *compita*, i. e. the spots of ground where in the parcelling out of agricultural allotments, divided by *semitae* or *viae*, one of these crossed another at right angles. At the point of crossing we learn that there was a kind of chapel with as many niches as there were allotments here touching each other, each niche containing the image of a Lar in historical times, and, as we may presume, the Lar himself in the spirit, before images came in.[1] What exactly was the relation of each Lar to the allotment he represented is not so easy to say ; but we shall not be far wrong if we guess that he was a protecting spirit, upon whom the family owning that bit of land could call for help, exactly as the Arval Brethren of the developed State called on the Lares as a whole, ' Enos Lases iuvate '. Thus we get a gap filled up in the category of spirits in whom the family was interested ; for if the Lares were spirits of the house and of deceased ancestors, where are we to look for individual guardians of the land belonging to that house, and once cultivated by those ancestors ? The interpretation of family deities cannot be rightly undertaken without a clear idea of the economy of the family (in which we include all members of the economic unit, free and unfree, all who worked on its land) ; and if we insist on bringing the Lares into the house in that early age of which I am speaking, we have no spirits left to perform the necessary duties of guardians of the family's land.

Yet the Lar, originally one for each family, did undoubtedly

spirits mentioned, but of these unluckily we know nothing certain (*Roman Festivals*, p. 136).

[1] See *Roman Festivals*, p. 279, where the references are given. Cf. Cic. *de Legibus*, ii. 19 ' lucos *in agris* habento et Larum sedes ' ; ib. 27 ' Nec ea quae a maioribus prodita est cum dominis tum famulis, posita *in fundo* villaeque conspectu religio Larium '.

find his way into the house : that is made certain by innumerable allusions in Latin authors of the literary age, among the earliest of which is a well-known prologue of Plautus, spoken by the Lar himself (*Aulularia*, 2 ff.) :

> Ego Lar sum familiaris ex hac familia
> unde exeuntem me aspexistis. hanc domum
> iam multos annos est quam possideo et colo
> patri auoque iam huiius qui nunc hic habet.

And this Lar seems to inhabit the *focus* ; for he goes on to say that the present owner's grandfather entrusted him with a treasure secretly, and buried it ' in medio foco '. A hundred other passages will confirm this evidence of the Lar in the house : and the question for us is, how did he come off the land and get a footing in the house ?

My own belief is that he came with the slaves of the *familia*. The *familia*, I need hardly say, was an economic unit settled on the land, including unfree members as well as free ; [1] and it is important to understand that the unfree, in early Roman days, would not be slaves drawn from distant regions, as in the later ages of the republic, but Italians, captives from neighbouring cities, or debtors condemned to slavery.

Had these slaves any share in the religious life of the economic unit ? Assuredly they had no part in the worship of Vesta and the Penates, or in the cult of the *di parentes* of the family. The hearth was the peculiar care of the daughters of the family, as the *penus* was of the materfamilias and the children ; and in what we know of the cult of Vesta and the Penates as embodied in the State worship of a later age, and in that of the ancestors at the Parentalia, there is no trace whatever of a share taken by any strange or unfree person. But it is not so with the cult of the Lar ; we know that slaves took part in the Compitalia, where the Lares of the *compita* were the object of worship, as well as in other festivals which were clearly descended from the religion of

[1] Cf. *Rel. Exp.*, p. 70. It is worth noting here that the adjective *familiaris* came to be used for a slave : Seneca, *Ep.* 47. 14 ' Dominum patrem familiae adpellaverunt, servos, quod etiam in mimis adhuc durat, familiares.' See other references in Marquardt, *Privatleben*, p. 172.

the farm, the Paganalia and probably the Saturnalia.   For
the Paganalia we have the evidence of Ovid :[1]

> Vilice, da requiem terrae, semente peracta :
>   da requiem terram qui coluere viris.

Tibullus is generally thought to be referring to this in a passage
on which I have commented elsewhere ;[2] in any case he is
speaking of one of the country festivals in which groups of
familiae joined :

> Tunc nitidus plenis confisus rusticus agris
>   ingeret ardenti grandia ligna foco,
> turbaque vernarum, saturi bona signa coloni,
>   ludet et ex virgis extruet ante casas.

And at the Saturnalia in December there can be little doubt
that the well-known custom by which slaves were treated
as being in a position of entire equality with their masters,
was descended from the religion of the farm.[3]

As to the Compitalia, which was a festival originally of
the rural folk owning allotments of land, under the old Latin
system of rectangular divisions separated by *semitae*, which
(as was said above) crossed each other at *compita*, there is
practically no doubt that unfree labourers took part in it.
Dionysius tells us that this was a privilege conceded to them
by King Servius Tullius in explicit terms, since the Lares
were pleased with the service rendered by these workers.[4]
He is giving a popular explanation of the Compitalia of the
city in his own time ; but that explanation itself has its
root in the old country practice, as may be seen if we compare
with it what Cato says in his treatise on agriculture about
the relations between the slaves and the Lar of the *compitum*.
In the fifth chapter Cato tells us that the steward (*vilicus*)
must not sacrifice 'in compito aut in foco' except at the
Compitalia ;[5] words which seem to me to mean that at the

---

[1] *Fasti*, i. 667. As the *vilicus* was usually himself a slave, there is little
doubt that slaves are here meant : cf. Wallon, *Hist. de l'Esclavage*, iii. 211.
[2] Tib. ii. 1. 21.   [3] *Roman Festivals*, p. 272.
[4] Dionys. iv. 14, *ad fin.*
[5] ' Rem divinam nisi Compitalibus in compito aut in foco ne faciat.'

Compitalia, and only then, he might sacrifice for the unfree
workers to the Lar at the *compitum* (*in compito*), or to the
Lar in the homestead (*in foco*), the ' aut ' suggesting that
where the Lar had already found his way to the house, there
the *vilicus* might follow him for the purpose of sacrificing.
So too his wife, the *vilica*, might and should adorn the *focus*
with a garland on *calends nones* and *ides*, and on the days
of the *lustratio agri* she might pray to the *Lar familiaris*
' pro copia ' ; representing the female slaves of the house,
she thus had a modest share in the worship of the Lar of that
economic unit (*familiaris*), but not in that of any other spirit
or deity.[1]   In all other rites of this unit the paterfamilias
alone had the right of sacrifice, except when he deputed this
duty to his steward.   As in the Anglo-Saxon manor the
duties of an absentee landlord were performed by the Gerêfa,
usually a *villanus* or serf, so in the frequent absence of the
Roman rural paterfamilias, becoming more constant as Rome
grew more powerful, his duties passed to the unfree *vilicus*.

It seems fairly clear, then, that the worship of the Lar at
the *compitum* or in the house came more and more distinctly
to be the right of the *vilicus* and his wife, and through them
of the slaves of the *familia*, perhaps even without the necessity
of obtaining leave or receiving orders to that effect from the
master (*dominus*) ; and thus the Lar came to be called
familiaris, which plainly indicated that in his cult the slaves
were included.   Now we know that it was the old custom
for the slaves to sit at the meals of the family on benches
(*subsellia*) ' below the salt ' ;[2] it was therefore quite natural
that they should see and worship there the only deity of the
farm to which they were closely attached.   What more
natural than that they should bring the Lar with them from
the *compitum* to the house, especially in the frequent absence
of the master ?

In other words, as the slaves came to be more and more

---

[1] *Cato*, 143 ' kalendis, idibus, nonis, festus dies cum erit, coronam in
focum indat, per eosdemque dies lari familiari pro copia supplicet.'

[2] Marquardt, *Privatleben der Römer*, p. 171.

distinctly recognized as members of the economic community
of which the house was the centre, the one deity whom they
had always worshipped on the land followed them into the
house. In this, as in a hundred other instances, a more accurate
knowledge of the details of Roman religion, once so much
decried and despised, will be found to have a most important
bearing on the social and economic history of the wonderful
Roman people.

FORTUNA PRIMIGENIA

It is quite in keeping with the tendencies of the time that
I am unlearning in my old age some of the settled conclusions
of my younger days. Lately I convinced myself that the
Romans did not see Jupiter in the triumphator, as I used
(more or less doubtfully) to think. Now I am going to retract
another opinion, expressed by me in print at least three times
over, viz. that Fortuna primigenia of Praeneste was the
firstborn daughter of Jupiter. I owe this change of mind
mainly to my friend Mr. Mackail, who interested himself in
the question after reading what I said of Fortuna in *Roman
Ideas of Deity*, Lect. III. I sent him Jordan's treatment of
the subject,[1] which has been meekly followed, German fashion,
by all who have touched on it since, including myself ; and
being quite free from traditional bias, he at once pointed out
that though Jordan rightly interprets the passages on which
alone we depend for our knowledge of the word *primigenius*,
he perversely arrives at a wrong conclusion as to the meaning
of the word itself. Jordan held that it means ' quicquid
primum genitum sit primaeque servet geniturae signum ',
and proceeds to argue that as a title of Fortuna, *primigenia*
must mean ' firstborn '. What brought him to this I will
presently explain ; but let us first look carefully into the
passages which he quotes from Varro to show us the meaning

---

[1] *Symbolae ad Historiam religionum Italicarum alterae :* Königsberg,
1885. See also my *Roman Festivals*, pp. 223 ff.

of this rare word. Varro seems to like it and to wish to save
it from becoming obsolete.

Varro, *R. R.* i. 40 ' Primigenia semina dedit natura,
reliqua invenit experientia coloni. Nam prima, quae sine
colono priusquam sata nata ; secunda, quae ex iis collecta
neque priusquam sata nata.' Nature has given the original
seeds ; the rest were discovered through experiments made
by the farmer. Virgil, in *Georg.* ii. 9 ff., seems to be following
this passage, in distinguishing wild plants from cultivated
ones by supposing that the former ' came of themselves ' ;
Varro's book was probably just out when Virgil was at work
on the *Georgics.* The same idea is found however in Lucretius,
ii. 1156 ff., and this famous passage, and indeed the idea
generally, seem to fall in with the favourite notion of a golden
age long past, about which Greek poets, Hesiod and Aratus, had
sung before him. Varro, of course, should have distinguished
more clearly between natural and artificial planting ; but it
is in any case plain that by *primigenius* he means ' natural ',
existing before man began to meddle with agriculture ; the
original seed of all, and therefore the most natural. Note
that the termination *genius* may here be rather active
than passive in meaning ; the original seed has a dynamic
principle within it. Certainly firstborn, in the ordinary sense
of that word, is not the meaning here. Nor is it the meaning
in Varro, *R. R.* ii. 2 init., where he says that this book is to
be devoted to the subject of stock, and that he will begin
with *primigenia pecuaria (res)*, i. e. the most ancient kind of
stock, for, as he goes on to explain, the sheep was the first
wild animal to be domesticated by man.[1]

Varro seems beyond doubt to have been fond of the word, for
in *de Ling. Lat.* vi. 36 and 37 he uses it four times in the course
of a few lines. He seems to have found the phrase *primigenia
verba* in a grammatical treatise by one Cosconius, who said
that of such ' original ' words there were in Latin about

---

[1] The word *primigenius* is here put into the mouth of Atticus, who takes
part in this dialogue ; and I incline to think that he is supposed to be
alluding lightly to the fondness of Varro for the word, exemplified in the
previous day's conversation (i. 40).

a thousand. From this Varro concludes that of words derived in various ways from these there were about fifty thousand. He then goes on to explain the sense he and his predecessor give to *primigenia verba*. ' Primigenia dicuntur verba ut lego, scribo, sto, sedeo, et cetera quae non sunt ab alio quo verbo, sed suas habent radices ', i. e. they are not grafted on or propagated from other words, but grow from their own root. ' Contra verba declinata sunt quae ab alio quo oriuntur, ut ab lego legis legit legam, et sic indidem hinc permulta.' He does not mean that *primigenia verba* are what we call roots, of which of course he knew nothing ; but what he believed to be the original forms, later modified by the ingenuity of man. As with the *primigenia semina*, the notion is unscientific, but we can understand clearly enough what he means. I may add here that the pedantic Emperor Claudius, when he doubled two of his legions (XV and XXII), gave to the original ones of these numbers the title *primigenia*.

Festus, representing Verrius Flaccus, had a gloss on *primigenius sulcus*, now hopelessly mutilated (Lindsay, p. 270), but Paulus preserved it in this form : ' Primigenius sulcus dicitur, qui in condenda nova urbe tauro et vacca designationis causa imprimitur.' [1] This must mean the first furrow made by the plough round the *urbs* that was to be, which furrow was to be enlarged afterwards into a foss. This, though not so useful as the other usages, tends to confirm what was said above of the active or dynamical meaning in the word ; seeds, words, foss, are all developed out of an original to which the epithet can be applied.

Lastly, Arnobius in the fourth century A. D. writes of *primigenios ortus* (ii. 61 and 70) ; but his text is uncertain and his meaning not very clear. I do not think that he throws any light on the meaning of the word ; and I know of no other occurrence of it in the least likely to help us. The meaning as Varro understood it is perfectly clear. If we apply it to Fortuna primigenia, the meaning of the title would seem to be, the Fortuna who (or whose cult) was the

[1] I do not know why Jordan, p. 6, says that this ' e Varronis libris fluxit '.

original of all the Fortunae afterwards suggested or devised by man's experience, the one that gave rise to the whole series. And it is not impossible that this may really have been the meaning. There were many Fortunae in Latium, among which she of Praeneste always retained her supremacy, or at any rate her claim to it. At Antium, where as at Praeneste she presided over something in the nature of an oracle, she had, so far as we know, no cult-titles. But since Jordan wrote his dissertation every one has followed him in translating (Fortuna) primigenia 'firstborn'. I must now explain why this was.

I feel fairly sure that Jordan would not have thus translated the word, if it had not been for the discovery, three years before he wrote, of an inscription from Praeneste which runs thus (Dessau, no. 3684 ; *C. I. L.* xiv. 2863) :

Orcevia Numeri nationu gratia *Fortuna Diovo fileia Primogenia* donom dedi.

Here Fortuna appears to our astonishment as the daughter of Jupiter, a position she claims nowhere else in Italy. There are indeed two later inscriptions at Praeneste in which she appears as *Iovis puero* (i. e. the daughter of Jupiter, by an old usage of the word *puer*, as it is generally understood) ; in one of these the word *primigeniae* follows, in the other it is absent. The Praenestines must have been most inconsistent people. The *older* inscription has the familiar *filia*, the later ones have the antique use of *puer*, meaning daughter. One man calls Fortuna *primigenia*, another does not. Still more astonishing is it that Cicero, who seems to have known something about the cults of Praeneste, declares that there actually was among them one of Jupiter puer, who was seated with Juno in the lap of his *mother* Fortuna, and was fondly worshipped by mothers (*de Div.* ii. 85 ; cf. *Roman Festivals*, p. 224). But this seems to be a case of confusion arising from a misinterpretation by Praenestines of statues and inscriptions, none of which were really primitive or of pure Italian origin. Even the oldest, the first quoted above, cannot well be earlier than the fourth century B. C., unless I am greatly mistaken,

E 2

and is probably still younger. It is hardly safe, where there is such confusion as this, to conclude that in Orcevia's dedication *primigenia* is to be taken with Diovo fileia, and understood in the sense of firstborn. Nor even if it must be so taken, as some will argue, should it be considered authoritative evidence of a common belief. Except this particular dedication, there is not only no ground for such a belief, but two special points which make against it.

1. It is certain that Fortuna is never mentioned or suggested by any Latin author as the daughter of Jupiter, and that no Latin deity was thought of, except after becoming Graecized, as the son or daughter of another deity. Praeneste was saturated with Greek influence, and Greek works of art were early introduced there ; after which, we know not how, some notion must have got abroad such as is expressed in these inscriptions. But it never spread beyond Praeneste ; when the great goddess of that city was taken to dwell in a Roman temple in 194 B. C., she went as Fortuna primigenia simply,[1] and no Roman ever suspected her of being Jupiter's child.

2. The word *primigenius* never means *firstborn* in Roman literature ; that I hope I have already proved. If it had ever had this meaning, why was it not retained ? why be content with the awkward ' natu maximus ' ? The make of the word does not suggest this meaning to us, nor did it suggest it to Romans. When Cicero in his *de Legibus*, ii. 28, is discussing the various forms of Fortuna, and their particular objects, he simply says of Fortuna primigenia that she is *a gignendo comes*—a new aspect of the deity indeed, and perhaps a fancy one, but with no relation whatever to firstborn children, or to the deity herself as any one's firstborn. Nor even at Praeneste (*Div.* ii. 85) does he know of *primigenia* in such a sense.

Without doubt Fortuna primigenia is the real title of the Praenestine deity, and until we have more explicit evidence we may let the Diovo fileia drop out. Without doubt too she

---

[1] The hopelessly mutilated gloss in Festus (p. 272, Lindsay), might have solved some difficulties, as Verrius knew Praeneste.

was *not* called *primigenia* because she was a firstborn daughter. What the title really meant was, so far as I can see, unknown to the Romans, like many other such cult-titles, e. g. Gradivus as used of Mars. We ourselves can only guess at it, and I confess that I have no definite conviction. I have already said that if we hold to the meaning of the word as Varro understood it, we should think of a Fortuna who claimed to be the original deity of the name, before man began to interfere with her, adding artificial titles such as *Fortuna huiusce diei, Fortuna muliebris, Fortuna virilis,* and so on ; as the first of the series, which gave rise to the rest, and therefore not standing in the relation of an eldest child to the younger ones.

On the other hand, there may be something in the ' *a gignendo comes* '[1] of Cicero. She may originally at Praeneste have been thought of as the equivalent of genius, the spiritual power which the Romans called Juno, attending on women as genius on men. This is what Mr. Mackail seems disposed to see in her. Or to use his own words in a letter to me, ' Fortuna primigenia would be the power which determines the whole movement of any life from its outset.' He refers to *Iliad* vi. 488–9, and *Od.* vii. 197–8 ; and there can be no objection in the case of a Praenestine cult in thus referring to Homer. This would fall in with the fact that at Praeneste and elsewhere Fortuna was specially worshipped by women, without doubt in special connexion with childbirth. Possibly she held at Praeneste the same place, or something like it, which Juno Lucina held at Rome and elsewhere ; for Lucina, I believe, is not known to have inhabited Praeneste, where Juno was of secondary importance. It is worth noting that there was a *Iunonarium,* i. e. a *cella* or shrine, in the great temple of Fortuna there.

I have not yet mentioned that the cult-title *primigenius* is found in a few inscriptions applied to Hercules, both at Rome and in the province of Baetica (*C. I. L.* ii. 1436, 1545, 2463 ; and Dessau, no. 3433), and that Jordan claims (op. cit., p. 8)

---

[1] If this reading be right, there is a lacuna immediately after *comes.*

that here too we are to understand it as firstborn (of Jupiter). I think that after what has been said above we may be sure that whatever it does mean in this instance, it certainly does not mean that.

PASSING UNDER THE YOKE

In ancient Italy, when an army surrendered in the field, there were three alternatives before the victors for dealing with the vanquished. First, they might put them to death ; there was nothing to prevent this but the feeling and tradition among Italian peoples in historical times against unnecessary bloodshed.[1] Secondly, they might keep them as prisoners of war, and sell them as slaves ; but in early times this was practically out of the question, partly owing to the difficulty of feeding and guarding them before they were sold, and partly because the machinery of sale, the slave-agents at hand and the slave-markets in the cities, had not then been invented. Thirdly, they might let their captives go free, with or without imposing conditions on them to be ratified by their State. This was really the simplest and easiest plan, and was adopted in the few cases recorded by Livy in which whole armies were captured.[2] But before the vanquished were dismissed, they were made to go through the ceremony of ' passing under the yoke ' (*sub iugum missi*), which Livy, when he first mentions it, explains as a kind of dramatized form of degradation. Two spears were fixed upright in the ground, and a third was fastened horizontally by each end to the tops of them ; under this extemporized arch the conquered army had to pass, disarmed, and apparently wearing nothing but an under-garment, probably the subligaculum, in later times the dress rather of slaves than of soldiers or citizens. Livy's language is explicit : ' ut exprimatur

---

[1] See Phillipson, *International Law and Custom of Ancient Greece and Rome*, ii. 253 ff. Liv. ix. 3 shows the feeling against bloodshed.

[2] Liv. iii. 28 ; ix. 6 ; x. 36.

confessio subactam domitamque esse gentem.' In historical times this was certainly the commonly received view, and it is still possible that it may be the true explanation. But there is real reason to believe that the passage under the yoke had originally another object and meaning. In the second edition of his *Golden Bough*, iii. 406, Sir James Frazer, after collecting a number of practices in which human beings or animals are passed through a space limited in some way on either side, suggested in a footnote that the passage under the yoke might have been a rite of purification, ' destined to strip the foe of his malignant and hostile powers before dismissing him to his home '. In the third edition of his work, vii. 194, he took up this suggestion and worked it out more fully in his text, bringing to bear on the problem of the yoke, (1) the *tigillum sororium*, and (2) the *porta triumphalis*. It happened that I was doing the very same thing at the same time in the *Classical Review* for March 1913. What I wrote then I reproduce now, with full acknowledgement to my friend Frazer of his original suggestion in his second edition.[1]

On the steep slope of the Carinae, just above the hollow where the Coliseum now stands, there was a small street called the vicus Cuprius ; and where it was crossed by another (*ad compitum Acili*), a beam (*tigillum*) stretched from one side of the street to the other, called the *tigillum sororium*. Festus, p. 380 (Lindsay), tells us that this had originally rested upon two other beams, like the spear under which the captured army passed ; and that it was set up in this manner by the father of Horatius, who in the legend had murdered his sister, after his acquittal by the people, and after certain sacrifices to Janus Curiatius and Juno Sororia, whose altars remained there to the latest age of Roman history.[2] But what was the

---

[1] In March 1914 I received from Professor Zachariae, of Halle a. d. Saale, an article written by him in the Berlin *Zeitschrift des Vereins für Volkskunde*, entitled ' Das Kaudinische Joch '. He too had reached the same kind of conclusion, unknown to me or to Sir James Frazer, taking a hint, as I had done, from the second edition of the *Golden Bough*.

[2] The best account of the position is in Hülsen-Jordan, *Röm. Topographie*, iii. 322 ff., where also the texts relating to the *tigillum* are quoted in full

object of this beam ? Livy, Festus, and Dionysius all agree
that Horatius was made to pass under it ' velut sub iugum
missus ', as an *expiatio* for the crime he had committed.
His acquittal by the people was not enough ; he was not,
by that method of procedure, ' liberatus omni noxia sceleris '
(Festus). Something had yet to be done in order to make
him fit to mingle with his fellow citizens, and what was done
was of a religious character. He is represented as having
his head covered, which is a sure sign of this, even if we
cannot trust the tradition about the two altars below the beam.
He passed under the beam, as under the yoke, and was then
clear of all *scelus* with the approval of the augurs.

I have used the Latin word *scelus*, not wishing to commit
myself to the notion that the thing thus got rid of was *moral*
guilt ; had it been that, our modern minds would naturally
suppose that it was wiped away by the acquittal. Far from
it ; the sister's blood had been shed, and no lay court could
possibly get rid of that stain. Horatius was undoubtedly
sacer, i. e. taboo, in an infectious condition, dangerous to
society. But in this peculiar form of passage under an arch
or *iugum*, the religious authorities were able to apply a method
of disinfection,[1] which in the language of a later age is naturally
spoken of as *expiatio* or purification. What the primitive
Romans may have believed that it effected can only be guessed
by one who studies carefully the evidence collected in the
Golden Bough.[2]

The second object in Rome which may be compared to the
iugum was the *porta triumphalis*. A victorious army,
before entering the city, had to pass under an arch or gateway

(Liv. i. 26 ; Festus (p. 380, Lindsay) ; Dionys. iii. 22. 7). For the two
altars below the beam see *Auct. de viris illustribus*, iii. 4. It is singular that
the beam itself seems to have been an object of worship ; the *Fasti Arvales*
have a note on October 1 : ' tigillo sororio ad compitum Acili ', Henzen,
Acta Fratr. Arv., p. ccxxxviii. It is easy to get out of one's depth in specula-
ting on these worships and their connexion with the *gens Horatia*, as
Pais does, *Storia di Roma*, i. 298 ff. My own opinion on these puzzling
points is expressed in my *Roman Festivals*, pp. 237 ff.

[1] See *Rel. Exp.*, p. 28.

[2] It will be found in *Balder the Beautiful*, ii. 169.

which was called by this name. Its exact position we do not know for certain, but it is quite clear from a passage in Josephus (*Bell. Iud.* vii. 5. 4) that it was in the Campus Martius, i. e. that it was an archway standing by itself outside the walls, and it is probable that it was close to the famous ara Martis, but separated from it by the stream called Petronia amnis, which had a religious importance of its own.[1] We may suppose that in ancient times the army was lustrated *in campo*, near the ara Martis, and that it then crossed the sacred stream and passed under the *porta triumphalis*. What this *porta* was like we do not know ; neither description nor representation of it survives. I may perhaps conjecture that the oldest surviving triumphal arch, that of Augustus at Rimini, was not wholly unlike it. When triumphal arches were first introduced as memorials of some military achievement, it is reasonable to suppose that they took the form of the old *porta triumphalis* familiar to Roman soldiers, and that a more elaborate style of ornamentation was only developed in course of time.[2] If we look at the arch at Rimini, of which there is a cut handy in the *Dictionary of Antiquities*, s. v. *arcus triumphalis*, we shall notice that the most striking part of it consists of two upright Corinthian pillars with an architrave laid across them ; within this is an arch proper built on the usual plan. I hope I am not too fanciful in suggesting that we may have here a reminiscence of the horizontal beam or spear resting on two upright ones. This was in fact the very oldest form of gateway, as one sees in the Lion gate

[1] See Hülsen-Jordan, op. cit., iii. 494 and references ; also Domaszewski, in *Abhandlungen zur röm. Religion*, pp. 222 ff. For purification water running from a spring was necessary ; Festus (p. 296, Lindsay) ; Liv. i. 45-6.

[2] Nearly all forms of Roman art are now thought to be traceable to Greek originals, and without doubt the ornamentations of the triumphal arches which have survived are Hellenistic ; but such a thing as a triumphal arch is not known in Hellas, and I believe that the idea is far more likely to be Roman. According to Servius on *Aen.* xi. 6, the original object of the arch was to supply an elevated position for trophies, which certainly formed a part of the ornamentations on the arches of later date. The question is discussed in a sensible way, though without anthropological knowledge, in Courbaud's *Le Bas-relief romain*, p. 370 ff.

at Mycenae, and thus a course of development may be traced from very primitive beginnings, to the most elaborately decorated archways of the Roman Emperors.

Now is there any common idea in the use of these three arches (or whatever we choose to call them), the *iugum*, the *tigillum*, and the *porta triumphalis* ? Let us compare the objects in the three cases, so far as they can be made out.

The object is clearest in the case of Horatius. He had to be cleansed from something dangerous and infectious, and the consummation of this cleansing is signified by his passage under an object which formed a limit between the region of the *sacrum* and that of the *profanum* ; he could not mingle with his fellow citizens if he were *sacer*, but the sacrifices and the passage under the *tigillum* effectually rid him of this burden. It was what has been well called a ' rite de passage ', and may safely be compared with those in which a human being passes through some divided object such as a cleft tree, or between two posts, in order to get rid of some disease or other trouble.[1]

The passage through the *porta triumphalis* may well have had the same meaning. The army was guilty of bloodshed, like Horatius, and had been moving about in places where there were strange beings, human and spiritual, with whom it would be unsafe to come in contact ; unsafe not only for the soldiers themselves, but for the citizens with whom they might mingle on their return. Even if we cannot exactly say that the returning host was *sacer*, we know that it needed lustration, and that it underwent this process immediately before passing through the *porta* ; which was exactly what happened to Horatius, according to the story.[2]

Lastly, let us return to the *iugum* of the three spears. I think we are now justified in assuming that there was a religious

---

[1] See Van Gennep, *Rites de passage*, ch. ii, pp. 19 ff. ; Frazer, *Golden Bough*, ed. 3 (*Balder the Beautiful*), ii. 169 ff. It is absolutely necessary to read these pages carefully in order to be convinced of the meaning of rites of this kind in different parts of the world.

[2] The same fear of the evil influence of an enemy is seen in the belief that spoils taken from him should be destroyed by fire, which has been elucidated by M. S. Reinach in his *Cultes, Mythes et Religions*, iii. 233 ff. I have discussed this in *The Death of Turnus*, p. 155 (*Aen.* xii. 938 ff.).

or magical element in this degrading ceremony. The many analogous examples collected in the *Golden Bough* strongly suggest it, and so also does the *tigillum sororium*, which plainly reminded the Romans, as we saw, of the *iugum*. And the passage through the *porta triumphalis*, though it is the passage of a victorious and not a surrendered army, had beyond doubt a religious or magical meaning, which should suggest an analogous one in the case of the *iugum*. Still there is a difficulty. What can have been the object of subjecting the captives to the same kind of ceremony as the murderer, or the victorious host ? Sir James Frazer thinks that it was to deprive them of their malignant and hostile powers before sending them home. I do not see that we can find a better explanation, though I might put it somewhat differently. They had to be brought out of one status into another ; they must not be any longer the same beings they were before the surrender ; just as in historical times the *dediticius* passed out of his former status into a new one, and became absorbed in the body politic of the conqueror, to be henceforward harmless.

NOTE ON PRIVATELY DEDICATED ROMAN ALTARS

I HAVE recently been asked a question which seems simple enough, yet is not after all very easy to answer. If a Roman in the provinces of the Empire wished to erect an altar, in fulfilment as a rule of a vow, how did he set about it ? How could he make it sacred, secure it against sacrilege ? Man does not erect altars to his gods unless he can protect them from harm ; how is this protection procured for the innumerable *ex votos* of the Roman provinces ?

It may be worth while to put together such evidence as I can collect on the subject of the dedication of altars whether at Rome or in the provinces ; in this way we may be able to answer, more or less directly, the question raised above.

Within the limits of the *ager Romanus* the transfer of an object to the gods, e. g. of a temple, altar, or *sacellum* of some kind, might be either public or private according as it was made over by the State under public law, or by an individual or a corporation *privati iuris*. If it were the act of the State, the process of dedication was completed by the *consecratio* of the *pontifices*, and the object became *sacrum*, i. e. it was taken out of the region of ordinary human usage, and became the property of the god to whom it was dedicated.[1] As usual in such solemn acts, the priest dictated the formula while the magistrate repeated it after him,[2] and the result, if the object were a temple, was a *lex*, or written covenant destined to guarantee the sanctity of the site and building for all time. How far the Roman pontifical authority and law spread beyond the Roman territory into Italy we do not know for certain ; in any case this could only happen if the Italian communities adopted it.

But *municipia* and *coloniae*, whether in Italy or the provinces, had their own religious authorities, pontifices and augurs,[3] and when the community wished to erect a temple or altar, these no doubt provided the necessary formulae. Did they also assist the private individual or corporation in a dedication, and thereby give it sanctity and security ? I find no

---

[1] Aelius Gallus ap. Festum (p. 424, Lindsay) ' Gallus Aelius ait sacrum esse, quocunque modo atque instituto civitatis consecratum sit, sive aedis, sive ara, sive signum, sive locus, sive pecunia, sive quid aliud quod dis dedicatum atque consecratum sit.' Gaius, ii. 4 ' sacrae sunt (res) quae dis superis consecratae sunt : religiosae quae Dis Manibus relictae sunt ' : sec. 5, though mutilated, seems to state that in order to be *sacrum* an object must be dedicated ' auctoritate populi Romani '. Cf. Liv. ix. 46. 7.

[2] Wissowa, *R. K.*, pp. 394 ff. ; Marquardt, pp. 145 ff., 270 ff.

[3] The plainest evidence is that of the Lex Coloniae Genetivae (*C. I. L.* ii. 5439, sec. 62 ; Dessau, *Inscr. Lat. Selectae*, ii. 1, p. 502). Toutain, *Cultes païens dans l' Emp. rom.* i. 277 ff., tells us that pontifices and augurs are not found in inscriptions of the three Gauls, Britain, Germany, and Rhaetia ; but in those provinces Roman towns were comparatively few. Where *municipia* and *coloniae* are in plenty, there is also plenty of evidence of the existence of these priesthoods.

proof of this in the provinces, but we may here admit the
evidence of certain inscriptions at Ostia, which was an ancient
colony and had its own priests.[1] Among these priests the chief
was the *pontifex Volcani et aedium sacrarum*, who was in charge
of all the temples of the colony, and whose permission seems
to have been necessary before statues could be erected in
sacred precincts or gifts of importance dedicated in sanc-
tuaries.[2] It is not unlikely that this priest superintended the
process of other private dedications.

But the legal result of these dedications, even when sanctioned by the local priesthood, was not as complete as it was
within Roman territory. The Roman lawyers assure us that
the objects dedicated could not become *sacra* in the proper
sense of that word, but were held to be *religiosa* only, like
burial-places and spots struck by lightning;[3] that is to say,
they were not made over to a deity as his property, but were
objects of reverence and awe without the legal protection
gained by *consecratio*. The word *sacrum* is of course found
in votive inscriptions all over the Empire, but when so used
it is not a term of Roman religious law.

[1] See Ruggiero, *Diz. Epigr.*, i, s.v. *aedes* and *ara*, who says that private
dedications did not need the help of a priest, but gives evidence of an
occasional instance of such help : e. g. *C. I. L.* vi. 746 ' ara posita asstante
sacerdote Secreusina Secundo ut voverant ' ; p. 412 ' aram posuit per
C. Fab. Germanum sacerd.' Cf. De Marchi, *La Religione nella vita domestica*,
i. 290. In the Roman *ius divinum* the pontifices and augurs seem to have
been called in to assist private individuals or families in religious details :
Cicero in his imaginary code (*Legg.* ii. 8. 20) says ' quoque haec privatim
et publice modo rituque fiant, discunto ignari a publicis sacerdotibus '.
Commenting on this in sec. 47, he reckons *vota* among the matters of private
religion over which the *pontifices* may have superintendence, together with
feriae, sepulcra, et si quid eiusmodi est. Cf. what Cic. says of the great
P. M. Coruncanius and of P. Crassus in *de Orat.* iii. 134 ' ut ad eos de omnibus
divinis et humanis rebus referretur.' *Rel. Exp.*, p. 281. From this we may
infer that the same held good of the priests in *municipia* and *coloniae* in
Italy and the provinces.

[2] For Ostia see Miss Lily Taylor's monograph on the *Cults of Ostia* :
Bryn Mawr monographs, xi. 15 ff.

[3] Festus, *l. c.* ; Marcianus, *Dig.* i. 8. 6, sec. 3 ' si quis privatim sibi
sacrum constituerit, sacrum non est sed profanum.' Gaius, ii. 7, seems to
imply that in this case the object was not even technically *religiosum*, but
was considered to be *pro religioso*.

Outside Roman towns, or within them on ground owned by an individual (*in privato solo*[1]), it was common enough for the private person to set up altars, temporary or permanent, or to dedicate any other object,[2] on land to which he had some kind of a legal title. When Cicero wished to erect a shrine (*fanum*) to his daughter Tullia in a public place, he had to purchase land to suit his purpose.[3] There is a curious case from older Roman history, of the erection of an altar within a sacellum *in a private house*, in order to be the rival of an older cult of a public character.[4] In the fifth *Eclogue* of Virgil we find shepherds erecting altars, apparently meant to be permanent, to Apollo and Daphnis.[5] There is another example in a poem of Martial ; the *vilicus* of an estate has erected altars to Jupiter and Silvanus, which the owner entrusts to a friend during his absence, with a request that he will perform all the necessary rites.[6] Such cases as this last illustrate the usual method of instituting private cults in Italy and the provinces.

Dedications by corporate associations, of a private character, of which there are very large numbers, stood on the same legal footing as those made by private individuals ; the objects dedicated did not become technically *sacra*.[7]

---

[1] It will be remembered that Augustus built his great temple of Apollo on the Palatine ' in solo privato ' ; the political meaning of this is well stated by J. B. Carter, *Religion of Numa*, p. 166.

[2] Great numbers of these were merely votive tablets or inscriptions, but many were *aedes* or *aediculae*, as well as *arae*.

[3] See my *Religious Experience of the Romans*, p. 385, and the letters quoted in notes 23 and 24.

[4] Liv. x. 23. The older cult was that of Pudicitia *patricia* in the Forum *boarium* ; the new one was to Pudicitia *plebeia* : ' in vico Longo, ubi habitabat, ex parte aedium quod satis esset loci modico sacello exclusit aramque ibi posuit.'

[5] *Ecl.* v. 65 ff. Note the expression *solennia vota*.

[6] Mart. x. 92 :

> Commendo pinus ilicesque Faunorum
> et semidocta vilici manu structas
> Tonantis aras horridique Silvani.

[7] Waltzing, *Les Corporations professionnelles chez les Romains*, ii. 434 ff. ; iv. 457 ff. ; De Marchi, *La Religione gentilizia* (*Il Culto privato*, pt. ii), pp. 134 ff.

They were protected from abuse simply by the fact that they were Roman, if they were in the provinces ; if in Italy, by their religious character. We may perhaps assume that though they were not the property of the deity *iure divino*, they were so regarded by the vulgar, and were truly *religiosa*, i. e. objects of reverence and awe. This was certainly the case with all those that were dedicated by soldiers under the licence, and when possible the supervision, of the Caesar or his representative.[1] Thus we may roughly say that there was little or no question of the mutilation or destruction of these objects throughout the Empire, since they were always Roman, and very often Roman in a military sense.

THE PONTIFICES AND THE FERIAE: THE LAW OF REST-DAYS

THE subject of Roman rest-days is an interesting one, for it helps us to understand not only the religious feeling of the Romans in regard to times and seasons, and the policy of the *pontifices* in dealing with that feeling, but incidentally throws sidelights on the life and work of the Roman farmer. It has been touched upon by Bouché-Leclercq in his book *Les Pontifes*, pp. 119 ff., and recently by Dr. Hutton Webster in his *Rest-days*, pp. 94 ff. and 121 ff. ; but there is room for further discussion of a subject still obscure in some points.

We all know the lines in the first *Georgic* (268 ff.) in which Virgil touches on the rule that *feriae* were rest-days, and on some of the exceptions .to that rule which were sanctioned by the *pontifices*.

> Quippe etiam festis quaedam exercere diebus
> fas et iura sinunt ; rivos deducere nulla
> religio vetuit, segeti praetendere saepem,
> insidias avibus moliri, incendere vepres,
> balantumque gregem fluvio mersare salubri.
> saepe oleo tardi costas agitator aselli
> vilibus aut onerat pomis, lapidemque revertens
> incusum aut atrae massam picis urbe reportat.

[1] See Domaszewski, *Religion des römischen Heeres*, p. 110.

I must make one note on this passage before going on. By
the words ' fas et iura ' Virgil undoubtedly means the action
of the *pontifices* in making or relaxing rules. It has been usual,
from Servius downwards, to explain the two words as meaning
religious and civil law respectively ; ' divina humanaque
iura ', as Servius puts it. But it is certain that the *pontifices*
alone had cognisance of these rules, and their *ius pontificium*
was a part of the *ius divinum* which governed all religious
matters. Virgil, who is not using technical language, adopts
the term *fas*, then just coming to be used in this sense, to
mean this pontifical law, and adds *iura* to make it more
intelligible to his readers.[1]

' Dies festi ', as Virgil calls them, or more strictly Feriae,[2]
were days made over to the gods, just as *templa* were the
definite spots of ground in which those gods had consented
to take up their abode. For this reason both days and places
were under the control of the *pontifices*, not of the civil
magistrates ; and the outcome of this priestly control was
known as *ius divinum* ('fas et iura', as Virgil calls it), or as
ius pontificium in reference to its regulators. I am not here
specially concerned with the primitive history and origins
of rest-days, for which I can now refer the reader to Professor
Webster's book just mentioned, and to his own and other
articles on Sabbath (primitive) in Hastings's *Encyclopaedia
of Religion and Ethics.* When Roman history begins, the
feriae and the *pontifices* are already there ; and any attempt
to trace them farther back must, in the present state of our
knowledge, be pure speculation. We may, however, be fairly
sure that whatever be the primitive origin of the institution
of fixed rest-days, the idea in the minds of the early Romans
was that these days had become the property of deities, and
that man honoured these deities by abstaining from work on

[1] On this meaning of *fas*, see Appendix IV to my *Religious Experience
of the Romans.*

[2] *Dies festi* is the wider and less technical expression, and might include
nundinae (markets) and *ludi.* *Feriae* in historical times was limited to days
dedicated to a deity (Serv. *Georg.* i. 268 ; Wissowa, *Rel. und Kult.*, ed. 2,
pp. 432 n. and 441 n.).

those days, just as he honoured them with sacrifices in their temples. We may indeed find an indication here and there that there were much older ideas at the root of the rules as the later Romans knew them, of which a word will be said later on ; at present I am dealing with the subject as it appeared to the Roman farmer in the two centuries from Cato to Columella.

Our earliest information about what might be done on *feriae* comes from Cato (*de Agric.* ii. 4, Keil). The owner of the estate is supposed to be telling his bailiff what he might or ought to have done, during his master's absence, better and more carefully than he has done. There were many things, for example, which he might have done in bad weather ; and then he goes on ' per ferias potuisse fossas veteres tergeri, viam publicam muniri, vepres recidi, hortum fodiri, pratum purgari, virgas vinciri, spinas runcari, expinsi far, munditias fieri '. This is characteristic of Cato, and doubtless of the Roman farmer generally in that age of money-making. No time was to be lost on the farm ; the slaves were not to be idle even on *feriae*, for there was plenty that they might do without transgressing the divine law. The examples of such work are interesting ; most of them are concerned with cleaning out and cleaning up, as distinct from starting new work. One or two are interesting for other reasons. The repairing of a public road seems to imply hard work, but if it was work made necessary by a proximity of the estate to a *via publica*, repairable by the neighbouring owners,[1] the bailiff should have been glad to get it done on days when important work on the farm was not possible. *Expinsi far* refers, I think, to the preparation of salt-cake for the daily domestic sacrifice ; if so, it was natural enough that the pounding should be done on

---

[1] This method of repairing roads is alluded to by Siculus Flaccus, *de conditionibus agrorum* (Gromatici, p. 146): ' Vicinales viae de publicis quae devertuntur in agros, et saepe ipsae ad alteras publicas perveniunt, aliter muniuntur, per pagos, id est per magistros pagorum, qui operas (slaves) a possessoribus ad eas tuendas exigere soliti sunt. Aut, ut comperimus, uni cuique possessori per singulos agros certa spatia adsignantur, quae suis impensis tueantur.'

days devoted to the gods. *Far*, in Cato's time, would hardly be used for ordinary bread ; in religious rites it survived, and was pounded in a mortar instead of being ground in a mill (*Roman Festivals*, p. 149). One other rule we learn from Cato which may be mentioned here ; it occurs in ch. 138. Oxen might be yoked on *feriae* for draught purposes, but mules, horses, and asses have no *feriae* ' nisi si in familia sunt '. What these last words mean I am not sure ; Professor Webster translates (p. 95), ' For mules, horses and asses there are no other holidays than those of the family '. The words would more naturally mean that the animals had no holidays unless they belonged to the *familia* in some special sense, e. g. lived in the homestead. Cato is probably using *familia* in its true sense, of the economic unit settled on the land. Of this unit the animals in question were certainly members ; but what animals were those which were not in the *familia* ? Perhaps an explanation may be found in the distinction drawn by Varro (*R. R.* ii. 6. 4) between the *villatica pastio* and the *pastio agrestis* ; the latter being far away, while the former was at or near the homestead.

We hear nothing more of the law of *feriae* until we come to the great Pont. Max. Mucius Scaevola, of whom Cicero has much to tell us in the *Brutus* : a man of fine character and liberal ideas of law. Macrobius tells us (i. 16. 10–12) that this man, when asked ' quid feriis agi liceret ', answered succinctly ' quod praetermissum noceret '. *Feriae* were made for man, not man for *feriae* ; if an ox fell into a drain or reservoir (*specus*), no one need scruple to pull it out on a *dies festus*. But at the same time he insisted that the old rule of sacred law still held good, that if a man knowingly broke the peace of the *feriae*, no *piaculum* could absolve him ; he became *impius*. Another Pont. Max., called simply Umbro by Macrobius, laid it down that no man was polluted who did any work ' ad deos pertinens or sacrorum causa ' (such perhaps as the preparation of the salt-cake), or anything ' ad urgentem vitae utilitatem respiciens '—an interpretation even wider than that of Scaevola. It is pretty clear that by this time the sting had been taken out of the old rigid rules ; the ancient scruples and superstitions were losing strength. Half a century later it is interesting to find that Cicero, when drawing up his imaginary code of religious law (which, by the way, he does not call *fas*), gives the law of *feriae* for the first time a quasi-moral meaning. 'Let contentions of every kind cease among the free members of a community, and let slaves enjoy these days as holidays ; for this purpose they were ordained at special times.'[1]

The policy of Augustus in matters of religion was to restore as far as possible the old feeling of duty to the gods ; and it may be that there was a revival of interest in the rules of pontifical law, which is perhaps shown in Virgil's lines. It is remarkable that far the larger part of our knowledge both of rules and exceptions comes from the agricultural writer Columella, who, though a Spaniard by birth, was a practical farmer in Italy in the generation next after Augustus, and wrote his book in old age under Nero.[2]

I will now examine what he and Virgil have to tell us about these rules. ' Pontifices negant segetem feriis saepiri debere ', says Columella ; but here Virgil differs. On this Keightley remarked, and probably with justice, that the poet must have been thinking of the mending of a fence, while the *pontifices* meant that you must not begin a new one. For Servius (Interpol) commenting on *G*. i. 272, says that any work was lawful which was not a beginning, ' quicquid fieri sine institutione novi operis potest '.[3] This is an interesting point, and may help to explain other rules. A moment's thought will show how important in a religious sense the Romans believed the beginning of any serious undertaking to be : the beginning of a literary work, an oration, a war, the foundation of a city, are among the examples that instantly occur to us ; and the

---

[1] Cic. *de Legibus*, ii. 8. 18, and 12. 29 ; *de Div*. i. 45. 102. Cf. Webster, *Rest-days*, p. 97.

[2] Schanz, *Gesch. der Röm. Lit.* (ed. 3), pt. ii. 2, p. 501. The passage of Columella is bk. ii. 22.

[3] Verrius Flaccus (*ap. Macr.* i. 15. 21) cynically observed that on this principle *feriae* were better suited for marriages of widows than of maids !

intense desire for good omens at the beginning of a journey
or a battle, points in the same direction. The association of
Janus with beginnings, though it may not have been primitive, will also help us here. We all know the emotion we
experience in taking a decisive step—in crossing a Rubicon,
as Dr. Marett has lately put it ; when once the work is begun,
the resumption of it never again suggests quite the same
feeling. In the second chapter of Dr. Webster's *Rest-days*, on
' tabooed days at critical periods ', plenty of evidence will
be found of the ' religio ' attaching to newness or beginnings
in many parts of the world at the present day.[1] Especially,
as we might expect, it is the important matters of food, war,
and so on, most deeply affecting the life of the community,
which have taboos attached to their beginnings ; and these
have descended to civilized peoples, in many cases, in the
form of religious rules of law. I cannot pursue the subject
here ; but it will not fail to interest a student of human nature,
seeing that it has its root in truth and fact.

Virgil says that sheep may be washed on a *dies festus* :
' balantumque gregem fluvio mersare salubri.' Here again
he has to be explained or corrected, but both Columella and
Macrobius are most anxious to save his credit. ' Maro
omnium disciplinarum peritus ', says Macrobius, ' sciens
lavari ovem aut lanae purgandae aut scabiae curandae gratia,
pronuntiavit tunc ovem per ferias licere mersari, si hoc
remedii causa fieret.' Columella lays special stress on the
word *salubri*, and is followed by Servius : they take it as
indicating that the poet thought of the washing as done for
medical reasons only, a remedy mentioned in *G.* iii. 441.
However this may be, the rule emerges that the important
operation of sheep-washing, occurring regularly at a certain
time of year, may not be done on a *dies festus* ; but a casual
remedy for scab may be applied at any time. Perhaps the
association of all medical remedies with religion in early
Rome and elsewhere had something to do with this exception ;
and we must also remember that no time was to be lost in

[1] See especially pp. 14–17, 32, and 34 ff.

applying the remedy, which would come under Scaevola's rule of ' quod praetermissum noceret '.

Virgil says ' Rivos deducere nulla Religio vetuit '. *Rivos deducere* is explained by Servius as *siccare* ; not to be taken as *irrigare*, which is expressed in this first *Georgic* by *inducere*, as in 106. What is meant by *deducere* is the drawing the water off the fields which have already been irrigated. Servius goes on to quote Varro as saying that it was ' contra religionem ' either to irrigate land or wash animals on *feriae*, because water-spirits (Nymphae [1]) ' sine piaculo non possunt moveri '. Varro is here reflecting a real *religio* about the use of fresh water, of which it unluckily happens that we have but few traces in Latium.[2] The distinction is between the pure fresh water, full of life and healing, which was let in on the fields from brook or river, and the water which had become stagnant after doing its work there. We may remember that only fresh running water was of avail for religious purposes, and that the Vestals fetched their supply daily from Juturna's spring. I take it that the used-up water had been abandoned by the spirits before it was drawn off ; they did not inhabit a farmyard pond, but, like trout, rejoiced in the living water of a running stream.

Columella tells us that you might on *feriae* cultivate a hired vineyard or olive yard, one, that is, which you undertake for its owner at a certain price. This exception has been explained as being necessary in order to enable the lessee to fulfil engagements within a specified time.[3] Or it may be that as Roman law originally recognized no other form of possession but absolute ownership,[4] other forms which came in later were more easily made subject to exemptions of this kind. There might be a difference of feeling about land not your own, which would therefore not be a part of the economic

---

[1] Varro used the word *Nymphae* because the Latin water-spirits were nameless (Wissowa, *R. K.*, p. 223).

[2] *Aen.* viii. 68, and a note in my *Death of Turnus*, p. 55 ff. Cf. Varro, *R. R.* i. 11.

[3] Bouché-Leclercq, *Pontifes*, p. 119.   [4] Gaius, ii. 40.

unit for which the Pontifical rules were laid down ; and this may possibly help to explain the distinction between animals which are or are not 'in familia '.

Columella also tells us that meadows might be mown a second time on *feriae*. This does not mean, I think, a second crop, of which I find no mention. It is explained sufficiently by Varro and Pliny.[1] After the hay was carried, it was usual to go over the fields again (*sicilire prata*), cutting off any bits that had been passed over by the mowers, such as tufts of grass and plants which run to seed and damage the field, like nettles and yarrow on our own dairy farms. The operation was therefore entirely subsidiary ; and the rule was one of common sense.

Among the many examples of light work which might be done on *feriae* is the spreading out (*pandere*) of apples, pears, and figs, in order to dry them in the sun for preservation.[2] You might also make cheese, and spread manure, though you might not cart or unload it. On the same principle you might lay up hay in lofts, though you might not cut or carry it. The reason seems to be, in these two last cases, that the easiest part of the process was allowable, but not the really hard work.

It is allowable, says Columella, to bring home young trees for planting ; but they must be carried on your own back, or on a pack animal, not in a cart or wagon. The yoking of bullocks and other draught animals seems to have been regarded as a serious undertaking ; for example, ' we read in the pontifical books ', says Columella in this same chapter, ' that mules might not be yoked on *feriae denicales* ', i. e. the tenth day after a death in the family (see also Cato, 138). Virgil seems to be alluding to this rule in the last three lines of the passage quoted above, where the ' agitator aselli ' was apparently driving a pack animal. The explanation here is perhaps that the use of wheeled vehicles was a comparatively late innovation on rural farms, and that it was not

---

[1] Varro, *R. R.* i. 49 ; Pliny, *N. H.* xviii. 259.

[2] See Varro, *R. R.* i. 57 ff., and Columella, xii. 14 and 15; the latter says that country people preserve these fruits as not the least part of their food in winter.

deemed advisable that they should be put in use, with the animals that drew them, on all days alike.

When the trees are brought home, they must not be planted on a *dies festus*, for work done above ground can alone be permitted. *You might not open the ground* on such a day. Here we come upon a survival of the very primitive idea that the bosom of the earth is sacred (i. e. holy, dangerous), and cannot be violated with impunity ; e. g. in making a clearing you must propitiate the spirits that may be dwelling there. For this idea see Cato, 139 ; and a good illustration of it may be found in the *Journal of Roman Studies*, 1916, p. 22, from Hose and MacDougall's *Pagan Tribes of Borneo*. There is also an allusion to it in Columella's poem, Book X, 58 ff.

You may do anything you like in your garden, says Columella, relating to pot herbs. I think that this follows the general rule that almost anything might be done on *feriae* at the homestead ; digging in your garden would disturb no spirits, for they were either by this time domesticated, or had retired to more uncultivated spots. He adds a curious prohibition about sheep which I cannot entirely explain. You might not clothe your sheep with skins. Here he seems to be alluding to a certain breed of ' jacketed ' sheep of which Varro tells us that they had to be protected by skins so that their wool might not be soiled. But the only place in Italy which he mentions for such sheep is Tarentum.[1]

Lastly, according to Columella, the sacrifice of a puppy, offered before certain operations forbidden on *feriae*, such as sowing, harvest, vintage, sheep-shearing, would insure you against the wrath of offended deities, if you found yourself compelled to break the rule. This is a good example of what I have elsewhere called sacrificial insurance. The Arval Brethren, if they had to take an iron implement into their sacred grove, offered a *piaculum* before as well as after this breach of religious rule.[2] Why on the farm the victim should be a puppy is not clear ; but puppies were not unknown in agricultural religion, e. g. at the festival of the Robigalia

[1] *R. R.* ii. 2. 18.   [2] See *Rel. Exp.*, p. 191, and references there given.

(see my *Roman Festivals*, pp. 90 ff.).[1] Perhaps the solution lies in the number of puppies in a litter that were not kept for training ; you selected the best, Varro tells us,[2] when they were quite young, and destroyed the rest. But it might be convenient to keep some for purposes of insurance !

Let us now consider these pontifical rulings as a whole. Professor Webster, in a footnote on p. 98, writes : ' the pontifical law in such matters was as minute, tyrannical, and absurd as the rabbinical ordinances relating to the proper observance of the Sabbath '. Here I cannot at all agree with him. The rabbinical ordinances were a much later development of law than the pontifical, relatively to the history of society in Judaea and Rome respectively ; they were the result of a curious passion for *minutiae* of tiresome and meaningless casuistry. ' The brief prohibition of work on the Sabbath which is found in the Pentateuch, and which hardly at all enters into detail, was in the course of time developed in so many-sided a manner as to form of itself an important branch of knowledge. For of course the Rabbis could not rest satisfied with simple prohibition. They must also accurately define what work was forbidden. And consequently they at last, with much ingenuity, found that on the whole thirty-nine kinds of work were prohibited, of which very few are anywhere alluded to in the older law.' [3] The thirty-nine prohibited works include the chief operations of agriculture, but descend to such things as making or untying a knot, sewing two stitches, catching a deer, and killing, skinning, and salting it, writing two letters, putting out a fire, lighting a fire, and so on. And each of those rules needed further discussion of their range and meaning ; e. g. to what kind of knots the rule applied ; and it was decided that the knot of camel-drivers and that of sailors was forbidden, both for tying and untying. What depths of absurdity can be reached by those who once launch on this kind of inquiry, may be

---

[1] Pliny, xxix. 58, notices the use of puppies ' placandis numinibus hostiarum vice ', as if it were a well-known practice.

[2] *R. R.* ii. 9.   Schürer, II. ii. 96.

THE LAW OF REST-DAYS

seen in Schürer's chapter on ' Life under the Law ' in his
Jewish People in the time of Christ, II. ii. 97 ff. I can see
little of this kind of absurdity in the rules we have been examining. Something of the same love of *minutiae* is seen in the
lists of the Indigitamenta ;[1] but in the practical matters of
farm work we expect and we find more good sense.

We may assume, I think, that in the earliest times there
were no exceptions to the ancient taboos on days made over
to deities ; no work at all could be done on those days, of
which in rural life there were probably not too many. This
seems to me to be suggested by the survival of primitive
ideas about the spirits of earth and water, and the strict
maintenance of the associated taboos even in the time of
Columella. I should imagine that the same rigidity attached
to the rules even after the city calendar was drawn up in the
age of the later kings. But when we come down to the
fourth and third centuries B. C., which is in other ways the
age of special pontifical activity, we find that though these
rules are fully kept up in theory, the growing difficulties of
the farmer are being gradually resolved by pontifical decisions
of which Cato a century later gives us some specimens. Whatever the share of the *pontifices* may originally have been in
fixing the rules, their work was now to discover the means
of relaxing them—a process in which I seem to see, from
the examples examined above, a considerable amount of
common sense.

This relief was called for, we may conjecture, mainly by the
exigencies of more extensive and more scientific farming.
The rules which could do no harm while the peasant had
only his two *iugera* of *heredium* and his rights of common of
pasture, were likely enough to hamper his activity when he
farmed 200 acres or more at a distance from Rome, or ran
large herds of cattle on the *saltus* of the hilly country. The
process of enlarging farms was exactly contemporaneous
with the period when pontifical activity was at its height,
when plebeians had a share in land newly acquired from

[1] *Rel. Exp.*, pp. 164, 286.

conquered enemies, and when even the Pontifex Maximus might be a plebeian. The chief result of these decisions was that many minor operations came to be ruled lawful on *feriae*, especially those which could be carried on at the homestead, in order to gain more time and labour for those of greater importance, such as sowing, ploughing, and harvest. Rules about beginning a new work, or such as might disturb the spirits of land and water, were retained, but subsequent work of the same kind, which involved no disturbance to the spirits nor scruple to the farmer, was allowed.

Whether an increase in the number of the *feriae* was also a contributory cause is a difficult question. The number in any case is hard to fix for a farm, for we do not know the exact relation between city calendars and rural ones. For early Latium, however, we may reckon sixty-one *feriae* of city life, with two or three more that were *conceptivae* (movable) and do not appear in the oldest city calendar, and further an unknown number of *feriae privatae*, i. e. those of the *gens* or family, such as *dies natales* and *feriae denicales*, all of which were under pontifical rule.[1] The whole number is not likely to have been less than 70 or 80 out of a total of 355 days, not counting *nundinae*, or the *ludi* of the city which became so numerous in later times. For real honest work on a big farm in the fourth and third century B. C. this number of holidays may well have been a serious inconvenience. Hence it was that not only light work and secondary work came to be allowed on *feriae*, but even more serious operations if *piacula* had been offered beforehand as an insurance against divine wrath. All this seems to me to show good sense.

By the time of Scaevola and Cicero a more liberal and generous interpretation of the old rules was general and acknowledged ; and though there may have been a revival of strictness under Augustus, as was suggested above, the ancient taboos gradually gave way everywhere. ' Necessitas feriis caret ', said Palladius in the fourth century of the Empire (i. 6).

---

[1] Wissowa, *Rel. und Kult.*, p. 433 ; Macrob. I. xvi. 7.

ON THE DATE OF THE
RHETORICA AD HERENNIUM

(*Rhet. ad Herenn.* iv. 54. 68)

IN 1880, at the suggestion of the late Professor Henry
Nettleship, I very carefully examined a now well-known
passage near the end of the fourth book of the *Rhetorica ad
Herennium*, with the object of determining whether it could
be referred to Marius, instead of to Sulla, to whom scholars
had till then been in the habit of referring it. On November 19
of that year I read a paper on the subject to the Oxford
Philological Society, giving reasons for my belief that the
person referred to is Marius, and that the date of the work
may be 83 or 82 B. C. The paper appeared in the *Journal of
Philology* for 1882, pp. 197 ff. ; it was the first of its kind
I ever published, and I remember that I took all possible
pains with it. It has occasionally been referred to in German
works, e. g. in the second edition of Teuffel's *Roman Literature*,
and also in the second edition of Schanz's great work on the
same subject. But there is no mention of it in the very
elaborate edition of the *Rhetorica* by F. Marx (1894).

I should not be disposed to go back on it now, but that
Marx, though he too, like most scholars, is now of opinion
that the passage refers to Marius, has found himself compelled,
by the rules of textual criticism which have been suggested
to him by his investigation of the MSS., to ʻ restore ʼ the
passage to very much the same lamentable condition in which
it formerly stood.

It occurs in iv. 54. 68, and is an example of *brevitas* in oratory
—a point to be noted carefully. It is preceded by another
example, to which I will return later on. In Kayser's separate
edition of the *Rhetorica* (1854), which was not improved on
by Baiter and Kayser in their joint edition (1860), it runs
thus :

Item : modo consul quodam is deinde primus erat civitatis. Tum proficiscitur in Asiam, deinde hostis est dictus, post imperator et populi Romani consul factus est.

Here the two most doubtful points are : (1) the obviously corrupt *quodam is*, and (2) the words *populi Romani*, which in an example of *brevitas* are as obviously absurd, and are the emendation of the early editors for *populorum*, the reading of the best group of MSS.[1] I proposed to read the passage as follows :

Item : modo consul quotannis deinde primus erat civitatis. Tum proficiscitur in Asiam, deinde hostis est dictus, post imperator populorum et consul factus est.

The correction *quotannis* (or *quodannis*) appeared on the authority of H. Jordan in *Hermes*, May 1881, midway between the reading of my paper and its publication. The reference to the six successive consulships of Marius seemed thus fairly well established, and since then there has been a general consensus, so far as I know, that Marius and not Sulla is the person referred to. And the *brevitas* of the example was undeniable.[2]

Marx however, though he agrees about Marius, spoils the *brevitas*, as it seems to me, as well as the neatness of the Latin. In his text the words appear thus :

Item: Modo consul quondam, is deinde primus erat ciuitatis ; tum proficiscitur in Asiam, deinde hostis est dictus, post imperator et postremo factus est consul.

Will any one maintain that ' Modo consul quondam ' is a natural way of alluding to six successive consulships of Marius only some twenty years before the *Rhetorica* was written ? or that ' is ' has any meaning in an example of

---

[1] See the edition of Marx, p. 373, and *Prolegomena*, p. 154.

[2] In a letter written to me at the time by the late Professor Robinson Ellis, which I have fortunately preserved, he says of my version : ' As an example of *breuitas* the sentence now becomes excellent : antithetical, and with just the amount of deviation from ordinary expressions which would strike an attentive reader... If *quodannis* is right, then I think, as I suggested at the meeting, there can be no doubt that *modo*, i. e. " just now ", " but recently ", is in antithesis to *deinde*.'

breuitas ? or that ' postremo ' is not superfluous for the same
reason, especially as Marius was elected to his seventh consulship only just after Cinna had illegally made him imperator ?
But Marx's canon of textual criticism compels him, it seems,
to spoil the passage thus. Let me explain.

The text of the *Rhetorica* depends on two groups of MSS.,
each of which may be taken to represent a lost archetype :
(1) an older group (ninth and tenth centuries) in which there
are *lacunae* ; and (2) a younger group (*c.* twelfth century)
constituting a complete text. If pp. 41–5 of Marx's *Prolegomena* are studied carefully, it will appear that the reading
of the older group M must under certain circumstances give
way to those of the younger group E, especially where the
former is corrupt. Now in our example M has ' Modo consul
quodam is ', and this is retained by Marx, except that he writes
quondam for *quodam*,[1] inserting the additional letter on the
evidence of his experience of M. The younger group E has
' quondam tribunus ', and this is also the reading of C, one
of the MSS. of group M. This last fact makes a difficulty,
and causes Marx to retain the reading of M as against that of
E (see *Proleg.*, p. 43), which is almost certainly wrong, for
to refer to the tribuneship of Marius in such a passage as this
would be surprising as well as superfluous. But in the last
words of the example E is preferred for reasons which I confess
I do not quite understand ; and ' postremo ' is read from E
instead of ' populorum ' from M. ' Postremo ' may seem
natural until we remember that we are dealing with an example
of *breuitas*, ' res tantummodo verbis necessariis expedita,' as
it is defined in this same chapter ; but when we bear that in
mind it becomes superfluous, and is indeed almost absurd, as
I will show directly. For *populorum*, on the other hand,
I can find a very good sense, appropriate to the time, and to
the facts of the life of Marius.

As it is now generally accepted that Marius and not Sulla

---

[1] This is in spite of the fact that on his own showing the word *quondam*
is nowhere found in the whole four books of the work. See Marx, index,
and *Prolegomena*, p. 154.

is the person whose public life is here briefly expressed, I need not reproduce in full the arguments I used in the *Journal of Philology* to prove this point. But as the last words of the example do not seem to me to have been correctly understood, I must advert to them for a moment ; I mean the words which in M run thus : ' post imperator et populorum consul factus est ', or as Marx would read them, ' post imperator et postremo factus est consul '.

First, the word ' imperator ', if Sulla be meant, is meaningless, or at least needs a justification which it has not yet found. It is true that Sulla was technically imperator from the day on which he left Rome in 87, to the day on which he resigned his Dictatorship in 79. But the word, if here used of Sulla, must be used in some such special and extended sense as was afterwards given it by Augustus ; and we have no evidence whatever that in this point Sulla anticipated the Empire. In the inscription on the equestrian statue, which (according to Appian, *B. C.* i. 97) ran Κορνηλίου Σύλλας ἡγεμόνος εὐτυχοῦς, we must understand ἡγεμόνος as meaning Dictatoris and not Imperatoris, since the latter word would have been rendered αὐτοκράτωρ by a Greek writer.[1] Marius, on the other hand, was furnished by the consul Cinna with the *proconsulare imperium* and the *fasces*, doubtless in order to give him, technically *hostis* as he still was, a definite position in the eyes of his soldiers ; illegally no doubt, and doubly so, as Cinna himself was not legally consul. But in the eyes of the Italians, who were to form the bulk at least of his army, and in the eyes of the Auctor of this work, whose leaning to the side of the *populares* is universally recognized, the title might well be accepted *de facto.* That it was conferred is stated by Plutarch in a passage too explicit to be the result of misapprehension, and probably derived from Posidonius, who was in Italy a few months later, and had an interview with Marius on his death-bed.[2]

Secondly, the mysterious word ' populorum ' can have no

---

[1] See Mommsen in *C. I. L.* i. 168.
[2] Plut. *Marius,* 41 ; cf. 45. H. Peter, *Quellen Plutarch's,* p. 103.

meaning if Sulla be the person spoken of ; but it fits in well enough with the position of Marius in the middle of 87, after he had been made imperator by Cinna. The army he got together, like those of Cinna, Carbo, and Sertorius, at this time, was composed of the Italian *populi* still in arms,[1] together with numbers of the new Italian *cives* who were discontented with the inferior position assigned them by the Senatorial government in a limited number of tribes. This campaign in fact, though commonly called the first Civil War, was only a new phase of the Social or Marsic War ; the new feature being that one party at Rome was now heading the Italians against the other. If we had the eighth and ninth decades of Livy, we should no doubt find, as we may guess from his Epitomist, that throughout the war the Italians were called ' populi Italici ', or ' populi ' only ;[2] and in an example of *breuitas*, framed by a person writing soon after the war, it would be perfectly natural to term a general at the head of an Italian army ' imperator populorum '. So I propose to read here ' Post imperator populorum et consul factus est '.[3] Marius became consul for the seventh time on January 1, 86, having been elected (or appointed by Cinna) but a short time after he had been made imperator ; thus the word ' postremo ', which Marx insists on reading, in spite of the unanimity of the M group of MSS., for *populorum*, is certainly superfluous, even to absurdity, in an example of *breuitas*.

Let me now turn to the example of *breuitas* which immediately preceded the one we have been so far discussing. The

[1] Liv. *Epit.* 80 (Samnium) ; Appian, *B. C.* i. 67 (Etruria). Cf. Kiene, *Bundesgenossenkrieg*, p. 298 ; Mommsen, *R. H.* (Eng. trans. iii. 317 ff.).

[2] Liv. *Epit.* 72 ' Italici populi defecerunt '. 73 ' Complures populi ad hostes defecerunt '. 75 ' L. Sulla . . . *aliquos populos recepit* '. 80 ' Italicis populis a senatu civitas data est '. 86 ' Sulla cum Italicis populis foedus percussit '. A writer of the age of the Auctor might well write *populi* simply and be understood at once.

[3] The transposition of the *et* from before *populorum* to follow it, may be justified by the muddle that had arisen at a very early date in the copying of these words.

latter, I may note, is now accepted as giving us the year 86, and the last consulship and death of Marius, as a *terminus ex quo* for the date of the *Rhetorica ad Herennium*.[1] But I am strongly inclined to think that we can make a more exact conjecture as to that date, if we carefully examine the first example in relation to the events of the time. I believe that it refers to the movements of Lucullus and his fleet, co-operating with Sulla, and providing for the safe progress of his army to the Hellespont in the spring of 84 B.C.

In Marx's edition the text of this passage stands thus :

Lemnum praeteriens cepit, inde Thasi praesidium reliquit, post urbem Viminacium sustulit, inde pulsus in Hellespontum statim potitur Abydi.

These few words, in spite of corruption, indicate clearly that some one with a fleet is watching the Thracian coast, trying to guard it from a hostile fleet by securing the two islands, Lemnos and Thasos, which (as Strabo says) lie immediately off it, and having the command of the Hellespont as his ultimate object. This at once suggests that some one else is approaching along that coast by the via Egnatia, for whom the naval commander is making his march safe. Now early in 84 Sulla was advancing from Greece by the via Egnatia, and had commissioned Lucullus, who after various adventures had established himself with a fleet off the Troad,[2] to clear the Aegean and the Hellespont of the forces of Mithridates. The situation is thus exactly that which is reflected in the words just quoted. Lucullus took Lemnos, occupied Thasos, then did two other things which the corruption of the text leaves obscure, and finally, exactly as Appian relates,[3] returned to the Hellespont, and seized Abydos on the Asiatic side, so as to prevent Mithridates from establishing himself there. With Abydos in Roman hands, the Hellespont was

---

[1] Schanz, *Röm. Litt.* i. 2 (ed. 3), p. 467.   [2] Plut. *Lucullus*, 3.

[3] App. *Mithridatica*, 56, implies that Lucullus seized Abydos in advance of Sulla, in order to secure the safe passage of the Hellespont for his chief. It was this passage of Appian that originally suggested to me that the Auctor is referring to these movements.

also theirs, and Sulla's march was secured. But there are
two textual difficulties here about which I must say a
word.

The first of these lies in the name Viminacium (M *uimina-
chium*[1]). Under the Empire there was a well-known city
of that name some 300 miles inland from the Hellespont,
on the Danube, which probably suggested itself to a copyist
who could not make out the name in his copy. But it was
unknown to the Romans of Marius's time, if indeed it existed
then at all. Lysimachia was adopted by Kayser; a city on
the isthmus of the Thracian Chersonese, and therefore in
one sense a key to the Hellespont; and the only city in these
regions, so far as I can discover, whose name ends in *machia*
or *achia*, the reading of M.[1] But I fear that Lysimachia must
be rejected, partly as difficult to reconcile with the MSS., and
partly as being probably too strong to be destroyed by a force
landing from a fleet. 'Sustulit', about which there is no
doubt, must mean total destruction; and Lysimachia did
not meet with this fate, for it is mentioned by Strabo as
existing in his time (vi. 54). It is more likely, I think, that
this town may have been some small one, on the Thracian
coast, a spot commanding the via Egnatia, of which the
name has vanished since its destruction. Anyhow, I have not
as yet been able to discover a name which can help us, on
that coast.[2]

[1] Three MSS. of group E have Bithynia, which is as impossible as Vimi-
nacia. Surely the name must have become hopelessly corrupted before
the date of the archetypes of either M or E. Lysimachia was the conjecture
of Spengel. Cf. Liv. xxxvii. 36. My friend Mr. J. A. R. Munro ingeniously
suggests that the words *post urbem* may conceal the name Pistyrum, a small
town opposite to Thasos which is mentioned in Herodotus vii. 109. In
that case Viminacium may conceal the name of some tribe in the genitive
plural; or the latter part of the word might be, as he suggests ... *ad lacum*.
An old pupil who has been much on that coast during the war, suggests
that *urbem* might be the town of Thasos, which threatened the garrison
that had been left there (*vi minacem* is his conjecture) and was promptly
destroyed.

[2] It was not in Thasos, as the words *praesidium reliquit* prove. It is
to be looked for somewhere on the Thracian coast between the Strymon
and the Hebrus.

The second difficulty lies in the word ' pulsus ', which might suggest that Lucullus had experienced a reverse immediately after the destruction of the town, whatever it was, and had been compelled to fly to his head-quarters. But *pulsus* is not in the MSS. ; those of group M have *sulsus*, all except C, which seems to stand by itself, and to give us occasionally the true reading. C has *rursus*, and this suggests to me *reversus*,[1] i. e. Lucullus then retraced his steps to the parts whence he had started to prepare the way for Sulla, and immediately seized Abydos, as we have seen. He had started from the Troad, where he had been watching the entrance to the straits, and having got into touch with Sulla, probably after the destruction of the little town, returned to the Helles-pont to await his arrival. We know that he then took Sulla across the strait, and that the interview with Mithridates followed which brought about a peace.

These events happened in the spring of 84. If the Auctor alludes to them, he had probably heard of them from some one serving in the fleet, and put them in at the very end of his work not long after they happened, perhaps the very next year. In any case we now have some ground for bringing our *terminus* down to the year 84.[2]

I may add that it seems to me not impossible that the author of this work, who had made no secret in it of his sympathy with the cause of the *populares* and Italians,[3] may have perished in the Sullan reign of terror which followed close on its publication. This would account in some degree for the mystery which has shrouded its authorship, and for the fact

[1] *Reversus*, I find, was adopted by Baiter and Kayser in the edition of 1860.

[2] Kayser (notes, p. 310) saw in iv. 52, 65 (example of *sermocinatio*) an allusion to an outrage at Larinum adverted to by Cicero in *pro Cluentio* viii. 25, which must have occurred in 83, after Sulla's return to Italy. But this cannot be proved from a comparison of the two passages : for in the former no names are given, and in the latter no details.

[3] Among other passages which indicate this conclusion I may note iv. 9. 13, 22. 31, 34. 46, and 55. 68. The name of Herennius, to whom the work is dedicated, also suggests Italian and Marian associations (Plut. *Marius* 5). See Schanz, op. cit., I. ii. (ed. 3), 471.

that we know of no subsequent work by the same hand. It is at any rate quite fruitless to attempt to identify the author with any individual known to have been living at a later date, whether bearing the name Cornificius (as used to be thought probable) or any other.

THE *LEX FRUMENTARIA* OF GAIUS GRACCHUS

THE details of this bill are clear as far as our knowledge goes, though that is but a little way. Corn was to be sold in the capital to any one applying for it at the rate of 6⅓ asses per modius ;[1] no one was to be excluded from purchasing at this price on account of position or means.[2] What amount any one could buy at one time is uncertain ; the amount needed by an individual was about five modii per month, and it is usually assumed[3] that this was the amount named in the bill. The average price of a modius is believed to have been about 16 asses or a denarius ;[4] but it was liable to great fluctuation, according to the fortune of the harvest. The price fixed by Gracchus may have been calculated as that to which the value of the modius might eventually be reduced, by careful development of the corn-growing industry, and of the means of regular transport to Rome.

Nothing is easier for a modern than to condemn this law as an unpardona le blunder, if not as a crime. When once the laws of political economy have been clearly formulated, it needs no appreciable mental effort to see that you cannot put an artificial price on corn, even within a limited space,

---

[1] Liv. *Epit.* 60, with Mommsen's certain emendation of ' senis cum triente '.

[2] This appears from the language of Cicero in *Tusc. Disp.* iii. 20. 48. Piso Frugi, a consularis, had applied for purchase at the cheap rate, though he had spoken against the bill.

[3] On the strength of a passage in Sallust (*Hist. Fragmenta*, iii. 61. 19, Dietsch).

[4] Marquardt, *Staatsverwaltung*, ii. 111, and note. For a good instance of fluctuation under Augustus, Dio. 56. 22 ff.

without producing serious moral and economic damage; [1] but in ancient times it was the urgent difficulty of the moment on which the legislator acted, rather than on reasoned consideration of causes and their effects. Even as late as the year 1800, believing that the country was threatened with starvation, Pitt, who had been brought up on Adam Smith, wished to put a guaranteed price on importations of grain, and was only prevented from doing so by the urgent remonstrances of Grenville.[2] To judge of Gracchus's policy fairly we must do more than simply state the fact that he brought the State power to act artificially on the price of corn in Rome, reducing it by more than one-half, thereby creating a heavy charge on the treasury, putting an unwholesome premium on life in the great city, and bribing the mob to support his other measures. We must endeavour to realize the difficulties he had to meet, and the amount of experience and knowledge which he could bring to bear on them.

His legislation comes at the end of a period which had been marked by the rise of new and populous cities under the rule of the Diadochi, and by a great increase in the population of many old cities. Beloch has compared this period with the nineteenth century in modern Europe, which has seen exactly the same phenomenon.[3] What the causes were in each case need not now detain us; the fact is sufficient that among the innumerable cities of the Hellenic world some developed in wealth and population to an extraordinary degree, while others sank into comparative insignificance. Hence arose new problems of administration, analogous to those which faced the commanders of large armies serving for a long period, as compared with the far simpler administration of the burgher forces of the city-states. The task of feeding the populations of Alexandria, Antioch, or Carthage, may not have been difficult, since the districts in which such cities were placed were rich in the fruits of the earth, and lent themselves easily

---

[1] Written before the War.   [2] Stanhope's *Life of Pitt*, iii. 244.
[3] *Bevölkerung*, p. 479. Cf. Pöhlmann, *Übervölkerung der antiken Gross städte*, ch. ii.

to the work of transport ; but the new mistress of the Mediterranean world was not so happily situated.

Italy, though capable of raising sufficient corn for its many
cities of moderate size, is in reality a peninsula of hill and
mountain, and must, even in the time of the Gracchi, have still
been largely occupied by forest and undrained marsh. At an
early period the inhabitants discovered that it was worth
their while to spend immense labour in draining the lakes
among their hills, in order to provide themselves with fertile
corn-land.[1] Even now the dwellers in some districts of the
Apennines live chiefly on meal made not of grain but of
chestnuts. The Italy of Gracchus's day could hardly do more
than feed its own country population ; for it must be remembered that the people lived almost entirely on grain, consuming but little meat, and that they used their sheep and
cattle chiefly for the production of wool and leather. Even
if the country could have been stimulated to a larger production of grain, the transport of it to Rome would have been
both difficult and costly ; for example, the great fertile plain
of Cisalpine Gaul, the most valuable corn-land in the country,
would have had to send its products to the Roman market in
vessels coasting round the heel and toe of the peninsula, for
a land-transport of three hundred miles over the Apennines
was practically out of the question. Yet the population of
Rome was steadily increasing, and at the end of the second
century B. C. was probably not less than half a million souls.[2]
And the causes operating to produce this result were so
intimately connected with the astonishing rise of the Roman
dominion, with slavery, with professional soldiery, with
commercial development, with the increase of capital and the
conveniences and luxuries of city-life, that to counteract

[1] See a very interesting paper by Prof. Tenney Frank, in the American
Economic Review, vol. ix, no. 2 (June 1919), on Agriculture in Early
Latium.

[2] Beloch (*Bevölkerung*, ch. ix, sec. 2) puts the population of the city in
the early empire at about 800,000, basing this conclusion on three several
methods of calculation. The same facts are not available for calculating
the population before Sulla's time. Beloch handled the same subject more
recently in Klio (iii. 490) and arrived at much the same result.

them successfully was almost as impossible as to renounce
that dominion itself. So at least it must have seemed to an
intelligent statesman of that day.

It may be indeed that a highly intelligent governing class,
with leisure to attend to home problems as well as to foreign
wars, might have done much to check the increase when
once the long struggle with Hannibal was over ; but that fatal
war inevitably led to others, distracted attention from
Italian problems, and warped and narrowed the policy of
the Roman aristocracy towards the Italian peoples who had
helped to prolong the struggle. The feeding of the great city
had to be done at haphazard, without reference to the economic
condition of the peninsula of which it was the political centre.
Long before the Gracchan age, and even before the Hannibalic
war, the aediles, whose duty it was to supervise the supply
of grain, had been used to procure the necessary quantity
from Sicily and Sardinia ; Sicily in fact paid its tribute to
the Roman state in this form, and was forbidden to export
corn to other countries.[1] With corn-growing possessions so
close at hand, whence the transport was short and safe, the
State might well be tempted to keep its growing city population comfortable and quiet at the expense of these provinces.
Cato had described Sicily as the store-cupboard of the Roman
people,[2] and its possession enabled the government to regulate
both the supply and the price of its chief product. The hungry
plebs usually expected a commander returning from a successful campaign to bring corn with him for their benefit ; we
have records of corn thus obtained being sold at nominal
prices even before the Hannibalic war, and again as soon as

---

[1] Marquardt, *Staatsverwaltung*, ii. 109, notes 3 and 4. Polybius (xxviii. 2)
says that the Rhodians, wishing to buy corn in Sicily, were unable to do
so without leave from Rome. On the importation of corn by Greek cities
long before this, see Dr. Grundy's book on Thucydides, ch. iii. I do not
think it has been noticed that Caesar, in describing his own difficulties of
supply during the campaign of Dyrrhachium, tells us that the inhabitants
of those parts, i. e. Dyrrhachium and Apollonia, consumed for the most
part imported grain (*Bell. Civ.* iii. 42).

[2] ' Cella penaria reipublicae nostrae, nutrix populi Romani ' : quoted
by Cic. *Verr.* ii. 2. 5.

it was over.[1] Such a case is mentioned by Plutarch as occurring during the first tribunate of C. Gracchus. A large
quantity of corn was sent by a propraetor from Spain for
distribution ; Gracchus himself persuaded the Senate to
have this corn sold and the value of it returned to the provincials from whom it had been stolen.[2] But was it not better,
he may have thought, to avoid all such dealings in the future—
dealings which were unjust to the provincials, and doubtfully
beneficial to the Roman plebs ?

Let us consider this question from his own point of view,
as we may reasonably imagine it. Was it not possible to
bring the price of corn permanently low enough to make it
worth no man's while to gain a temporary popularity by
treats of this kind, for which the treaters themselves paid
little or nothing ? Was it not possible so to organize and
manipulate the existing supervision of the corn-supply by
the State, as to solve, for the time at least, the problem of
keeping the huge population of the city alive and in good
humour ? Was it really necessary to leave such dangerous
work to the mercies of individual capitalists, or even to the
inexperience of yearly changing aediles, guided by their own
intuitions rather than by permanent legal regulations ? It
should not be forgotten that these aediles might have from
time to time to encounter special difficulties, the result of
bad harvests or the neglect of their predecessors. Just before
the first tribunate of Gracchus an extraordinary plague of
locusts had done irreparable damage to the crops in Africa ;
and it has been suggested that this was one of the immediate
causes of Gracchus's action.[3] We know how in later times

[1] The instances are collected in Marquardt, op. cit., p. 110. A reference to
the bibliography of the subject given in the same work, p. 106, note 4
(which might now be considerably enlarged), will serve to show how carefully this matter has been investigated.

[2] Plutarch, *Gaius Gracchus*, ch. 6. This was at the moment of Gracchus's
greatest personal influence. The stroke was a fine one : he would get the
grain, gain credit with the provincials for righteous dealing, and at the
same time baulk the personal ambition of the propraetor Fabius.

[3] Nitzsch, *Die Gracchen*, p. 393. The plague of locusts is mentioned in
Liv. *Epit.* 60, and by Orosius, v. 11, where it is placed in the year 125 B. C.

the security of the corn-supply became a matter of the utmost moment, not only as affecting the lives and temper of the Roman plebs but the political situation of the moment and the ambitions of public men.

I have long been convinced that Gracchus's object was not merely, as is so often assumed by historians, to ' bribe ' the hungry plebs into acquiescence with his legislative projects, but (1) to prevent sudden and violent fluctuations in the market-price of corn, which were dangerous both politically and economically ; (2) to stimulate the production of corn in Italy, in harmony with the spirit of his brother's agrarian law, and in immediate connexion with his own ;[1] to keep the agricultural population on the land, and to facilitate the transport of their produce and its safe warehousing at Rome. Let us consider these two points separately, though in my view they are two parts of one and the same scheme.

1. We have in the history of our own country a good example of the acceptance by a State of the policy of maintaining a fair and steady price for the staple food of a nation, at a period when economic circumstances were apt to produce sudden and unwholesome fluctuations. Mr. R. E. Prothero (Lord Ernle), in his *History of British Farming*, has shown how the English Government in the seventeenth and eighteenth centuries, though they had no such dangerous circumstances to contend with as the Roman Government in Gracchus's time, yet found it desirable to do what they could to maintain ' a just price '.[2] ' When prices were below a certain level, foreign imports were practically prohibited, exports of home-grown corn permitted, and the quantity of production stimulated by bounties. When home prices rose above a certain level, the bounties ceased, exports were prohibited,

See also Dr. Greenidge's *History of Rome*, p. 205. For a modern parallel see this book, p. 165.

[1] In my view the corn-law and the land-law of C. Gracchus were both passed in his first tribunate and about the same time. Dr. Heitland is of the same opinion (*Roman Republic*, ii. 301–2) ; but he differs from me in thinking that the two laws were irreconcileable with each other, from the point of view of the agrarian interest, and that Gracchus did not perceive this.

[2] Prothero, *English Farming Past and Present*, pp. 255 and 257.

and imports of foreign corn admitted duty free or at reduced
rates.' This was the method, which differed of course from that
of the Roman legislator, but the object was essentially the
same in both cases. Prices of corn both in England and ancient
Italy, owing to difficulties of transport and warehousing, were
much more sensitive then than now to fluctuations in the yield
of harvests. Again, in Italy as in England, the amount of
corn produced (even if we include Sicily in the former case)
was as a rule not much more than was needed for the population, and when a bad harvest was anticipated or realized,
corn might run up to panic prices. Thus the general aim of
legislators, as Mr. Prothero puts it for England, was to
maintain an abundant supply of food at fair and steady
prices ; and to save the country from violent oscillations
between cheapness and dearness. It is interesting to find
that among the practical steps taken for this end, one at least
is found in ancient Rome as well as in modern England.
' The erection of public granaries, in which farmers might
store the surplus of one year against the shortage of the next
was borrowed from Holland, and urged on the country by
Royal proclamation. In 1620 the King's Council wrote
letters into every shire . . . to provide a granary or storehouse,
with stock to buy corn, and keep it for a dear year.' We are
expressly told by Plutarch, whose authority for this biography
was unquestionably a contemporary one,[1] that Gracchus
paid special and personal attention to the erection of granaries,
and this must have been with the same object of keeping the
supply as constant as possible.

2. It may be argued that Gracchus could not have meant to
stimulate production by this bill, since it lowered the price
of corn by more than one-half in the city, and would thus
rather discourage agrarian effort. But I doubt if this argument will hold good. I take it that the ordinary small holder
under the Gracchan legislation would not usually look on the

---

[1] Plutarch, *C. Gracchus*, ch. 6. For an excellent and judicious investigation of the value of Plutarch's lives of the Gracchi, see the introduction
to Mr. G. E. Underhill's edition, 1892. Cf. *English Hist. Rev.*, 1905,
pp. 212 ff.

Roman market as his main object ; but after a good harvest he would be only too glad to sell to the government what grain he had beyond the needs of his family or of the nearest town, even if the price he could obtain for it were not a high one. And that government might be willing to pay him more for the corn than they could get for it in Rome under the *lex frumentaria.* In any case the grower would benefit, if he could only get his corn conveyed to Rome for deposit in the public granaries ; and this seems to have been the object of Gracchus's road-making, on which Plutarch lays so much stress. Of his own *lex agraria* we know nothing, though we may be fairly sure that it practically re-enacted his brother's and set the agrarian commission on its feet again ; but we do know the important fact that it was accompanied by a *lex viaria* (road-law), and Plutarch describes the way in which this was carried out under Gracchus's personal super-vision.[1] These roads must have been meant to assist the small farmers who were to benefit under the agrarian laws ; the assistance they would most naturally need would be that of increased facility for transport from their farms to the great roads.[2] I think, therefore, that I am justified in concluding that roads and granaries taken together with the corn-law and the agrarian law are all parts of a plan for the encourage-ment of the Italian corn-grower by enabling him to find eventually a market in the capital, after supplying the needs of his own household or locality.

Now supposing that these were the more spacious aims of Gracchus, apart from the narrower and immediate one which is usually ascribed to him, it is none the less inevitable that we should condemn his method. He no doubt honestly thought that he could fix the price of corn in the city, just

---

[1] Plutarch, *C. Gracchus,* ch. 7.

[2] Such a law was attached to (or was a part of) the *lex Servilia Rulli* in 63, and again to another *lex agraria* which failed to pass, in 51 B. C., Cic. *ad Fam.* viii. 6. 5 : ' (Curio) transfugit ad populum et pro Caesare loqui coepit : legemque viariam, non dissimilem agrariae Rulli, et alimentariam, quae iubet aediles metiri, iactavit.' The concurrence here of a *lex viaria* and a *lex alimentaria* is significant.

as long afterwards Diocletian fancied that he could fix prices
for articles of all kinds. If we compare such a policy with
that of the English Government to which I referred just now,
we see the blunder at once. The English policy was an honest
attempt to keep prices at a reasonable average by adjusting
the imposition of duties and bounties to the economic circumstances of the moment. It may be compared to the
action of a coxswain who keeps a straight course by moving
the helm first to one side, then to another, as tide, current,
and wind act upon his boat. But Gracchus, living in the
infancy of State-navigation, would seem to have known no
better than to tie the tiller-ropes fast, in the expectation
that the boat would go straight ; he fixed by law a permanent
price, hoping that it might be possible to abide by it. But
there is no doubt that he miscalculated the cost to the State
and the drain on its resources, though there is some ground,
as we shall see directly, for thinking that he did not neglect
to make some estimate of it. And there is also no doubt
that he failed to see that less scrupulous leaders of the 'people',
exaggerating his policy, would sooner or later be ready to
feed the city-mob entirely at the expense of the State—as
actually in due time happened.[1]

All this seems to us so strange, especially to beginners in
the study of Roman politics who have some chance acquaintance with political economy, that I have often been at pains
to try to realize for myself and my pupils not only the conditions of the problem before Gracchus, but the mental equipment he could bring to bear on it. We are so apt to think
of these crises of ancient history simply in terms of modern
life, and to judge of the actors in them by modern standards
of experience, that it may be worth while to ask how a man
of such remarkable ability and integrity as Gracchus can have
been so curiously misled.

First, I would point out that there was then no political
philosophy in existence which took into account this particular

[1] The facts will be found put together in Marquardt, *Staatsverwaltung*,
ii, loc. cit.

difficulty of life in great cities. The old Greek thinkers dealt with the πόλις, the city which ideally at least needed no support from without ; [1] and those of the Hellenistic period did not greatly trouble themselves about the practical problems of government. Thus the Roman statesman, even if educated, like the Gracchi, by Greek philosophic teachers, had no intellectual inheritance to draw upon in such matters ; nor indeed had he any sound tradition of Roman experience to work on. Experience had indeed shown that the senate and magistrates had so far been able to feed the *plebs urbana* and keep it quiet by means of an unlimited power of organization ; but when the reforming statesman arose, and was brought into conflict with that oligarchy, compelled to figure as the leader of the sovereign people against it, *he himself became inevitably responsible both for the order and for the food-supply.* Yet Gracchus, in facing these difficulties, at one of the most critical moments of Roman history, had no experience to guide him but that of his political opponents, and no organization but such as he could create by the force of his own genius. Later legislators, Sulla, Caesar, Augustus, being backed by military force, had both time and organization at command ; but Gracchus was in the peculiar position of being in opposition yet forced to govern, and unable to reckon for certain on having sufficient time to think out and work out his problems. Here, as in almost every political question of the age, we see the utter inadequacy of the machinery of the city-state to cope with the difficulties of an imperial system. It was empire that had produced the vast increase of the city population, and it was by means of empire that that population was destined to be fed ; [2] yet the constitution

[1] The Greek remedy for over-population was colonization, and this was recognized by Plato (*Laws*, 708 B). But the problem of feeding a city-population does not seem to have attracted the attention of philosophers, though if Dr. Grundy is right (Thucydides, ch. iii) they must have been aware of it. In the Hellenistic age the mainland of Greece was suffering from depopulation ; the over-populated cities were far away, and the philosophers of the post-Aristotelian schools do not seem to have been interested in their difficulties.

[2] The treasury was filled mainly from the provinces, and the corn supply

remained that of the city-state with its yearly changing magistrates, and the only hope of efficient administration seemed to lie in the permanent council, the senate. At one moment it looked as if Gracchus were about to overpower this oligarchic council by sheer weight of ability and by the courteous tact which distinguished him ; [1] but in fact he had no chance against its traditions and prejudices. Yet it is not unlikely that if he had been able from the first to dominate or reform it, no permanent *lex frumentaria* might have been needed.

Again, if Gracchus could have had time and the means of organization, his true policy would have been to police the city adequately, as Augustus afterwards did ; to check the growth of slavery, and consequently of manumission ; to encourage industrial undertakings in the city, as well as agricultural activity in Italy ; and to organize the foreign corn-supply effectively, so as to keep the natural price permanently low, while holding fast to the principle that the State should not expend its wealth on the maintenance of its ' unemployed '. But for the moment, as it must have seemed to him, the one necessary condition of getting any of these reforms started was to keep the sovereign mob comfortable at any price. The treasury was full, yet the citizens were almost untaxed, and the temptation was great. Counteracting measures might follow, agrarian bills, colony bills, road-making bills, the eventual result of which might be to relieve the treasury of its new burden. It may be that he saw the necessity of such measures as antidotes to the corn-law ; at any rate he devoted to the execution of them such an amount of personal energy as suggests this strongly. But for the moment he was compelled to find cheap corn for the people, because for the moment they were masters of the situation.

If he seriously believed that he was thus creating a permanent charge on the treasury, he was certainly to be blamed, and if he hoped to avoid it he was as certainly over-sanguine ;

itself tended more and more to depend upon Sicilian, African, and Egyptian harvests.

[1] See the story about the corn from Spain in Plutarch, *C. Gracchus*, ch. 6, and the description of his relation to the senate there given.

but we must remember that we have none of those speeches in which he developed his policy and defended it.

'Read his speeches', wrote Cicero in a memorable passage, 'and you would call him a veritable *patronus aerarii* '.[1] This makes it more than probable that he had gone carefully into the financial question; and to me it also suggests that he was devising schemes for neutralizing the drain on the treasury by so developing the production and transport of corn, as to bring down the price at Rome by natural instead of artificial means.

In conclusion, I would raise the question whether these alimentations, as we may call them, were really so vicious in their consequences as is generally assumed. That they constituted a serious evil no one can deny ; but I am inclined to think it possible that they saved Rome from still worse evils. When the government of an empire is concentrated in a single city, and that city is in the power of an ignorant, hungry, and idle mob, the statesman can only be described as sitting on a volcano. Until military organization and discipline could be brought to bear on it, till the centre of political gravity could be shifted away from it, the danger was chronic and extreme. Bad government and the lawless population of Alexandria brought the Empire of the Ptolemies to ruin ; bad government and an unfed populace might have done the same for the Roman Empire. No Roman statesman for a century after Gracchus was able to counteract the tendencies which kept this great mass of population crowded in the city ; for all of them circumstances were too strong, and all but Sulla acquiesced in the Gracchan remedy. It was an ugly running sore in the Roman system, and no physician could be found to attack the cause at its root. All that could be done was to prevent the disease becoming mortal ; and though he probably had higher aims, this seems the result of Gracchus's policy.

[1] *Tusc. Disp.* iii. 20, 48. Cicero is here contrasting the words and acts of Gracchus. But Gracchus was no mere rhetorician, as we know from Cicero's own evidence (*Brutus*, 126 ' grandis est verbis, sapiens sententiis, genere toto gravis '), and this passage must be taken as indicating a serious attempt to deal with the financial aspect of his bill.

THE *CARMEN SAECVLARE* OF HORACE AND ITS PERFORMANCE, JUNE 3RD, 17 B.C.

THE great object of Augustus in celebrating Ludi saeculares in 17 B. C. was to encourage the belief in himself and the consequent active loyalty to himself, as the restorer of the *pax deorum*—the good relation between the divine and human inhabitants of Rome. So far he had tried to attain this end by the ancient usual and proper means, i. e. by carrying out the various regulations of the *ius diuinum*, so many of which had long been neglected. But in that year he determined to undertake a special celebration, with the design of more effectually stamping the impression already made on the minds of the people ; and it so happens that we have more detailed knowledge of this celebration than of any other Roman rite of any period. This is fortunate, for it stands on the margin between an old and a new régime, like the *Aeneid* of Virgil, who had died two years earlier : that great religious poem was just becoming known, and there is an allusion to it in the hymn of which I am going to speak.[1] The Ludi were the outward or ritualistic expression of the idea immortalized by the poet, that a regeneration is at hand of Rome and Italy, in religion, morals, agriculture, government : old things are now to be put away,[2] a new and glorious era is to open. Henceforward the Roman was to look ahead in hope and confidence, trusting in Augustus, the Aeneas of the actual State.

Thus the study of the ritual of this festival is in every way most instructive, and every one can study it for himself in the several sources from which our information is derived : in the account given by Zosimus,[3] in the Sibylline oracle

---

[1] Line 40 ff.

[2] For the meaning of *saeculum* and *saeculum condere*, see Mommsen, *Röm. Chronologie*, ed. 2, p. 172, and Wissowa, *Abhandlungen zur römischen Religions- und Stadtgeschichte*, pp. 200-2.

[3] Zosimus, ii. 5 : the oracle is in ii. 6. Both are printed in Wickham's Horace in the introduction to the *Carm. Saec.*

which he has fortunately preserved, in the hymn sung on the last day of the Ludi, and in the inscribed *Acta* of which a great part was discovered in 1890 by the Tiber bank near the Ponte St. Angelo.[1] Soon after the publication of this latest source, it was discussed from three several points of view at one of the most interesting meetings of the Oxford Philological Society which I have ever attended. I do not remember that any of us who took part in that discussion laid stress on the new light which it threw on the performance of the *Carmen saeculare* : but it soon became apparent that it had a direct bearing not only on the performance but on the matter and composition of the hymn, and would give rise to controversy on these points. For whereas up till then we only knew that it was sung on the Palatine,[2] before the temple of Apollo which Augustus had lately built there ' in priuato solo ', we learnt from the *Acta* (line 147) that it was sung also on the Capitol : *Sacrificioque perfecto pueri XXVII quibus denuntiatum erat patrimi et matrimi et puellae totidem carmen cecinerunt* (i. e. on the Palatine) *eodemque modo in Capitolio. Carmen composuit Q. Horatius Flaccus.*

Mommsen in commenting on this in *Ephemeris Epigraphica* VIII, where he published the inscription, insisted that the *argumentum* of the hymn forbids us to suppose that the whole of it was sung both on the Palatine and on the Capitoline, for only the middle part of it, where Jupiter and Juno the Capitoline deities are rather obscurely hinted at, is suited to the Capitol, while Apollo and Diana (who was associated with Apollo in the Palatine temple)[3] are prominent both at the beginning and end. The first part, he contended, was sung on the Palatine, the middle part on the Capitoline, and the last part again after the return of the choirs to their original station. As to singing *en route*, he did not express a definite opinion.

---

[1] *Ephemeris Epigraphica* VIII, 255 ff., contains the text and Mommsen's commentary. Dessau, *Inscript. Selectae*, ii. 1. 282, does not give the whole document. *C. I. L.* vi. 32323.

[2] So Zosimus, who adds that the hymn was sung both in Latin and Greek : but of this we have no confirmation.

[3] Propertius, ii. 31. 15. It also seems to be implied in Plin. *N. H.* xxxvi. 13.

This view gave rise to a good deal of controversy, as will be seen by reference to the last edition of Wickham's Horace ; but it has recently been reasserted by Wissowa, who in reprinting a paper written in 1894 about the Ludi added a note in which he declared that the threefold division of the *Carmen* 'springt in die Augen', that lines 37–52 belong to the Capitoline worship, all the rest to that of the Palatine, and assumes that what belongs to each temple area was necessarily sung there. He too declines to speak with confidence about singing during the procession from one area to the other.[1]

It may clear the ground if I state my reasons for believing that the hymn was not sung in procession at all. True, such singing was not unknown at Rome. In 207 B. C. a choir of twenty-seven virgins sang a *carmen* in Saturnian verse of Livius the poet, as they went in procession from the shrine of Apollo in the Campus Martius to the Forum, where they stopped and danced in a peculiar manner with a rope,[2] and thence proceeded, whether singing or not Livy does not say, to the temple of Juno Regina on the Aventine, which had been struck by lightning. This performance, as Diels has observed in his *Sibyllinische Blätter*,[3] stands half-way between the old semi-magical singing and dancing of the Salii and the Fratres Arvales, and the singing of our *Carmen*, which was really only a *carmen* (so to speak) by courtesy, having no magical intent whatever,[4] and, as being in Greek lyrical metre, does not

---

[1] Wissowa, *Gesammelte Abhandlungen zur römischen Religions- und Stadtgeschichte*, p. 206 and note. Mommsen in *Ephemeris Epigraphica*, viii. 256.

[2] Liv. xxvii. 37 'Septem et uiginti uirgines, longam indutae uestem, carmen in (i. e. addressed to) Iunonem Reginam canentes ibant : illa tempestate forsitan laudabile rudibus ingeniis, nunc abhorrens et inconditum, si referatur. . . . A porta (Carmentali) Iugario uico in forum uenere : in foro pompa constitit : et per manus reste data, uirgines sonum uocis pulsu pedum modulantes incesserunt.' Diels, *Sib. Blätter* 91, puts this rope-dancing down as Greek, not Roman, and connects it with the ropes which occur in lists of articles paid for by the ἱεροποιοί in Delian inscriptions.   [3] p. 91, note 1.

[4] For the original magical meaning of the word, see Jevons in *Anthropology and the Classics*, pp. 94 ff.

suggest dancing in the sense of any old Roman religious practice. Rhythmic movements of some kind there certainly were, as I hope to show directly, but in the two sacred areas, not in procession from one to the other. And further, the words of the *Acta* seem to me explicit : the hymn was sung on Palatine and Capitoline, and nothing is there said of any point between the two. Practically too there would have been serious difficulty in marshalling fifty-four boys and girls, if they sang as they went down the steep hill from the Apollo temple to the Sacra via, along that irregular way and through the narrow fornix Fabianus into the Forum, and finally up the steep ascent to the temple of Jupiter. Gardthausen, in his work on Augustus,[1] suggested that they might have stopped at particular points to sing, e. g. in the Forum : but there is nothing in the hymn or the *Acta* to support this— no deity of the Forum is mentioned, nor did the Forum play any part in the religious rites of the Ludi. Once more, if the children had to sing in procession, accompanied as I presume they were by instruments,[2] careful rehearsal would be needed more than once : and if this were done in public as it must have been, it would destroy the novelty of the performance on June 3. We know from *Odes* iv. 5 *ad fin.* that Horace took pains with his rehearsing : but he says nothing there that can suggest processional singing. It is far better, I think, to accept the words of the *Acta* as giving us the simple fact. They are in other matters curiously explicit, and it is unlikely that in this one particular they should have been unnecessarily concise. I prefer even to accept the literal statement that the hymn was sung right through once on the Palatine and once on the Capitoline, and that the performance came to an end there. At any rate we will for the moment assume that the children were not compelled, after singing nineteen stanzas in one place and the same number at another

---

[1] *Augustus und seine Zeit*, vol. i, pt. ii, p. 630. Ferrero, *Greatness and Decline of Rome*, v. 94, note, is right in objecting to this kind of interpretation.

[2] *Aenatores* are mentioned in line 88 of the *Acta* : but these belong to another part of the Ludi. I imagine that the boys and girls were accompanied by tibicines.

nearly half a mile away, to plod back again and go through them all once more at the original starting-point.

But how are we to reconcile this limitation of the places of performance to two, with the contents of the poem itself ? In order to explain how I think this may be done, I must digress for a moment, and consider what the instructions must have been which Augustus gave to his poet-laureate. We must not of course imagine that on such an occasion Horace was left to himself. I suppose there is no bit of Latin poetry which has more constantly been in my mind than this hymn : and the impression it always gives me is that Augustus wrote out in prose what he wanted put into it, and that his laureate did this with consummate skill and *concinnitas* ; but the result, for me at least, is that it is as flat as such compositions usually have been. Nay, it is occasionally prosy, as e. g. in the fifth and sixth stanzas. Recently Signor Ferrero has glorified it as a most magnificent poem, full of inspiration, in language which suggests as great a want of judgement in literary, as he so often exhibits in historical, criticism.[1] At any rate the inspiration came from Augustus and not from the poet's native genius.

First, I should like to point out (though it does not directly concern our problem) that Augustus clearly wished Horace to combine in the hymn the three ideas of *religion, morality, and the fertility of man, beast, and crop*. The Princeps, I have long been confident, had grasped the fundamental idea of the old Roman worship, still alive in the hearts of most Italians, that this general fertility, without which the State could not go on and prosper, depended on the dutiful attention (*pietas*) paid to the divine beings who had taken up their abode in farm or city : ideas which covered the ordered life and religion both of family and State—both morality and religious duty. All these three ideas will be found duly expressed in the hymn.[2]

Secondly, Horace must have had instructions not to mention Augustus personally—that would be unnecessary,

[1] op. cit., v. 90 ff.   [2] e. g. in lines 13 ff., 29 ff., 45 ff., and 57 ff.

H 2

owing to the prominent part taken by him in the whole ritual of the Ludi ; but to give his poem a strong Apolline colouring, which was much the same thing as giving it a strong Augustan colouring, so completely had Augustus by this time come to be associated with the god whom he had settled close to his own house on the Palatine and on his own land. This of course suited Horace exactly as a poet, and he expresses his satisfaction in *Odes* iv. 6. 29 ff. I think it is quite possible that he went a little beyond his instructions ; for Apollo and Diana are far more prominent than Jupiter and Juno of the Capitol, who are only alluded to, not named.[1]

No doubt it was part of Augustus's policy to put the great Jupiter of the republic somewhat in the background as compared with his own Apollo : this can be proved in many ways :[2] yet I half suspect that Horace here went a little beyond what was required of him. The Capitoline deities had as a matter of fact been so far, i. e. up to the third day, on which the hymn was sung, more prominent in the ritual than Apollo.

Thirdly, Horace must have been told that the hymn must contain allusions to *all* the deities invoked in the ritual during the three previous nights and two days, as well as those of the third day. Now offerings had been made on the first night, at the underground altar of the Tarentum, near the Tiber bank, to the Moirae, on the second to Ileithyia (or the plural), and on the third to Tellus or Ceres :[3] and these all duly appear in stanzas 4 to 8 inclusive. Then by day the sacrifices had been offered to the Capitoline deities—and they

[1] i. e. in 45–52.

[2] See e. g. J. B. Carter, *Religion of Numa*, pp. 166 ff., who has many interesting remarks on the Apollinism of Augustus.

[3] In line 29 it is tempting to write Tellus with a capital T : but here Ceres seems to be performing her part as deity. The two run very closely together throughout the early history of the Roman religion : see my *Roman Festivals*, pp. 73 ff., Wissowa, *Rel. und Kult. der Römer*, pp. 192 ff. Mr. Stuart Jones has drawn my attention to Petersen's very interesting suggestion of a connexion between this stanza and the slab from the Ara Pacis in the Uffizi at Florence ; see Petersen, *Ara Pacis Augustae*, pp. 48 ff. : Mrs. Strong's *Roman Sculpture*, p. 42.

too are here, though somewhat obscured, in lines 45 to 52. These Capitoline deities are followed by Fides, Pax, Honos, &c., of whom we do not hear anything in the ritual : but this point I must for the moment postpone. Then Apollo and Diana come to the front again, and the hymn ends with a kind of summing-up of all the deities, Jupiter, Apollo, and Diana being mentioned by name.

The result of all this is that to a casual reader the hymn is a jumble of divine names, Roman and Greek, with Apollo appearing oftener than the rest, and almost abruptly in lines 33 and 61. Even when we have learnt all about the ritual and the policy of Augustus, it is very hard to divide the poem intelligibly : and I confess that no threefold division of it has ever ' sprung into my eyes ', as into Dr. Wissowa's.[1] Those five stanzas concerned with the deities of the night-ritual absolutely forbid it. So far as I can see, it runs thus : (1) an Apolline introduction or proodos of two stanzas, with an invocation of Apollo as Sol, which I will explain directly ; (2) five stanzas concerned with the deities of the nightly worship at the Tarentum ; (3) a return to Apollo for three stanzas ; (4) an appeal to the Capitoline deities, whom we identify by the white victims in line 49, followed by two apparently rather irrelevant stanzas about the prestige of Rome and her virtues ; (5) another return to Apollo and Diana ; and a concluding stanza, summing up the whole. How are we to reconcile all this apparent confusion with the singing of the hymn on Palatine and Capitoline only—i. e. on two sites with which Jupiter and Juno, Apollo and Diana were respectively alone concerned ? To sing of Jupiter or the Parcae or Tellus at the temple of Apollo on the Palatine

---

[1] *Abhandlungen*, p. 206, note 1, quoting Vahlen, whose paper I have not been able to see. Wissowa seems to take the whole down to line 36 as standing together and Apolline (p. 207, note). But to me lines 13 to 32 are plainly in honour of the deities of the Tarentum, though Ileithyia is introduced first instead of second, perhaps in order to run her into a dim kind of identification with Diana Lucina, or Juno Lucina, or both. This would suit the last and Apolline day of the festival : and we must note that the Tarentine deities are not now Dis and Proserpina, i. e. sinister deities of the underworld, but helpful ones (Wiss. 208).

would seem inappropriate, if we assume that the whole hymn was gone through there, as the *Acta* plainly imply ; and still more inappropriate would it seem that Apollo and Diana and the deities of the underground altar should be celebrated in the precincts of the great Jupiter of the Capitol.

The solution of these difficulties which I now propose for criticism has been suggested by a consideration of the nature of the two sites on which we know for certain that the hymn was sung : combined with the further consideration, in which no doubt every one will agree with me, that this hymn was not sung by two choruses of boys and girls standing stock still all the time, but making certain movements like the simple evolutions of the Greek chorus. This is now made clear by line 21 of the *Acta*, which probably belongs to a letter of Augustus to the quindecemviri datable some three months before the festival. This left plenty of time for choir training, and the inference is that there was plenty to learn. The words of Augustus's letter show that there was more than learning the hymn by heart ; the necessary steps are to be taken ' ad carmen canendum *chorosque habendos* '. Here some kind of evolutions must be meant, if not exactly dancing.[1] We cannot certainly know what those movements were ; but we may be sure that they would add to the interest and pleasure both of performers and spectators : and perhaps what I am going to say about the nature of the two sites will help us in guessing at some of them.

The only possible site of the temple of Apollo, says Hülsen,[2] is at the north-eastern corner of the Palatine. But there are serious objections to this view, and of late the conviction has been growing that the real site was where the temple of Jupiter Victor is generally supposed to be, overlooking the Forum Boarium and the Circus Maximus, whence there is an uninterrupted view over the Campus Martius, with the Capitol in the foreground a little to the right—a point of importance for my interpretation of the *Carmen*, as will be

---

[1] For Horace's use of the word *chorus*, see *Odes* iv. 7. 6 ; i. 4. 5. Cf. Propertius, ii. 2. 28.   [2] Jordan-Hülsen, *Röm. Topogr.* iii. 72.

seen directly.   Ovid suggests this site strongly in the lines in
his *Tristia* (iii. 1. 59 ff.) in which he imagines his book arriving
from Tomi and climbing up to this temple :

> Inde *tenore pari* gradibus sublimia celsis
>   Ducor ad intonsi candida templa dei.

The words *tenore pari* must mean ' going straight on ', equivalent to *uno tenore*, as Professor A. C. Clark suggests to me.
As Ovid's book is supposed to enter the Palatine by the temple
of Jupiter Stator from the *sacra via*, and to arrive first at
the *domus* of Augustus, it would have to turn sharp to the
left if the Apollo temple were on Hülsen's site, but would
go straight on if it were beyond the *domus* at the western
edge of the hill.   Here was space enough for a grand area,
enclosing the temple to north, south, and west, and in this
open space a few very simple movements would enable the
chorus to command every other site of religious or historical
interest in the city, now adorned in all directions with new
or restored buildings.   There was no building as yet on the
Palatine that could interfere with this view.   A little to the
right was the Capitol, with its own splendid temple, rising
above the Forum ; and beyond that again, plainly visible in
the distance just to the left of the Capitoline hill, was the site
of the Tarentum, where the midnight ceremonies had been
held.   Let us now apply our knowledge of this splendid
prospect to the subject-matter of the *Carmen*.

At once we see that the first three stanzas hang together,
and contain a happy allusion to the view from the area :
' possis nihil Roma uisere maius.'   But they contain also
another allusion, which (so far as I know) has not been noticed
in this connexion.   On the *fastigium* of the temple there was,
as Propertius tells us,[1] a figure of Sol with a quadriga :

> Tum medium claro surgebat marmore templum
>   Et patria Phoebo carius Ortygia.
> In quo Solis erat supra fastigia currus . . .

If we suppose that the first two stanzas were sung by the
united choirs in position, or as they wheeled into position on

---

[1] Propertius, ii. 31–10 (ed. H. E. Butler) foll.

the area, facing the view, we may safely conjecture that when they reached the third stanza they would wheel again to face the temple and Sol looking down from his *fastigium*. If the real sun were shining at the time the effect of this fine stanza would be very impressive. It is in my humble judgement the best in the poem :

> Alme Sol, curru nitido diem qui
> Promis et celas, aliusque et idem
> Nasceris, possis nihil urbe Roma
> Visere maius.

As they sang these last words the choirs may have wheeled again to face the prospect of the city. If so, they would then be in the right position for celebrating the next group of deities, those of the Tarentum and the nightly rites, who must of course be taken before those of day and light, as in the order of the festival.

With what movements, if any, the following five stanzas were sung, which plainly refer to the nightly rites, invoking the female deities there worshipped, it is impossible to say. They may have all been sung by the girls, and softly : they are certainly not so well suited to the boys. Nor would it be easy to explain why there are so many of them—five in all—if Augustus had not given his poet strict orders to bring in the *lex de maritandis ordinibus* [1]—a task accomplished deftly in that prosaic stanza to which I referred just now. Doubtless Horace was very glad to get back to Apollo in the next group of stanzas, to which I now turn.

The more closely I examine the hymn, the more convinced I become that it is purposely written so as to keep its Apolline character persistently in the minds of the audience ; three of its five parts are Apolline—the first, third, and fifth : in be-tween these we have the deities of the Tarentum and those of the Capitol. This reversion to the Apolline character would be emphasized, at the point we have now reached, by a movement of the choirs which would bring them once more into position facing the temple.

---

[1] This lex Julia had come into effect the year before that of the Ludi, viz. 18 B. C.

There is a difficulty here as to how far we are to consider this reversion to Apollo and Diana as continuing. Wissowa [1] would limit it to one stanza, putting a full stop (I suppose) after *puellas*, and connecting the four following stanzas together as Capitoline, i. e. as addressed to Jupiter and Juno. By general consent the last of these, beginning ' *Quaeque uos bobus ueneratur albis* ' is so addressed : for the white heifer was the special victim of Jupiter, and was never offered to Apollo : the *Acta* inform us that Jupiter and Juno had on the two previous days been propitiated with *boues pulchri* and *pulchrae*, while to Apollo had been offered only *cakes* of various kinds. There is also a strong opinion (Mommsen, Vahlen, Wissowa) that the stanza immediately before this one, ' *Di probos mores, &c.*', belongs to the Capitoline deities, and with this I agree, seeing that *probi mores*, and the general well-being of the *gens Romula* would be much more naturally connected with Jupiter and Juno than with Apollo and Diana. But I cannot, with Wissowa, begin the Capitoline part with ' Roma si uestrum est opus ' ; Apollo was the protecting god of Troy, and the way in which he is treated in *Odes* iv. 6, written at this same time, seems to me to make it clear that Augustus wished to encourage the idea that Rome was in a legendary sense at least the work of Apollo. I should therefore put a full stop after *relictis*, and there end the Apolline diversion : and imagine the choirs turning towards the Capitoline temple in front of them to begin—perhaps after a pause—the address to Jupiter and Juno with ' Di, probos mores docili iuuentae '.

With this must be connected, not only the next stanza, about which there is no doubt, but that which follows it ; in both these we have a distinct expression of the imperial idea, and the mission of Rome in the world, and this idea could be associated with no other deity than Jupiter Capitolinus, and with no other temple than his. Every outward sign of the Roman *imperium* was thus associated in the minds of the people, and Augustus must have known well enough

[1] *Abhandlungen*, p. 207, note.

that any change in this could only be very gradually accomplished.

I will also hazard a conjecture that the fifteenth stanza, with the names of Fides, Pax, and other deified abstractions, belongs to this Capitoline section of the hymn. The abode of Fides, an ancient goddess, was on the Capitol, and there is hardly a doubt that she was closely connected with Jupiter. Wissowa thinks that she was an offshoot from the ancient Dius Fidius, who must be identified with Jupiter.[1] The notion in Augustus's mind, which Horace had here to reproduce, was, I think, to lay stress on the Pax Romana, which must rest on the basis of treaties and good faith ; and I look upon Fides as here playing the part of a *callida iunctura*, connecting Pax, Honos, Virtus, and Pudor, with the great deities of the Capitol. Pax was in Augustus's head at this time, just hovering, so to speak, on the verge of deification, as may be seen in Tibullus i. 10 : and the Ara Pacis was begun only four years later.[2] Honos et Virtus, though separated in the hymn for metrical reasons, must go together as they always did at Rome ; their character is military, and they suggest Mars and the warlike virtues, which would otherwise be unmentioned in the hymn.[3] The Pax Romana, let us remember, depended on these virtues as well as the domestic ones. Lastly, Pudor would probably have been Pudicitia if the metre had admitted of it ; the latter was the female family virtue at Rome, and here I think we may see a compliment to Livia, and through her to the Roman matrons. Valerius Maximus not long afterwards, in the preface to his sixth book, *de Pudicitia*, thus addressed her : ' Tu prisca religione consecratos Vestae focos incolis, tu Capitolinae Iunonis

---

[1] *Rel. und Kult.*, p. 129 ff.   [2] Wissowa, *R. K.*, p. 334.

[3] Wissowa, *R. K.*, pp. 149 ff. It used to be supposed that there was a temple to these deities on the Capitol (see e. g. Burn, *Rome and the Campagna*, p. 193), the work of Marius. The site of Marius's temple is, however, uncertain, though this passage of the *Carmen* might be used to support the old hypothesis. The best-known temple was near the Porta Capena : and it is probably of this temple that Dio Cassius writes (liv. 18) that Augustus in this year 17 B. C. fixed the date of its festival on May 29 ; which is almost the same thing as saying that he rebuilt it.

puluinaribus incubas, tu Palatii columen augustos Penates sanctissimumque Iuliae genialem torum adsidua statione celebras.'

This brings us to the end of the Capitoline section of the hymn as I understand it, all of which would be sung with the great Capitoline temple as the most conspicuous object in view. Then we return once more to Apollo and Diana, the choir wheeling round so as to face the temple behind them, and possibly turning towards the Aventine at line 69. Here with great skill the poet introduces Apollo as *augur*, probably in allusion to the *augurium salutis*, which Augustus had revived in 29 B. C.,[1] and with the physical welfare of the people still more distinctly in lines 63 and 64. The verbs become indicative,[2] anxious prayer changes to confident assertion : and the prosperous future of Rome is thus happily associated with the Augustan Apollo at the end of the performance on the Palatine. The nineteenth and last stanza, which sums up the whole ceremony as Horace and his choirs are about to return to their homes, could not, I think, have been sung here ; it was kept to the real end of the performance, was added as an odd or lucky number, and would be more appropriate to the temple which was still the spiritual home of the idea of Roman greatness. Towards that temple the procession would now make its way, down the steep ascent to the Sacra via, and so through the Forum up to the area Capitolina. Let us now in the last place shortly consider how the hymn was adapted to this site as perfectly as to the other.

The area Capitolina was even larger than that of the Apollo temple, and the view from it was equally magnificent ; these two religious sites were in fact the only two in which the choirs would have had ample space for evolutions, and from which at the same time they would be able to see

---

[1] Dio Cass. li. 20 ; Suet. *Aug.* 31. We know hardly anything about this antique ceremony : but the language of Dio in xxxvii. 241 shows that the word *salutis* (Wissowa, *R. K.* 525) is not the deity Salus, but the health of the people : cf. Cic. *de Legibus,* ii. 21 ' augures . . . salutem populi auguranto.' The medical character of Apollo is apparent in lines 63–4.

[2] See Wickham's commentary.

almost every other important religious site in Rome. A good idea may be formed of the size of the Capitoline area from Lanciani's map to scale of the Sacra via,[1] which includes both the Coliseum and the Capitoline ; there it will be seen that the area is at least as large as the whole space occupied by the Coliseum. The temple stood in the middle of it, which accounts for the somewhat astonishing fact that (at one time) chariot-races—a mild form, I presume—used to be held here at the time of the Latin festival.[2] As time went on other temples were built here, but there was plenty of room for meetings of Comitia up to the end of the republican period. If we apply these facts to the performance of the *Carmen* here, we see at once that it could be gone through with motions as perfectly appropriate as on the Palatine.

The new temple of Apollo, which they had just left, was in full view across the Forum Boarium and the Velabrum, with the quadriga of Sol on its *fastigium*—probably in its newness the most brilliant object in sight. Doubtless the choirs would be facing it as they sang the first three stanzas. The site of the Tarentum across the Campus Martius was of course visible from the southern end of the area, and here the choirs would be during the next five stanzas, while they would wheel again to the west when they reached the second Apolline passage. They would be drawn up in front of the great temple during the Capitoline stanzas that follow, and would wheel about once more for the three Apolline ones with which the singing had concluded on the Palatine.

There would then remain the nineteenth stanza, summing up the whole performance :

> Haec Iouem sentire deosque cunctos
> spem bonam certamque domum reporto,
> doctus et Phoebi chorus et Dianae
> dicere laudes.

This is an extremely clever stanza ; Horace contrives to bring in Jupiter as after all the presiding genius of Rome,

---

[1] In his *Ruins and Excavations of ancient Rome*, fig. 72.
[2] Plin. *N. H.* xxvii. 45.

upon whose good will the future of the State depends, and as also the presiding deity among all the rest—*dei cuncti*, of all of whom, including Apollo, there were statues in the area Capitolina.[1] To me it seems impossible that this concluding stanza should have been sung anywhere but in that area. But at the same time Horace has most dexterously managed to make the final touch an Apolline one, as would in fact be fitting on a day especially dedicated to the Augustan Apollo. Phoebus and Diana are not here alluded to as the controllers of the destinies of Rome, but as the deities in whose honour the choirs, now about to disperse, have learnt and sung this hymn.

Beyond doubt this last stanza was sung by both boys and girls. How the rest of the *Carmen* was distributed between them I think it is impossible to determine, though many attempts have been made. I have made attempts myself, but never reached a satisfactory conclusion : we simply have not the necessary data. I have found it much more interesting and instructive to myself to correlate the divisions of the hymn with the two sites in which we know it was sung, and the views from them.

It is difficult to realize to the full, even for one who has been constantly occupied with the religious side of Roman life, how intensely local all Roman worship was—how intimate the association between place and cult.[2] It was in fact a perfectly right instinct that prompted Mommsen and others to assume that the Apolline part of the hymn must have been sung on the Palatine, and the Jovian part on the Capitoline, and thus even to strain the plain words of the inscription, ' Eodemque modo in Capitolio . . .' But it was clearly impossible to carry out such a principle logically on this June 3 ; for to do it the choirs would have had to make a pilgrimage

---

[1] Servius, *ad Aen.* ii. 319. The statue of Apollo here was a remarkable one, thirty cubits high, brought from Apollonia by M. Lucullus, as Pliny tells us *N. H.* iv. 92 and xxxiv. 30.

[2] The same holds good in the case of Ludi, which were in origin only a form of cult. The ludi Romani e. g. were in the cult of Jupiter, and originally took place on the dedication day of the Capitoline temple, the ides of September. The Megalesia were celebrated before the temple of Magna Mater, ' in ipso Magnae Matris conspectu ' (Cic. *Harusp. Resp.* 24).

of about a mile and back right across the Campus Martius
to the Tarentum, and there to sing, in broad daylight instead
of at night, the stanzas appropriated to the Tarentine deities.
Yet to leave these out would have been to violate the plan of
Augustus for including in the last performance all the deities
invoked in the festival. Instead of this Augustus chose the
two finest religious sites in Rome, from each of which everything could be seen that was to be alluded to in the hymn,
for the complete performance ; so far yielding to popular
feeling and conviction as to fix the second and last performance
for the Capitoline, the real religious centre of the whole
empire : but astutely taking care that the interest of this
third day's entertainment should be closely connected with
himself and the new régime, and that the religious colouring
of the ritual and the hymn should be emphatically Apolline.
Nothing could please his poet better :

> Spiritum Phoebus mihi, Phoebus artem
> carminis nomenque dedit poetae.

ON THE *LAVDATIO TVRIAE* AND ITS ADDITIONAL FRAGMENT

(*C.I L.* vi. 1527)

ALL students of Roman law know the inscription which
goes by this name ; and that part of it which raises a compli-
cated question of legal inheritance is to be found in the later
editions of Bruns's *Fontes Iuris Romani*. The whole series
of surviving fragments, partly preserved in the Villa Albani
in the original marble, partly in the form of copies made long
ago of fragments now lost, contain a record of domestic life
of exceptional human interest ; the heartfelt utterance of
a husband on the death of a wife absolutely devoted to him
for forty-one years, and addressed, unlike all other *laudationes*,
to herself and not to an audience. The portrait which he
draws of her is no rhetorical exaggeration, but mainly a record
of facts, and she lives in it for ever as a woman of extraordinary

energy, ability, and good sense, yet a real tender-hearted unselfish woman, devoted to her household duties and to the interests of her husband and her relations, unfortunate only in having never borne him a son. The most touching passage in it is perhaps that in which, apparently after the death of an only daughter, he records how she implored him to divorce her and raise up seed by another wife ; he breaks out into a passionate protest against the very thought of such treachery to one who had rescued him by her prudence and self-devotion from imminent dangers, and had lived with him in unbroken harmony for so many years.

For a study of this famous inscription, which may almost count as a fragment of Roman literature, something had been done before 1863 when Mommsen took it in hand, but he for the first time made it intelligible as a whole. He read a paper on it to the Berlin Academy, which was published in a separate form, and is now reprinted, with the additional fragment which is chiefly the subject of this paper, in the first volume of his *Gesammelte Schriften.* This fragment was found at Rome in 1898 near the Via Portuense, and was first published in the *Notizie dei Scavi* of that year by Vaglieri ; it has since been printed with a short commentary by O. Hirschfeld in the *Wiener Studien* for 1902, who also inserted it in its proper place in the whole inscription as editor of the volume of Mommsen's works just mentioned. There can be no doubt that it belongs to the *Laudatio Turiae.* Though it consists of only ten lines, none of which seem to contain more than about three-quarters of the original ones, i. e. the latter part of each line, it seems to fit very naturally into a large gap in the middle of the whole inscription ; but it does not entirely fill this gap, for it does not join on at either end to the text as we have it. It gives us the only letters we possess of the original heading, which can be completed (U)XORIS ; but unluckily the wife's name is not preserved with it. We must therefore wait for further discoveries in order to make absolutely sure of the identity of this wonderful woman. Up to 1898 Mommsen and most scholars have accepted the view that the lady was Turia, wife (as we know from Val. Max. 6. 7. 2) of a Q. Lucretius, whose romantic adventures in the proscriptions of the year 43 are recorded by Appian, *Bell. Civ.* iv. 44. But both Vaglieri and Hirschfeld insist that this new fragment puts that view out of court, on grounds, as I think, by no means convincing. I propose to show in this paper why I think that the new fragment adds to the probability that Mommsen's view was the correct one, and that the lady was actually Turia, wife of Q. Lucretius Vespillo.

In order to explain the place which the new fragment should take in the inscription as we have it, it is necessary to understand that the *Laudatio* obviously consisted of two parts, roughly answering to the two parts of the surviving fragments, which are divided, as has been said above, by a gap which may have been a considerable one.[1] In the first part, which is mutilated at the beginning, the chief topics are the prudence, energy, and unselfishness of the wife in rescuing her father's will from an attack made on its validity by her relations, and the way in which she and the speaker dealt with the patrimonium they thus inherited ; these matters are only interrupted by two paragraphs[2] in which he speaks of the long period of their happy married life, and of his wife's many domestic and other virtues. This digression looks to me as if the speaker thought that he was getting too legally technical, and that the *laudatio* proper was not sufficiently obvious. However this may be, it is, I think, quite clear that in this first part of the document he never really travels beyond the beginning of their married life ; according to an almost certain completion of the text[3] (line 3), the marriage had not taken place when the parents of the wife were suddenly murdered together (perhaps by their own slaves, as Mommsen suggested), and the affair of the will

---

[1] The most convenient edition of the whole inscription is now that in Dessau's *Inscriptiones Selectae*, vol. ii, pars. ii, pp. 924 ff.

[2] Lines 27–36 in Dessau, p. 925.

[3] 'Orbata es re(pente ante nuptiar)um diem utroque pa(rente in penatium soli)tudine una oc(cisis).' It is hard to see how the first five words can be otherwise completed.

must have happened soon afterwards, whether when the speaker and his wife were still only betrothed or actually married is uncertain. But before we reach the end of part i, the details of the management of the patrimonium clearly show that the marriage has been completed. Then comes the gap which is imperfectly filled by the new fragment.

The second part, before the discovery of the new fragment, began with a mutilated passage which seems to refer to a return from absence or exile, which the husband owed quite as much to the energy and *pietas* of his wife, as to the clemency of some one in power ; and as the well-preserved succeeding paragraphs tell the story of a wonderful escape, of the vain efforts of the wife to persuade Lepidus to carry out the restitution accorded to her husband by Octavian (Caesar Augustus, as he is called by anticipation), of the brutal conduct of Lepidus, and the final *clementia* of Caesar, it has been assumed, and perhaps rightly, that this powerful person was Octavian himself. The *laudatio* then proceeds to the happy time of peace after Actium (' pacato orbe terrarum, restituta republica '), the want of children, the proposed divorce, and the speaker's horror at the bare idea of it, and the death of the wife ; ending with words which in a religious sense have not obtained the attention they deserve : ' te di Manes tui ut quietam patiantur atque ita tueantur opto.' [1]

I now give the correct text of the new fragment, from Hirschfeld.[2]

U XORIS
subsi DIA · FVGAE · MEAE · PRAESTITISTI · ÓRNAMENTIS ·
    CVM · OMNE · AVRVM · MARGARITAQVE · CORPORI
  trad IDISTI · MIHI · ET · SVBINDE · FAMILIÁ · NVMMÍS · FRVCTIBVS
5   *a* DVERSARIORVM · CVSTODIBVS · APSENTIAM · MEAM · LOCVPLETASTI
    ITIS · QVOD · VT · CONARERE · VIRTVS · TVA · TE · HORTABATVR
    VNIBAT · CLEMENTIÁ · EORVM · CONTRA · QVOS · EA · PARABAS
  v ÓX · TVA · EST · FIRMÌTATE · ANIMÍ · ÉMISSA.
    RTÍS · HOMINIBVS : Á · MILONE · QVOIVS · DOMVS · EMPTIONE
10   EXV[L] · BELLI · CIVÌLIS · OCCÁSIONIBVS · INRVPTVRVM
        defe NDISTÍ · DOMVM · NOSTRAM

[1] See my *Religious Experience of the Roman People*, p. 389.

[2] As printed in Dessau, op. cit., the fragment is further conjecturally completed, but without any gain of certainty.

From the position in this fragment of the word (*U*)*xoris*, the only one we as yet possess of the original heading of the inscription, and obviously the last one, it is clear that Hirschfeld was right [1] in placing this fragment in the big lacuna between the two main portions of the *laudatio* as we have it. But what was the size of the gap between the end of this and the beginning of the next fragment we cannot be sure. The one ends with a fairly clear indication of an attack on a house belonging to the pair, warded off by the wife in her husband's absence ; the other begins with an allusion to a return of the husband from exile or enforced absence. It has been assumed both by Vaglieri and Hirschfeld that they follow close on one another and refer to the same circumstance, viz. the escape of the husband from the proscriptions of 43 B. C. This seems to me to be quite impossible. It has arisen, I think, simply from unconscious prepossession in favour of the story as it was formerly known to us. They refer, I feel sure, to quite different times and events, and after a careful revision of this paper (in 1918) I am still more confident. That Dessau had an inkling of the truth I am also inclined to think ; for at the end of the new fragment he indicates a considerable gap.[2]

Let us consider this fragment a little more closely : in spite of the loss of a considerable part of each line, its general bearing is pretty clear. First, we have a *fuga* of the husband ; secondly, at his departure his wife gave him as *subsidia* all the gold and pearl ornaments she had about her. It is futile to connect this, as Hirschfeld does, with the story of a certain Acilius told by Appian (4. 39), who persuaded the soldiers to whom he was betrayed to take a communication to his wife, on promise of a rich reward : she gave them all her jewels, and they procured his escape to Sicily. In the husband's own account she gave the jewels *to himself*—' tradidisti mihi ' —which is a very different thing. Next we find her sending him slaves (*familia*), money, and *fructus*, in his absence.

---

[1] Mommsen's *Gesammelte Schriften*, i. 403.
[2] ' Perierunt non pauca.'

This is quite out of keeping with the hairbreadth escapes of 43, and would have been apt rather to attract attention to the man than to effect his security. As we read through the long list of escapes in Appian, it is clear that it was with the utmost difficulty that the proscribed eluded notice, hiding themselves, often ineffectually, in all sorts of holes and corners ; and of those who reached Sicily safely we are told that they were glad to receive food and clothing at the hands of Sextus Pompeius. I may add that the words ' apsentiam meam locupletasti ' also seem to me ill suited to a time of such imminent peril for the fugitives, when hardly any part of the empire was without its spies and assassins.

Again, the words that follow in lines 6, 7, 8, though they are by no means clear in detail, evidently refer to some effort on the part of the wife undertaken on behalf of her husband ; and if this is to be explained of the part she played after he was proscribed, the speaker has told the same story twice over in a most unnatural way, for he immediately proceeds to tell it again in lines 14 to 20 of the next fragment. If on the other hand we could explain it of some earlier danger and escape, the order of events in the *Laudatio* which is in the main presented through all that remains of it, would be sufficiently preserved.

But the most effectual proof, as I think, that he is here speaking, not of 43 B. C. but of an earlier time, lies in the mention of Milo in line 9 of the new fragment as if he were alive at the time spoken of. ' Mirum ', says Dessau in a note, ' orationem reverti ad annum ' 706 (48 B. C.) ; but it is not *mirum* at all, unless you insist on referring the new fragment to 43, with Hirschfeld and Vaglieri. Milo was killed in the spring of 48 B. C. after being recalled by Caelius Rufus from his exile at Massilia in order to join him in a mad sedition against Caesar's government and legislation (Caes. *Bell. Civ.* iii. 20-2). Caesar's own account of this miserable business is unluckily very corrupt, but the story can be made out in outline with the help of Dio Cassius (42. 24). It would seem

that when Caelius was ejected from Rome, he went to Campania and was there joined by Milo, who still had in his pay
the remains of gladiatorial bands which he had formerly
collected there; that they made a combined but futile
attempt on Capua, and that Milo was then sent south to the
region of Thurii ' ad sollicitandos pastores ', while Caelius
attacked Casilinum. Or it may be that Milo had left Campania
before the attempt to surprise Capua. But in any case it
is clear that Milo, as Dio Cassius says,[1] gathered a band of
desperadoes together, and roamed southwards seeking whom
he could devour ; in Bruttium he began to open the *ergastula*,
and met his death in an attempt on Cosa.

It seems to me hardly possible to refer the imperfect lines
9, 10, 11 of the new fragment to any other event than this.
The wife [2] is in a country house, as we are entitled to guess
from the fact that she supplied her husband with *fructus* as
well as with slaves and money. Milo may have had a grudge
against the pair for having bought cheap either this identical
villa, or some other house which had formerly belonged to
him and was sold cheap after the forfeiture of his property
by exile. We know something about such sales from Asconius
(*in Milonianam*, p. 54, ed. Clark), and from Cic. *ad Att.* v. 5 ;
Fam. viii. 8. 3. Milo apparently attacked the house, which
was successfully defended by the wife.

On this interpretation the whole of the new fragment would
refer to the events of 49 and 48 B. C. But if so, it will be
asked what was the *fuga* of line 2, for which the husband
received from his wife so much provision in the form of jewels
and gold, and during which she supplied him with slaves,
money, and *fructus* ? Let us notice (1) that in line 5 she
is evidently represented as having eluded or corrupted
' adversariorum custodes ', and that *adversarius* is exactly
the word which would be used of one side at the opening of

---

[1] Ἐς τε τὴν Ἰταλίαν ἀφίκετο, καὶ πολλοὺς ἀνθρώπους, τοὺς μὲν βίου δεομένους,
τοὺς δὲ καὶ τιμωρίαν τινὰ δεδιότας, συλλέξας τήν τε χώραν ἐκακούργει κτλ. 42. 24.

[2] I use the word ' wife ' for convenience : as will be seen directly, it is not
clear whether the marriage had as yet taken place. The completion,
(*defe*)*ndisti*, is almost certain.

a civil war, but not of assassins going about to catch and slay the victims of a proscription ; [1] (2) that in lines 4 and 5 of Part I, the husband is spoken of as being in Macedonia soon after the sudden murder of the parents of the wife, while her sister's husband Cluvius had gone to Africa ; (3) that if this fragment refers to the events of 49 and 48, the *clementia* spoken of in line 7 can hardly be other than that of Julius himself, of whom the word is so often used from the very outset of the civil war.   Putting these things together, we may divine, not with certainty, but with great probability, as I think, that the *fuga* was nothing more than a flight of the husband from the country house at which they were staying when the war broke out ; if it was the one attacked by Milo in the following year, it would probably be between Campania and Bruttium, and open to Caesar's troops marching in pursuit of Pompey to Brundisium.   We may guess that the husband reached Brundisium safely and crossed with Pompey to Macedonia ; the wife remained, and was treated with courtesy by Caesar's orders, after a display of the spirit and courage that was natural to her (' quod ut conarere virtus tua te hortabatur : vox tua est firmitate animi emissa '). This is indeed guesswork ; but it is entirely in keeping with the part of the lines left to us, and inconsistent with nothing that is recorded in the rest of the *laudatio*.

In any case, if it be true that this fragment refers to events having nothing whatever to do with the proscriptions of 43, and can be itself referred with confidence to 49 and 48, we are now in a position to recast our ideas both as to the date of the marriage and the identity of the pair.

On both these points we may now, in my view, safely return to the conclusions of Mommsen in his paper of 1863.   As regards the first, Mommsen put the marriage between 48 and 42 B. C.   The pair were certainly married at the time of

---

[1] It is interesting to find that this word is used no less than four times by Pompeius himself in his dispatches to Domitius preserved in Cic. *Att.* viii. 12 ; i. e. it is used of the opposite party and its leader in January 49, the very time to which, as I believe, the first lines of the fragment refer.

the proscriptions, which took place in the autumn of 43. At the time of the murder of the parents they were probably not married but only betrothed; but the condition of the first few lines of Part I, on which this conclusion is chiefly based, is not such as to make it quite certain. If however it is correct, the marriage remained uncelebrated while the future husband was in Macedonia, and a legal defence of the will, as well as the defence of the house alluded to in the new fragment (a house perhaps left them by her father) took place also during the period of betrothal. As Mommsen assumes, on the return of Caesar from the east in the autumn of 47, the affianced husband received a free pardon, like Cicero and so many others; or possibly this was after the battle of Pharsalia. The marriage would naturally follow, and we should not be far wrong in putting it at the end of 48 or some time in 47. As they were married for 41 years (as he tells us in line 27), this would bring the date of the death of the wife, and of the *laudatio* itself, to 7 or 6 B. C.

Secondly, as regards the identity of the husband, we may return to the hypothesis, recently discarded by Vaglieri and Hirschfeld, that he was that Q. Lucretius Vespillo whose adventures in the proscription of 43 are recorded by Appian and Valerius Maximus; for what the *laudatio* tells us of these adventures is not changed, according to my view, by anything in the new fragment. It may be as well to recapitulate the evidence for this identification, especially as the story of Lucretius's escape is incidentally of singular interest.

Caesar in *Bell. Civ.* iii. 7 mentions that on arriving off Oricum from Brundisium he found Lucretius Vespillo and another man in command of eighteen ships from Asia, i. e. a part of Pompey's fleet; and this exactly suits the statement of the *laudatio* that the speaker had gone to Macedonia while his wife's sister's husband, C. Cluvius, had passed to Africa— the two provinces where operations were being carried on by the Pompeian party in 49–48 B. C. This however is rather a confirmatory point than a matter of substantial evidence.

The real argument lies in a comparison of the accounts of

Appian and Valerius Maximus of the escape in 43, with the hints afforded by the *laudatio*. What the *laudatio* tells us is this : ' Why (he says) should I pluck from my inmost thoughts once more the story of my rescue ? how you sent me a sudden message of warning, how you repressed my *audacia,* and when I yielded to advice, you prepared *fida rece(ptacula)*, with the knowledge only of Cluvius and your sister.'

Appian's story is as follows : Lucretius was wandering in the country with two faithful slaves, and being in difficulty for provisions was trying to return to his wife in Rome, and had actually arrived at the gate, when he saw a troop of soldiers coming out. It suddenly occurred to him that this was the very place where his father had been arrested[1] in the Sullan proscription, and he slipped into one of the tombs that there lined the road. One of his slaves had hurt his leg, and he was leaning on the arm of the other when this happened. While they were hiding here they were surprised by some tomb-wreckers (what a picture here of the insecurity of the times !), and to these the slave gave himself up to be stripped while Lucretius fled to the gate—the soldiers having now presumably disappeared. At the gate, one reads with astonishment, he waited for the slave, shared his clothes with him, and reached the house in safety. There his wife hid him between the ceiling and roof of a chamber until the storm had passed over. Valerius Maximus, who gives the name of the wife as Turia, merely tells how he was hidden ' intra cameram et tectum cubiculi ' at the great peril of his wife, who shared the secret with one handmaid only.

Now the only contradiction between these combined accounts and the story of the *laudatio* is in the statement of Valerius Maximus that no one knew of the hiding-place but the maid, while the *laudatio* speaks of Cluvius and his wife being in the secret. This however is not a serious difficulty ;

---

[1] Appian does not say that he was killed. If that had been so, the son would have been forty when he himself was proscribed, and could not have been married till he was about thirty-five, which is perhaps unlikely.

we may assume that the maid was the only person *in the house* who knew, but that Cluvius and his wife were acquainted with the fact also, as being either in Rome or not far away. In any case Valerius Maximus was careless in regard to detail. Appian's account agrees strikingly with that of the *laudatio*, if we may assume that Lucretius was making for Rome on the advice of his wife, instead of exposing himself to his enemies in the country districts. She sent him a sudden warning and repressed his rashness, preparing meanwhile a safe hiding-place in their house in Rome. The return to the city was obviously made by night and in disguise ; this is suggested by the mention of the tomb-wreckers, and the changing of the clothes with the slave at the gate ; thus though the peril was undoubtedly great, it was less exactly to be described by the word *audacia* than the attempt to escape from Italy, which brought so many to their end.

This identification is of course by no means certain, but it may hold the field until another fragment is discovered. No other of Appian's many stories of wonderful escapes tallies in any degree with the *laudatio* ; and the whole tenor of the document shows that the speaker was a sufficiently important person to have been included in such a collection of stories. If he was Lucretius Vespillo, he held the consulship in 19 B.C. ; and here Hirschfeld has raised the objection that there is no mention of the consulship in the *laudatio*. But with singular and touching delicacy, the speaker throughout keeps himself in the background, attributing his wealth, his safety, his happiness, entirely to the wonderful woman he celebrates. Once, indeed, when he is speaking of their joint management of their property, he breaks off with the words, ' of this I will say no more, lest I should seem to be claiming a share in your praises ' (Part I, line 40). Could such a man have dreamt of referring to his consulship while recalling the happiness of his domestic life ?

Supposing that my reasoning holds good, I would reconstruct the whole astonishing story as follows : Turia's parents were murdered at the very outbreak of the civil war in January 49, at a time when we might naturally expect such things to happen. Shortly afterwards Lucretius, then affianced to her, had to leave Italy and act under Pompey in Epirus. Turia, left behind in Italy, with only her sister to help her, whose husband Cluvius had gone to Africa, also to fight on the Pompeian side, had now to face a series of dangers and difficulties, all of which she overcame by her wonderful courage and address ; she traced out the murderers of her parents and secured their punishment ; she obtained the protection of Caesar during his march through Italy to Brundisium ; she contrived to smuggle supplies to the absent Lucretius ; and resisted and finally defeated an attempt to upset her father's will, under which she and Lucretius were the chief if not the only inheritors. The next year, 48 B.C., during the attempted revolution of Caelius and Milo, she was attacked by the ruffian following of the latter in a villa in the country and contrived to beat them off. At the end of that year, or some time in 47, Lucretius returned like Cicero to Italy, and obtained a pardon from Caesar. The marriage was now celebrated, and until Caesar's assassination they presumably lived in tranquillity.

When a second triumvirate was formed and the proscriptions began, Lucretius's name appeared on the lists, whether at the instance of Octavian or Lepidus is not clear ; the restitution came from Octavian, and the conduct of Lepidus suggests that he had a personal spite against the pair. Then followed the extraordinary escape I have already described, which must have happened at the end of 43 or beginning of 42. For some months Lucretius must have been kept in concealment of some kind, for when at last an edict was obtained for his restitution, Octavian the author of it was absent ; he had gone to the campaign of Philippi, and his departure seems not to have taken place till the summer of 42. Turia took this document to Lepidus, who was consul and in charge of Rome and Italy, and was received, according to her husband's account, with insults and even with blows. The return of Octavian at the end of the year set this matter right ;

and Lucretius hints that Lepidus's brutality was not forgotten by him.

The rest of the story, which is of unique interest as a picture of Roman domestic life, does not properly belong to the subject of this paper.[1] It is to be hoped that other fragments may be discovered which may help to complete it, and may afford us a more certain identification of the husband and wife ; and this is not impossible if, as Vaglieri thinks, the original site of the inscription was in the locality where this new fragment was found, viz. the Via Portuense on the right bank of the Tiber.

AN UNNOTICED TRAIT IN THE CHAR-
ACTER OF JULIUS CAESAR

CAESAR did fewer foolish things than most men with his opportunities have done ; so far as we can judge from his own writings and the accounts of those who knew him, a want of practical wisdom was not one of his weak points. But on one occasion, early in his political life, he did what seems to us a foolish thing, and one which no one has ever attempted to explain as a wise one. I am thinking of the revival of a quaint antique and semi-religious procedure for the condemnation[2] of Rabirius in 63 B. C. The circumstances are familiar, and have been discussed recently in this country by the late Master of Balliol in his *Problems of Roman Criminal Law*, and by Dr. Hardy in the *Journal of Philology*.[3] The leaders of the popular or Marian party, Caesar and Crassus, wished to make it highly unsafe to put Roman citizens to death without trial under the ' last decree ' of the Senate, or in any other way, in times of political excitement. They did not so much want to impugn the legality of that decree

[1] See *Social Life at Rome in the Age of Cicero*, pp. 158 ff.

[2] The *condemnation*, because it is quite clear that the duumviri did not judge the case, but only pronounced sentence (Liv. i. 26).

[3] Strachan-Davidson, *Problems of Criminal Law*, i. 188 ff. Hardy in *Journal of Philology*, xxxiv. 12 ff.

(*senatus consultum ultimum*), for that would have been almost impossible ; [1] but to make it dangerous for the consul to take violent action under it. They wanted, no doubt, to impress this deeply on the minds of the city population, and Caesar hit upon the plan of reviving a curious and obsolete procedure, which would bring the possible results of such political violence and murder vividly before their eyes. The only example of the use of this procedure known to us dates from the age of the kings, and is embodied in the legend of the victorious Horatius, who slew his sister on his return from battle. For this murder he was not tried, but straightway condemned ; the king appointed two duumviri to perform this duty, being unwilling, Livy says, to undertake such an ill-omened job himself.[2] A *lex horrendi carminis* governed the procedure. The duumviri were to pronounce sentence ; against this sentence the condemned man might appeal to the people ; if their verdict went against him, ' caput obnubito, infelici arbori reste suspendito, verberato vel intra pomerium vel extra pomerium '.[3]

This procedure belonged to an age when civil law had not yet been fully disentangled from religious law. The words last quoted make it probable that Horatius was a *homo sacer* in some sense, and the sequel to the story shows how difficult it was to restore him to the condition of an ordinary citizen ; for this point, which does not bear directly on our present subject, I may refer to p. 72 of this volume.[4] What could have induced Caesar to imitate this strange, semi-religious ritual ? Was it simply that it gave him an opportunity to exhibit the *infelix arbor*, or, as Cicero calls it, the *crux*, in

[1] This follows from the acquittal of Opimius, in 121 B. C., for killing C. Gracchus, under the *senatus consultum ultimum*. See e. g. Heitland's *Roman Republic*, ii. 318. Hardy, op. cit., pp. 16 ff.

[2] Liv. i. 26 ' Rex, ne ipse tam tristis ingratique ad vulgus iudicii ac secundum iudicium supplicii auctor esset, concilio populi advocato, Duumviros, inquit, qui Horatio perduellionem iudicent, secundum legem facio.' I suspect that the Rex appointed duumviri in order that the sacred kingly office might not be polluted.

[3] Liv. i. 26. 6 : Strachan-Davidson, op. cit., i. 135 ff.

[4] Cf. *Journal of Roman Studies*, i. 58 ff.

the Campus Martius, with the executioner (*carnifex*) who was to do the ugly work, unless the victim were acquitted on appeal ?[1] Certain it is that, having found the old Rabirius, who was said to have killed Saturninus in the disturbances of the year 100, Caesar and Crassus, with Labienus as their agent, contrived to pass a law which revived this old procedure ; that Caesar and a relative of the same name were appointed duumviri under it, that they condemned Rabirius, and that on his appeal the Senate interfered and declared the whole foolish proceedings to be invalid.[2] (The speech of Cicero, of which we have a considerable part, was delivered in an ordinary trial before the tribune and his *comitia tributa*, and with this we are not concerned.) At the moment of condemnation, and before the Senate had quashed the proceedings, it seems possible that *crux* and *carnifex* were actually on view in the Campus. Yet the desire to *imponieren* seems hardly sufficient to explain why a sane man like Caesar should have chosen to go back to such primitive practice. Nothing else that we know of him in that year 63 shows any parallel to such injudicious statesmanship.

I think that there are traces in Caesar of a tendency, common at the time, to take an interest in ancient procedure, especially that of religion ; and it is possible that for once he may have been tempted to give this intellectual interest a practical application. It would be interesting if we could discover whether he was already *pontifex maximus* when he condemned Rabirius ; but it does not seem possible to determine this. It is, however, in any case likely that his thoughts were running on the probable vacancy, and the duties of the office, for which he and his mother seem to have been equally desirous.[3] It is worth remembering that Varro dedicated his great work on the religious antiquities of Rome to this *pontifex*

[1] Cicero seems to imply this in *pro Rabirio*, secs. 10, 11, 16. So, too, Strachan-Davidson, i. 197.

[2] So Hardy, op. cit., p. 28. Strachan-Davidson thinks that Cicero interfered, either as consul or through the agency of a tribune.

[3] ' Cum mane ad comitia descenderet, praedixisse matri osculanti fertur, domum se nisi pontificem non reversurum ' (Suet. *Iul.* 13).

maximus, which he would hardly have done if Caesar had shown no interest in such things. It is also worth remembering that, as a boy, Caesar had been, presumably by his family, intended to fill the most ancient of Roman priesthoods, and that a Flamen Dialis was daily and hourly engaged in *caerimonia*. I have elsewhere casually suggested that, as in the case of C. Valerius Flaccus, recorded by Livy as happening about a century earlier, the object of the family may have been to keep the lad out of mischief.[1] On the other hand, it is possible that Caesar's mother Aurelia, who seems to have shared with him his ambition to be the head of the Roman religious system, may have been one of those good ladies who venerate all forms of priesthood, and are ready to dedicate their sons at an early age to the lifelong service of the religion of the State. Undoubtedly these things were arranged within the family in collusion with the *pontifex maximus*, as in the case of the Vestals ; and it is noticeable that, according to Suetonius, the Flamen Dialis *destinatus* was immediately provided with a wife, young as he was, doubtless because the office could only be held by one who had a Flaminica ready to assist him in his duties.[2] Incidentally, I may remark that it was this wife Cornelia who saved Caesar for the world. As she was Cinna's daughter, Sulla ordered the boy to give her up, which he promptly refused to do, and was at once deprived of his priesthood (or, rather, the prospect of it), and of his wife's dowry and other property. Suetonius evidently thinks of the priesthood as an honour which Caesar would have been glad to retain ; but even if Aurelia looked at it in this light, it does not follow that at the early age of fifteen the boy was not glad to be safe from the shackles of such an office.

A few years after this (69 B. C.), when delivering an oration at the funeral of his aunt Julia, he dwelt on the fact that she was descended, on the mother's side, from a rex, Ancus

[1] *Religious Experience of the Roman People*, p. 343. According to Velleius ii. 43, Caesar had been made a *pontifex* during his absence in Asia as a young man, and hurried home to Italy to take up the office, which suggests that he was in earnest about these priesthoods.

[2] Suet. *Iul.* i, *ad init.* Frazer, *Adonis*, &c., p. 409.

Marcius, and on the father's side from Venus, the reputed ancestor of the gens Julia. His comment on this, as quoted by Suetonius from the original, is remarkable : ' Est ergo in genere et sanctitas regum, qui plurimum inter homines pollent, et *caerimonia* deorum quorum ipsi in potestate sunt reges.'[1] The use of the word *caerimonia* here is peculiar : it seems to mean that the Julii had an inherited instinct for looking after the cult of the gods—an instinct which, perhaps, the devoted Aurelia discerned in her son.[2] The whole sentence, a good specimen of the Attic style, breathes the young man's feeling that the Roman State cannot dispense with its gods, and that *caerimonia* is necessary in order to keep them in full vigour of benevolence.

On the whole, then, I think it quite possible that in the imprudent revival of the obsolete procedure of the duumviri Caesar may have been prompted by this instinct for *caerimonia* ; or, if I may be allowed a little latitude of conjecture, I should guess that Aurelia suggested to him a course which he was not unwilling to take. She was at this time living in his house, and her anxiety about *caerimonia* is well illustrated in the affair of the Bona Dea in the following year, when (as Plutarch tells us) she took all possible pains to prevent any disturbance of the rites. When Clodius was discovered she put an end to them at once : evidently she had the lead in the house at the time.[3] I have little doubt that the divorce which followed was also the work of this strong-minded mother.

But apart from these indirect inferences we have a story, which seems quite worthy of credence, that many years afterwards Caesar again had in his mind a piece of antique ritual, when he punished two mutinous soldiers in 46 B. C. Though the story is told only by Dio Cassius,[4] it cannot have

[1] Suet. *Iul.* 6.
[2] It is worth remembering that the Julii were charged with the care of the cult of Veiovis at Bovillae. *C. I. L.* i. 807, and Wissowa, *Rel. und Kult. der Römer*, ed. 2, p. 237.
[3] Plutarch, *Caesar*, ch. 9, is very explicit about this. Whence did he get his information about Caesar's private life ?
[4] D. C. xliii. 24.

been invented by him. These two men were put to death, the historian says, ' in a sort of priestly fashion '. ' I cannot explain it ', he goes on, ' for no Sibylline verse or other oracle is quoted for it ; but the fact is that they were sacrificed (ἐτύθησαν) in the Campus Martius in the presence of the pontifices and the Flamen Martialis, and their heads were afterwards fixed up on the Regia.' It has long been recognized that this strange and barbarous procedure closely resembles that of the sacrifice of a horse to Mars on the Ides of October, which I fully discussed in my *Roman Festivals*, p. 241. After a chariot-race in the Campus Martius, the near horse of the winning pair was sacrificed to Mars ; the tail was cut off and carried to the Regia (the official residence of the *pontifex maximus*), and the warm blood allowed to drip on the hearth there. The head was also cut off and decorated with cakes ; and formerly there was a fight for it between the men of the Via Sacra and those of the Subura. If the former carried off the prize, they fixed it on the wall of the Regia ; if the latter, on the Turris Mamilia.

Caesar himself took part, according to Dio Cassius, in the quelling of this mutiny, which was especially dangerous as taking place at Rome, where his position was not too secure. Dio puts it in the year 46 ; and in that year Caesar returned to Rome from the African war on July 26, and stayed there till after November 26, when we hear of him in a letter of Cicero.[1] He was thus beyond doubt in the city, as Dio states, at the time of the mutiny, and I am much inclined to suspect that the sacrifice of the mutineers took place on the Ides of October, and concurrently with that of the horse, or as a substitute for it. The motive was perhaps much the same as in the case of Rabirius, to make an impression on the city mob, who might easily be infected with the spirit of mutiny. We may doubt whether in either case the desired effect was produced. I do not think that Caesar was ever at home in

---

[1] Cf. *de Bell. Afr.* 98, and Cic. *ad Fam.* vi. 14 ; which letter is dated A. D. 5 Kal. *intercalares priores* (two intercalary months were that year inserted between November and December).

the city, or understood its motley population ; as I have said elsewhere,[1] they knew little of him, and had received no great benefits from him. Augustus understood them far better, and made no such strange attempts to frighten them into acquiescence.

There is yet another curious story of Caesar, which may be set by the side of these two examples of perverted *caerimonia*. It was said that when he crossed the Rubicon he ' consecrated ' a number of horses, and set them free to wander where they would. Suetonius tells us that in the days preceding his assassination these horses persistently refused to eat, and even shed abundant tears ; he seems in this chapter to be depending on the authority of Cornelius Balbus, Caesar's intimate friend and secretary.[2] The legend of their refusal to eat seems to be alluded to in the fifth Eclogue of Virgil, and was adduced by H. Nettleship as evidence for the identification of Daphnis in that poem with Caesar : [3]

> non ulli pastos illis egere diebus
> frigida, Daphni, boves ad flumina ; nulla neque amnem
> libavit quadrupes nec graminis attigit herbam.

But why did Caesar release these horses, and to what god did he consecrate them ? Is this, after all, only one of the legends which gathered round a famous event ? It may be so ; but, on the other hand, it is not a common form of marvel, but looks rather as if it had a bottom of truth, and we may note that Asinius Pollio was with him at the time, who afterwards wrote a history of the Civil Wars.[4] If the horses were consecrated at all they were consecrated to Mars, for whom he had a special regard, and to whom war-horses were sacred.[5] But it is difficult to fathom his motive, or even to be sure of the fact.

In the last place, let us note that in his somewhat elaborate

---

[1] *Roman Ideas of Deity*, p. 118.   [2] Suet. *Iul.* 81.
[3] *Ancient Lives of Virgil*, p. 40.   [4] Plutarch, *Caesar*, 32.
[5] *Roman Festivals*, p. 330. Caesar seems to have been fond of horses, and rode one of which Suetonius tells strange things (*Jul.* 61), and which would allow no one to mount him but Caesar. He afterwards placed a statue of this horse in front of his temple of Venus Genetrix.

account of the civilization of the Gauls great prominence is given to religion (*natio admodum dedita religionibus*), and especially to the Druids and the details of their human sacrifices, as well as to their gods.[1] Even now this account forms a considerable part of what we know about early Celtic religion.

There is then, I think, some reason to believe that Caesar, among his many various interests, included the *caerimonia* of deities at Rome and also elsewhere ; and that once or twice in his life he translated his interest and knowledge somewhat strangely into practical procedure. This does not mean, of course, that he was in any sense ' superstitious ' : what interested him was the ritual of State or tribe. He may have had his trifling superstitions. Pliny tells us[2] that after a certain carriage accident he always used to repeat a sort of spell three times when he took his seat—but this he may have done just as I take off my hat to a magpie. As we might expect, we have it on good authority that he never allowed a *religio* to alarm or delay him in any undertaking about which he had made up his mind : when in his African campaign the victim fled from the sacrificing priest, he went none the less determinedly to meet his enemy.[3] But of serious ritual he thought without contempt, and the careful pains which Augustus bestowed on this department of State activity may, after all, though we have not been used to think so, be due in some measure to his uncle's precepts. As Dr. Hardy reminds me, the uncle was as careful in the constitution of his colonies of the maintenance of *caerimonia* as Augustus himself could have been ; of this his *lex Ursonensis* gives abundant proof.

[1] *De Bell. Gall.* vi. 13–19.
[2] *Nat. Hist.* xxviii. 21.
[3] Suet. *Iul.* 59 ' Ne religione quidem ulla a quoquam incepto absterritus unquam vel retardatus est.'

ANCIENT ITALY AND MODERN BORNEO: A STUDY IN COMPARATIVE CULTURE[1]

THE valuable work of Messrs. Hose and McDougall on the *Pagan Tribes of Borneo* was published in 1912, and contains an account of the methods of divination practised by some of these peoples. In compiling it the authors had been led to consult Smith's *Dictionary of Classical Antiquities,* so striking did the parallelism appear between the augural practices of Borneo and those of ancient Italy. And they were not mistaken ; the parallelism is even stronger than they suspected, and induced me to write a notice of the book in the *Journal of Roman Studies,* in order to call the attention of students to the subject.[2] Since then I have again gone carefully through the work, and noted a number of other points in which the habits of the one people remind me of the other. It seems worth while to bring these together.

But before doing this, I must profess myself both unable and unwilling to theorize on comparative evidence of this kind. These singular analogies may arise naturally from the fact that those tribes of Borneo are now in much the same state of culture as were the earliest Latin settlers and their ancestors of the pile-dwellings and *terremare* of northern Italy.[3] It is primarily on these earlier stages of Italian life,

---

[1] Read to the Oxford Anthropological Society, April 1915.

[2] *J. R. S.* ii (1912), 269 f.

[3] For example, the Kayans, &c., live chiefly by agriculture, but they also keep domestic animals, particularly the pig (the favourite sacrifice), and they hunt wild animals, pigs, deer, &c. See Hose and McDougall, chs. vi and ix. That the peoples of the pile-dwellings and terremare were in much the same condition as regards their food is proved by the remains of it which have been found. Seeds of cultivated plants have been discovered among the earliest of these settlements, and the people seem to have become more agricultural as the settlements became more permanent. They had domesticated the pig, but continued to hunt it in its wild form. In the terremare we find evidence of distinct advance on the same lines : the people practised agriculture more elaborately, but had not ceased to be hunters. Peet, *Stone and Bronze Age in Italy,* chs. xiii and xiv ; Modestow, *Introduction à l'histoire romaine,* ch. iv.

wood was sometimes used instead of bone or horn. Wood
was occasionally hardened by burning in the age of the pile-
dwellings : and the same practice is found in Borneo ; ' for
the defence of a house short sharp stakes of split bamboo
are thrust slantingly into the ground, so as to present the
fire-hardened tip towards the feet of the coming foe '.[1]

Of the government of the old Italian long houses we of
course know nothing ; but it is none the less interesting
to examine that of the more advanced tribes in Borneo. Each
house has a chief and, if there is more than one house in
a village, the village has a chief ; but the most instructive
fact is that the chiefs and their families form a social class
like the patricians at the head of the community.[2] The
members of this class rarely marry outside it, and special
attention is paid to their methods of marriage, a fact which
reminds us of the patrician *confarreatio*. Cohabitation of
men of the upper class and women of that below is not unknown,
but the men will eventually marry into their own class. The
members of this upper class can be distinguished by the
superiority of their personal appearance as well as by their
dress ; but the origin of the class and its chieftainships does
not seem to be known. They do not appear to be of different
blood from the rest,[3] though some of them claim divine
descent, nor do they seem to have attained their position by
skill in ' magic ' ; there is nothing here to support Frazer's
theory of the origin of kingship. The government of the chiefs
has the three characteristic features of the old Roman kingship, i. e. they are leaders in war, in religion, and in the settlement of disputes and the punishment of the guilty. The

[1] See Peet, op. cit. 355, 297 ; H. and McD. i. 161. For the practice of
hardening wood in the fire see my *Roman Festivals*, p. 203, and Skutsch in
Classical Quarterly, 1910, p. 270. I find that it is familiar to anthropologists,
and I have been shown spears thus hardened in the Pitt Rivers Museum
at Oxford. For the smearing with blood, Professor Reid sends me an
interesting parallel in Ammianus, xix. 2, 61.

[2] There are three classes in all : the lowest consists of slaves, mainly
belonging to the upper class, and the middle class of all other members.
See H. and McD. i. 68 f.

[3] But see ii. 10.

moderation and good sense with which all this work is done, and the comparative absence of savagery and magic, suggest that the tendency we sometimes meet with to interpret Greek and Roman practices by reference to those of such primitive populations as the Australian aborigines, is apt to be misleading, and that there is need of more careful comparative study of peoples in a more advanced social condition.

I may note in passing one or two other characteristics of these chiefs, which will further help us in forming an idea of the intellectual condition of the ancestors of the Latins. They have a natural gift for oratory, and frequently use it in their deliberations : and they preserve the traditions of the history of their tribe, for at least several generations back.[1] How far they preserve them accurately we cannot tell ; but the fact is worth noting just now, when there are signs that we are beginning to criticize the destructive criticism of the last century or so, which brushed away all old Italian tradition as worthless.[2] It is as well to reflect that the members of the upper class, from which the chiefs were drawn, were both in Borneo and in Italy educated by their own experience and that of their ancestors ; they had religious, military and judicial duties to perform, and in performing them must have learnt much. There is no sign in either country that they were intellectually petrified, merely the creatures of collective habit ; there was room for individuality to ripen and fructify. As Professor Conway has lately said, the ' unknown Roman statesman who shaped the Roman constitution ' is surely the great Valerius Publicola, if we are to treat tradition with any sort of respect. The reader of *The Pagan Tribes of Borneo*, and especially its twentieth chapter, will find such a chief as Publicola in Tama Bulan of the

---

[1] H. and McD. i. 63 and 68. Other points relating to the chiefs and their class will be mentioned below. A photograph of a chief haranguing his followers will be found opposite i. 70.

[2] See e. g. Professor Conway in *Classical Review*, 1914, p. 275. Of course in ancient Italy the great difficulty is to distinguish what is Greek in origin from genuine Italian tradition, and especially in matters of religion. In civil history and law we are rather better able to see through the mist.

Kenyahs, not to speak of others.[1] In writing of peoples of
this stage of civilization it is preposterous to talk of ' repré-
sentations collectives ' or ' mentalité prélogique '.[2] At every
turn we have the clearest evidence of individual character
and its value.

The functions of the chiefs in three departments, war,
jurisdiction (if I may use the word), and religion, may suggest
a convenient division of the rest of my subject-matter.
Whatever is done of importance in these departments is done
by the chiefs and members of their families, i. e. the upper
class, as by the patricians in earliest Rome, who were doubtless the descendants of an upper class of chiefs and their
families in the age of the pile-dwellings and the *terremare*.

About the customs of war there is not much to say, but
it is interesting to find that enlightened chiefs are gradually
overcoming the savagery of former years, and initiating
a pacific policy destined to put an end to sudden raids, and
so to set an example to modern Europe.[3] Nothing definite,
however, in the nature of a ' ius fetiale ' seems as yet to have
been noticed. Except in the matter of head-hunting, which
seems not to have been an ancient practice of this people,
and is now dying out, war is not accompanied by special
cruelties among the higher tribes. Prisoners are eagerly
taken by the Kayans, and become slaves, but are kindly
treated, and as in ancient Latium, often form a part of the
family life.[4]

It is curious to find the classical ' testudo ' in use among
the Kayans. ' If a strong party determined to attack a house
in face of an alert defence, they may attempt to storm it in
broad daylight by forming several compact bodies of about
twenty-five men. Each body protects itself with a roof of

[1] Conway, loc. cit. ; H. and McD. index, s. v. Tama Bulan.

[2] Individuality is everywhere apparent in Hose and McDougall's book.
Even dancing, which is so often represented nowadays as the result of
' collective mental action ', is often performed by a single person (e. g. ii. 157).
For the ' mentalité prélogique ', &c., to which allusion is made above,
see e. g. Lévy-Bruhl, *Les Fonctions mentales dans les sociétés primitives*, ch. iv.

[3] H. and McD. ii. 205.

[4] ibid. i. 184. For head-hunting, see end of ch. x.

shields held closely together, and the several parties move quickly in upon the house simultaneously from different points, and attempt to carry it by assault.'[1] Compare the ' testudines ' as sculptured on the column of Marcus Aurelius, in Schreiber's *Atlas of Classical Antiquities*, plate 44, fig. 8.

There is evidently a certain kind of sacredness (for want of a better word) about warfare among the Bornean tribes, especially at its commencement : the warriors are subject to strict taboos throughout the raid or campaign.[2] Two of these show that curious instinct for avoiding new things and adhering to old ones, which is familiar to all students of old Italian religion ; they must use only their home-made earthen pots, and fire must only be made by friction.[3] They were clearly thought to be in a ' holy ' or dangerous state, a belief which might easily be illustrated from other parts of the world, and which has been fully dealt with by Sir James Frazer in *The Golden Bough*.[4] But the most curious ceremony is that which the men undergo who are to take part in the actual attack. Some distance from the village to be attacked ' two solid platforms are built about twenty feet apart, and a large beam is laid from one to the other. The chiefs and principal men take their seats on the platforms, and then every man of the party in turn approaches this beam, the fighting leader coming first. If he is willing to go through with the business, he slashes a chip from the beam with his parang and passes under it. On the far side of the beam stands a chief holding a large frond of fern, and as each man passes under, he gives him a bit of the leaf.'[5] The magic properties of fern are well known,[6] and here probably the idea is that some special protection would be gained by carrying it about the person. But the passage under the beam also, in all probability, contributed to this result ; here the last

[1] H. and McD. i. 181.   [2] ibid. i. 170 f.

[3] See e. g. Henzen, *Acta Fratrum Arvalium*, pp. 26 and 27 ; Wissowa, *Rel. und Kult. der Römer* (ed. 2), p. 160. For the making of fire by friction at Rome cf. Festus (p. 94, ed. Lindsay).

[4] See *G. B.*, pt. ii (Taboo, &c.), pp. 157 f.

[5] H. and McD. i. 171.   [6] *G. B.* ii. 66 f.

edition of *The Golden Bough* is again helpful in convincing
us that the passage through an aperture or under an arch
or beam enables a man or a host to get rid of evil influences.[1]
In another paper I have discussed this question in connexion
with the passing of a conquered army under the yoke in
ancient Italy, and of the return of an army into the city
through the Porta triumphalis.[2] We do not know for certain
that a Roman army *setting out* for a war had to pass under any
kind of arch ; but we do know that it had to be ' lustrated '
on its return in the Campus Martius ; and it is possible that
the so-called temple of Ianus, which was really a double
archway always standing open during war-time, may have
been a survival from a time when the host actually passed
through an arch on its way to a campaign.[3]

Turning to the administration of justice, we find that
custom, sanctioned by religion, and collective responsibility,
are the chief agents among the Kayans in enabling the chiefs
to perform this part of their duties without much difficulty.[4]
There is ample opportunity for the tact and ability of an
individual chief like Tama Bulan, but the real foundation
of justice is in the community itself. The following sentences

[1] *G. B.*, pt. vii, vol. ii, pp. 189 f.

[2] See above, p. 70 ff. ; cf. *G. B.*, pt. vii, vol. ii, pp. 193 f.

[3] See Domaszewski, *Abhandlungen*, p. 222 : he seems to guess that the
army originally passed out under this arch, and later on, after the building
of the ' Servian ' wall, by the Porta Carmentalis (cf. the story of the Fabii,
Ov. *Fasti*, ii. 201 ; Liv. ii. 49 ' infelici uia, dextro iano portae Carmentalis,
profecti ad Cremeram flumen perveniunt '). Dom. as usual gets out of his
depth here, but his main suggestion is worth attending to. This porta had
two iani or passages (Wissowa, *R. K.*, ed. 2, p. 104), and so had the Ianus
Quirinus or Ianus bifrons. Is it possible that this feature had some relation
to the exit and return of an army ? Note that according to Wissowa this
is the real meaning of the term Ianus geminus, the double head being now
proved to be later. I find an interesting fact from India bearing on this
matter : ' In northern India it is a common charm to drive the cattle under
a rope fixed over the village cattle-path, and among the Dravidians of
Mirzapur two poles and a crossbar are fixed at the entrance of the village
with the same object, i. e. to protect them against disease ', &c. (Crooke,
Folklore of Northern India, ii. 299).

[4] H. and McD. at the beginning of ch. xx. The whole of this chapter is
of very peculiar interest.

may help us to realize the conditions of social life in a Latin community like early Rome, where the basic principle of justice lay beyond all doubt in the minds of the people, that is, of the upper class, known to us in Rome as patricians. ' The principle of collective or communal responsibility of the household ' (i. e. of the ' long house '), ' which is thus recognized in face of the spiritual powers, as well as in face of other communities, gives every man an interest in the good behaviour of his fellows, and at the same time develops in him the sense of obligation towards his community. The small size of each community, its separation and clear demarcation by its residence under a single roof, its subordination to a single chief, and its perpetual rivalry and conflict with other neighbouring communities of similar constitution, all these circumstances also make strongly for the development in its members of a strong collective consciousness, that is to say, of a clear consciousness of the community and of his place within it, and a strong sentiment of attachment to it.' [1] The authors add that a member can hardly leave the community even if he would : he would be an outcast, without helm or sail, and he would find it almost impossible to gain admittance to any other community.[2] All these facts explain ' how smoothly the internal life of the community generally runs, how few serious offences are committed, how few are the quarrels, or the instances of insubordination towards the chief, and how tact and good sense can rule the house without inflicting any other punishment than fines and compensatory payments '. And the same class of facts, if we think of them as existing in early Latium, will help to explain the nature of the authority of the paterfamilias, and of that higher form of the same broadly based authority, conferred by the patrician body, which we know as that of the Rex.

There are, however, occasionally serious crimes, breaches

---

[1] H. and McD., pp. 194 f.

[2] In early Italy this was not so, as Professor Reid reminds me ; the provisions for a *ius exilii* were already elaborate.

of taboo, the most dreaded of which is incest, and these are held to bring grave peril to the house, and danger to the crop of *padi*.[1] The same feeling can be recognized in early Rome in the belief that crime disturbed or violated the ' pax deorum ', and that the deity concerned would punish the community unless some expiatory step were taken to re-establish the right relation between the human and divine inhabitants of the city.[2] At Rome this was done by making over the criminal, the man who had broken taboo, as ' sacer ' (cursed and consecrated) to the deity whose special rights he had violated, with the result that any one might put him to death who was so disposed.[3] At this point we find a remarkable similarity of feeling among the two peoples with whom we are concerned, in the dislike of shedding blood even in these cases of punishment for sinful crime. I have noticed this in my paper on the original meaning of the word ' sacer ' : the harvest thief is hung ; the man who had suffered ' consecratio capitis et bonorum ' might be thrown from the Tarpeian rock ; the guilty vestal was buried alive ; and the ' parricida ' was sewn up in a sack and cast into the water. For incest in Borneo the usual punishment is, strangely enough, also to shut up the offenders in a wicker cage and to throw them into the river.[4] This is a substitute for an older punishment which involved the shedding of blood, for this was felt to be *the blood of the community*. It may be that the strength of communal feeling, which was extremely strong in ancient Italy, may there also help to explain the intense dislike of shedding human blood, either in punishment or sacrifice or in the two combined. The idea that the blood of the individual is the blood of the community has been long familiar to us.[5] In Borneo even the process of cupping, which involves some loss of blood, has to be atoned for by an offering made to the patient by the surgeon. Kayans have no scruple in shedding the blood of their enemies, but

---

[1] H. and McD. ii. 196.

[2] *Religious Experience of the Romans*, pp. 272 f.

[3] See *J. R. S.* i (1911), 59. [4] H. and McD. ii. 196.

[5] See e. g. Robertson Smith, *Religion of the Semites*, pp. 254 f.

they rarely go to war with other Kayans : and the shedding of
Kayan blood by Kayans is of rare occurrence. To shed human
blood, even that of an enemy, in the house, is against custom.[1]

I now turn to the subject of religion proper, where our
comparison is in some points of remarkable interest. In
writing of the religion of the early Romans I have insisted
that their beliefs must be considered as essentially animistic ; [2]
and that, though showing traces of the survival of ideas which
Dr. Marett has described as animatistic, they were on their
way to develop something in the nature of deity out of their
world of spiritual agents. The Romans in fact were fairly
well advanced in their conception of the supernatural. The
same is the case with the Kayans and Kenyahs of Borneo.
' They may be said to attribute a soul or spirit to almost
every natural agent and to all living things, and they pay
special regard to those that seem most capable of affecting
their welfare for good or evil. They feel themselves to be
surrounded on all sides by spiritual powers, which appear
to them to be concentrated in those objects to which their
attention is directed by practical needs . . . we may say that
they have differentiated from a *continuum* of spiritual powers
a number of spiritual agents with very different degrees of
definiteness. Of these the less important are very vaguely
conceived, but are regarded as being able to bring harm to
men, who must therefore avoid giving offence to them, if they
should by ill-chance have been offended. The more important,
assuming individualized and anthropomorphic forms and
definite functions, receive proper names, are in some cases
represented by rude images, and become the recipients of
prayer and sacrifice.' [3]

This language might be used with little alteration of the
earliest Roman religion as I have described it in my sixth
Gifford lecture ; and that description may gain some force
from the comparison with another people not so far behind the

[1] H. and McD. ii. 199.

[2] See *Religious Experience of the Romans*, ch. vi.

[3] H. and McD. ii. 2, note.

early Latins in general culture. Life, soul, power, animation, or whatever we choose to call it, is the essential characteristic of the spirits of the Kayans and Kenyahs, as it was of the old Roman 'numina':[1] and *inanimate* objects were not supposed to be endowed with such powers by either people. There is no true worship of stocks and stones. Before every Kayan house there stand wooden posts, very roughly carved to indicate the head and limbs of a human form. 'But the post cannot be called an idol : it is more of the nature of an altar.' Perhaps the faint traces that we find at Rome of a tendency to make images of a deity, e. g. Pales,[2] should be explained in this way : as I wrote of them some years ago, 'it is hardly safe to take them as genuine examples of iconic worship'. Or the stone of Terminus may be compared with these curious objects (survivals from a preanimistic age, or an age of animatism, as Dr. Marett calls it) ; whether any spirit or 'numen' was thought actually to be resident in the stone, may be doubtful, yet that stone was also in some sense an altar, as is shown by the fact that when first set up as a boundary-mark it was sprinkled with blood and adorned with garlands.[3]

In one point, which is of importance in estimating the process of the development of deity out of a vague world of spirits, the religion of the Kayans and that of the Romans are strongly contrasted. The former have no priesthood ; not even in their chiefs do we see the characteristics of the true priest. Neither have they permanent temples, which are usually found in conjunction with a priesthood. The fact seems to be that priesthood arises where there is a fixed and permanent settlement on the land, and where a 'numen' or deity is caught and isolated on a particular spot, which becomes his own property, and so needs an agent or official.[4]

---

[1] H. and McD. ii. 3; *Rel. Exp.*, p. 119 ; *Roman Ideas of Deity*, p. 27, &c.

[2] *Rel. Exp.*, pp. 147 and 165, note 7, and Tibullus, ii. 5, 27.

[3] See my *Roman Festivals*, pp. 325–6.

[4] H. and McD. ii. 74 ; *Rel. Exp.*, p. 123. See also A. Lang, Gifford Lectures, *The Making of Religion*, p. 284 ; Robertson Smith, *Rel. of the Semites*, pp. 104–5.

The Romans and their Latin cousins were beginning to be definitely settled when we first catch a vague glimpse of them : Latium had at least some communities that we may call cities, of which the sites were never afterwards changed, nor the habitations of their deities. But the Borneo tribes are more in the condition of the pile-dwellers of the Italian lakes; their houses and villages, though often unchanged for long periods, are not as yet bound to the soil by any passionate regard for it. This is probably the reason why priest and temple are not found among them in any true sense of the words ; and this makes it seem strange that they should have got as far as they have in the direction of anthropo-morphic deity. But this may be the result of contact with other peoples.

Though the process of god-development is of some interest to us, it is hardly so with the gods thus developed. There is one, Laki Tenangan, who seems to be in some sort a supreme and intertribal deity ; but little is known of him, and that little does not show any real analogy with Zeus or Iupiter.[1] He is not a god of the sky, nor of the thunder ; but his title Laki seems to answer to the Graeco-Roman use of the word 'father', as applied to deities, i. e. his power can be used benevolently, and he is not unwilling so to use it for mankind.[2] So with the other gods of the Kayans and Kenyahs, who can be approached through the birds of omen, as I will explain directly, or by way of messages or prayers sent through the channel of sacrificed animals.

On the other hand, the great mass of spiritual beings, the Toh, are thought of as hostile to mankind. They are wild and have not been reclaimed : but ' those of the locality in which a man dwells are regarded by him as less dangerous than those of other parts : for experience has shown him that in the neighbourhood of his own village he may behave in certain ways with impunity, whereas in distant regions all

[1] H. and McD. ii. 6 and 10 f.
[2] ibid., ii. 6, where this is proved by reference to the sacrifice and prayer offered to this god.

is uncertain '.[1] This is simply the feeling of ' religio ', gradually soothed away in settled habitations, but recurring as they are left farther and farther behind, e. g. by an army, as I have described it more than once in my Gifford lectures.[2] Nothing can show more conclusively the importance of *permanent* settlement in the mental development of mankind.

This is illustrated too in one detail which reminds us of the early Latin settler. In clearing a patch of jungle for sowing *padi*, a few trees are usually left standing on some high point of the ground, in order not to offend the Toh of the locality, who are believed to use them as resting-places.[3] We may aptly compare this with the instructions given by Cato to the Latin farmer for making a new clearing ; he is to offer sacrifice and to pray the unknown spirits of the wood or trees to excuse the liberty he is taking : and when he proceeds to dig the ground, he is to take further steps to set himself right with the spirits.[4]

Midway between the gods and the Toh are spirits of a higher order than the latter, i. e. those attached to men or animals, alive or dead ; but they do not seem to throw any new light on ancestor worship or the idea of Genius, as we might have expected. True, the description given of the ' secret helper ' of an individual, which occurs mostly among the Sea-Dyaks, rarely among the tribes we are specially concerned with, is of great psychological interest ; but it does not seem as yet to be sufficiently investigated to enable us to compare it with familiar Greek and Roman beliefs.[5] The most instructive point about it is perhaps the strong proof contained in it of the development of the individual as distinct from the group.

I proceed in the last place to consider the system of divination among the Kayans and Kenyahs, which affords such striking points of comparison with that of the Romans and

[1] H. and McD. ii. 25.

[2] *Rel. Exp.*, pp. 41, 316, and many other passages (see index). See above, p. 8 ff.

[3] H. and McD. ii. 23.   [4] Cato, *de Agric.*, ch. 139, and see above p. 87.

[5] H. and McD. ii. 90 f.

Etruscans that it caused the authors to look up the details of the process in ancient Italy. They suggest, though with all due caution, that the two systems had a common root : that ' while the Aryans carried the system westward into Europe, the Indonesians, or some Caucasic people that has been merged in the Indonesian stock, carried it eastward '.[1] The bird whose flight is most important in augury is a hawk (Haliastur intermedius). In the work we are examining (ii. 52) is a most interesting account of the way in which this bird is consulted. A party of Kenyahs under Tama Bulan are about to undertake a journey, with the object of making peace with another tribe. The record is in the form of a diary, and the writer very naturally remarks at the end that he felt as if he had just lived through a book of the *Aeneid*.

After the chief had been purified with water and the blood of pigs, three men of the upper class—patricians in fact, who alone can take the auspices [2]—sat under an extempore shelter and searched the sky for hawks. After a while they caught sight of a hawk high up and far away, and began to try and persuade it to fly towards the right. This they luckily accomplished ; then they settled down to watch for another that should fly towards the left, and a third which should circle round and round. ' In about half an hour two hawks had obligingly put in an appearance, and behaved just as it was hoped they would behave ; and so this part of the business was finished.' What followed, i. e. sacrifice and prayer, also has its interest for us. Tama Bulan, though a trifle unwilling to perform these ancient rites, nevertheless had to act in a priestly capacity, like the Roman rex : he sprinkled on the congregation the blood of the victims (a practice obsolete in historical Rome), and recited a prayer in a rapid murmur, like the priests of Iguvium (*tacitus precator*).[3] ' Meanwhile four boys were pounding at two big drums to keep away from the worshippers all sounds but the

---

[1] H. and McD. ii. 255.   [2] *Rel. Exp.*, p. 304.
[3] Jevons in *Anthropology and the Classics*, pp. 94 f. ; *Rel. Exp.*, p. 187. Tama Bulan seems to have disliked the magical character of such praying.

words of their own prayers.' So at Rome the priest covered his head with his toga, and tibicines played all the time in order that no unlucky sound or word might be heard which would make it necessary to start afresh with a new victim. Here the Borneo practice seems useful in dissuading us from abandoning this old interpretation of the veiled head in favour of one of which the Romans themselves knew nothing at all, viz. that it was a sign of separation and consecration.[1]

A still more remarkable parallel with Roman custom is the consultation of Bali Flaki, the divine hawk, before sowing and harvesting the rice crop.[2] On some quiet spot by the river bank, what is called a ' tegulun ' is set up, i. e. a horizontal pole supported about a yard above the ground by a pair of vertical poles. The augur lights a small fire beside the ' tegulun ', and sits on the ground behind it, so as to see through it a square patch of sky, and waits until a hawk becomes visible on this patch. When the hawk becomes visible he waves it towards the left : ' for he knows that if it flies towards the left he will prevail over his enemy, but that if it goes to the right his enemy is too strong for him. Here we plainly have the old Italian ' templum ' of augury, the rectangular space marked out by the ' lituus ', within which birds might be observed ;[3] and here too we find the rule which both in Borneo and in Italy applied to some birds though not to all, that the left was the auspicious side. Then again we have ' oscines ' as well as ' alites ', e. g. the woodpecker has two notes, one of which is lucky, the other unlucky.[4]

[1] See *Rel. Exp.*, p. 195, note 35, and references there given. Add *Aen.* iii. 405 f., which leaves no doubt as to the Roman interpretation. So too Serv. ad loc.   [2] H. and McD. ii. 56.

[3] The templum was a rectangular space, af which the frame, so to speak, was an imaginary one; but I suspect that it was originally the space visible from the door or opening in the operator's tabernaculum, which would naturally be a rectangular one; cf. von Jhering, *Evolution of the Aryan* (Eng. trans.), p. 364.

[4] H. and McD. ii. 59. At Rome there were many minutiae in the doctrine of omens from oscines : here too the Black Woodpecker (*Picus Martius*) was an important bird in augury. Festus (Lindsay, p. 214). On the subject generally, see Bouché-Leclercq, *Hist. de Divination,* iv. 199 f.

If the augur has secured good omens from other birds, his men will avoid hearing the woodpecker by singing and rattling their paddles on the side of the boat, which seems to savour of Roman ways, if it cannot be exactly paralleled at Rome. We may remember that the famous Marcellus of the second Punic war used to ride in his litter with the blinds drawn down, so that he should not see anything of evil omen.[1]

The method of divination by examination of a victim's liver is also of great interest for students of old Italian religion. The sacrifice of a pig, the commonest victim, is always accompanied by such an examination, and Messrs. Hose and McDougall have given us a photograph of two Kayans in the act of inspection.[2] It does not appear that they are trained experts, like the *haruspices*; but these were the result of a long period of development, and we have to look for a closer parallel in the earliest form of the religion of Rome, before the Etruscans had passed on their elaborate code of doctrine to the Roman augurs.[3] As in early Rome, the liver was marked out in certain divisions. ' The rule generally followed is to identify the under surface of the right lobe with the territory of the party that kills the pig and makes the inquiry ; the adjacent part of the left lobe with the territory of any party involved in the question, which adjoins that of the first party ; and the under surface of the caudal extremity with that of any remoter third party.' It is interesting to note that the omens thus obtained are held to be the answer of the god to the prayers carried to him by the spirit of the pig ; and also that the killing of a pig is always the occasion for,

---

[1] Cic. *Div.* ii. 36. 77.   [2] ii. 80.

[3] Wissowa maintains (*R. K.*, ed. 2, pp. 418 f.) that the Romans did not examine the entrails with a view to divination, except to see whether the god would accept the victim, till they learnt the art from the Etruscans ; but I do not feel quite convinced on this point. (Wissowa states the same view in his article on Roman divination in Hastings's *Encycl.* iv. 824.) The appearance of the liver seems everywhere to have been looked on as a message from the deity ; what that message was, whether simply approval of the victim or communication of a more detailed character, is difficult to determine in each case. Some good remarks on this subject, based chiefly on Thulin, op. cit., will be found in Prof. Halliday's *Divination in Greece*, pp. 192 f.

or occasioned by, some religious rite, and even if the occasion is not primarily a religious one, the victim is invariably charged with a message to a god.[1]

We do not find here any system so highly elaborated as that of the Etruscans, illustrated as it now is by the famous bronze liver of Piacenza, as well as by the work of Martianus Capella, and indeed now also by our knowledge of the Babylonian science of hepatoscopy.[2] But the method of dividing the surface of the liver is the same in principle in both systems, though the Etruscans divided their livers into seats of deities instead of into territories belonging to the parties in a quarrel : and the Borneans seem to be in a fair way of developing their methods with something like Etruscan extravagance. On the whole we find an extraordinary growth of this pseudo-science in distant Borneo, in Babylonia, and in ancient Italy, such as is not found, so far as I know, in any other part of the world. What conclusions, if any, are to be drawn from this I will not attempt to guess, unless it be to suggest that we are to see in the mental build of these three peoples, or the

---

[1] H. and McD. ii. 64. The authors seem to have no doubt about this ; the message is carried, they say, by the spirit of the pig. But this purpose of sacrifice is rare, so far as I know. It is found in connexion with human sacrifice in Greece, but not in Italy. There is the famous case of the Getae in Thrace, who sent a messenger by sacrifice every five years to their god Zalmoxis, telling him what they were in need of (Herodotus, iv. 94) : and Herodotus tells us that they expected to go to this god themselves after death. Again in Euripides (*Hec.* 422–3), Polyxena, about to be sacrificed, asks what message she is to bear from Hecuba to Priam and Hector : which according to Mr. Lawson (*Modern Greek Folklore*, &c., pp. 340 and 346), who found the same idea in the island of Santorin surviving at the present day, was no mere poetic conceit, but a feature of the popular religion. Lastly, in *Aen.* ii. 547 (also quoted by Mr. Lawson), Pyrrhus makes Priam a messenger at the moment of his slaughter : ' referes ergo haec et nuntius ibis Pelidae genitori.' It seems not unnatural that the idea should spring up in connexion with human sacrifice, but I do not find it associated with ordinary animal sacrifice : is it possible that in Borneo it may be a late interpretation of animal sacrifice combined with prayer, and with the answer of the god in the liver of the sacrificed victim ? Messrs. Hubert et Mauss in their essay on Sacrifice (*Mélanges d'histoire des religions*) do not reach this view, though once or twice they approach it, e. g. on p. 124.

[2] Thulin, *Martianus Capella und die Leber von Piacenza*, p. 7 ; Hastings's *Encycl. of Religion and Ethics*, iv. 784.

upper classes among them, considerable resemblance to each other.

In conclusion I will add two or three points of some interest which have not been noticed in this paper so far :

1. *Marriage.* The ceremony is described as a blending of symbolical capture with actual purchase (ii. 174). In the Roman ceremony these two elements are also to be traced as survivals. The subject is too elaborate for me to dwell on it here : but see my article on Roman Marriage in Hastings's *Encycl. of Religion and Ethics.*[1]

2. *Initiation at puberty.* There is no elaboration of ceremony for this purpose in Borneo, as among the Australians and other primitive peoples, and (according to Miss Harrison) among the Greeks.[2] At Rome too we know of no such practice, unless the change of toga can be regarded as a survival of it.

3. *Mythology.* Though the Kayans, &c., are fond of stories, and possess a mythological instinct, their myths, like those of ancient Italy, have little or no relation to religion and the gods.[3] Roman divine myths are of Greek origin : the Borneans have none, properly so-called.

4. *Magic.* ' The Kayans dislike and discourage all magical practices, with the exception of those which are publicly practised for beneficent purposes, and have the sanction of custom. In the old days they used to kill those suspected of working evil by magic. There are no recognized magicians among them.' [4] The same dislike is a characteristic of Roman life, where magic was excluded from state ritual except in

[1] In the Roman ceremony we have the simulated rape of the bride at the deductio, the parting of her hair with a spear, and the lifting her over the threshold of the bridegroom's house, together with the legend of the rape of the Sabines. For the similar rites of the upper class among the Kayans, see H. and McD. ii. 172 f. But there is no actual trace of exogamy among either people, apart from these forms, which may be explained, as Mr. Crawley first showed us, in quite a different way. See his *Mystic Rose*, pp. 350 f. There was, of course, no actual purchase at Rome, but the form of *coemptio* may suggest that it was in use at some remote time, though personally I doubt this : see my article on Roman Marriage in Hastings, *Encycl. of Rel. and Eth.*, vol. viii.

[2] See her *Themis*, ch. i and elsewhere.

[3] H. and McD. ii. 136 ff.   [4] ibid. ii. 115 f.

the form of meaningless survivals, and practised privately under precautions taken by the State. See my *Roman Religious Experience*, pp. 49 and 107 (cf. index s. v. Magic).

5. The intimate relation (a quasi-religious one) of Bornean women to the seed-corn and its growth, and in fact to all agricultural operations, finds illustration rather in Greece than in Italy,[1] but we may aptly remember that the deities of Italian agriculture were mostly female, Tellus, Ceres, Pales, Ops, Vesta, Feronia (probably), Venus, Flora, and Pomona : a fact not without bearing on the question. In historical Rome the women did not work in the fields, as in Borneo, but the idea of a close connexion between that sex and the fruitfulness of grain seems to have survived in these female deities.

PARALLELA QUAEDAM

THE PLAGUE OF LOCUSTS IN 125 B. C. : AND A MODERN PARALLEL

Two years before the first tribunate of Gaius Gracchus, the Roman province of Africa, then the chief source of the corn supply of Rome, was ravaged by a terrible invasion of locusts.   The fact is well attested ; Livy probably described it at some length, for his epitomist (Ep. 60) devoted a sentence to it : ' Pestilentia in Africa ab ingenti locustarum multitudine et deinde necatarum strage fuisse traditur '.   We can gather further details from Julius Obsequens's book of *prodigia* (ch. 30, ed. Jahn), from St. Augustine (*Civ. Dei.* iii. 31), and from Orosius (v. 11).   All these accounts probably owe their details chiefly to Livy ; but as Augustine and Orosius were both intimately connected with the African province, the one

---

[1] H. and McD. i. 111. Here we are in touch with the idea of the vital principle in the seed, which is carried over from one harvest to another through the seed-corn, and is, so to speak, immortal. It may be at the root of many practices still here and there surviving, as I have suggested in 'Mundus Patet ', above p. 33 ff.

as a native, the other as an immigrant in early life, it is just possible that they may have picked up some traditions of the disaster still floating about at Utica or Carthage. The most curious feature in their account is the fact—for such, as I shall show, we may call it—that the swarms of locusts were blown out to sea by a sudden storm and drowned. Then, as the story runs, they were washed up on the shore by the waves, and as their numbers were boundless along a great reach of coast, the result was a poisonous miasma which produced a terrible pestilence. Orosius shall speak for himself :

At vero quanta fuerit hominum lues, ego ipse dum refero toto corpore perhorresco : siquidem in Numidia, in qua tunc Micipsa rex erat, octingenta milia hominum, circa oram vero maritimam, quae maxime Carthaginiensi atque Uticensi litori adiacet, plusquam ducenta milia perisse traditum est.

He adds that 30,000 soldiers, the garrison of the province, were wiped out ! That he did not get these numbers from Livy is sufficiently clear from the story of the 30,000 legionaries ; but on the whole we may assume that there was a pestilence at the time, to which the stench of the dead insects in some way contributed : so much seems to be proved by the words of the epitomist of Livy.[1] Whether the corn supply of Rome was affected by the visitation we do not know for certain ; but Nitzsch in his monograph on the Gracchi (1847) went so far as to suggest that C. Gracchus found in it a good opportunity for his *lex frumentaria* ;[2] and it is quite possible that in the following year, 124, when Gracchus was canvassing for the tribunate, the question of supply and of prices was brought home to him in this way.

My modern parallel is from South Africa, and was luckily recorded by a man of an accurate and scientific habit of mind. Sir John Barrow, afterwards F.R.S. and Secretary to the Admiralty for some forty years, happened to be at the Cape in 1796, on his way home from Lord Macartney's mission to China, and was the first Englishman to travel as far as the

[1] Cf. Joel, ii. 6 ff. ; Tristram, *Nat. Hist. of Bible*, p. 314.
[2] p. 393 ; cf. Greenidge, *Hist. of Rome*, p. 203

Orange river, at a time when the country was in our hands
for a few years before being returned to the Dutch at the
peace of Amiens.   In his autobiography he wrote as follows
of a locust plague of that year :

The present year was the third of their continuance in this
part of the colony.   Their last departure, with its result, is
described as rather singular, and it was confirmed by the
inhabitants of the lower part of the colony.   All the full-
fledged insects were driven by a tempestuous north-west
wind into the sea, and afterwards thrown back upon the beach,
where they formed a bank three or four feet high, between
the mouths of the Bosjesmans river and the Beeka, a distance
of nearly fifty miles ; and our present company assured me
that when this mass became putrid, the stench was sensibly
felt in several parts of Sneuwberg (p. 181).

The Sneuwberg range is about 150 miles as the crow flies
from the mouth of the Bushman river.   The stench must have
been quite enough, one would imagine, at the coast, to be the
contributory cause of a pestilence, but of this Barrow gives no
hint.   We must, however, remember that the coast in question
was at that time very thinly populated as compared with
that of Roman North Africa in 125 B. C., where for the last
twenty years a Roman population had been adding itself
to that of Carthaginians and Libyans.

But whether or no the pestilence was due to the locusts,
the heaping of the dead locusts on the shore, and the stench
thereby occasioned, are fully and independently confirmed
by Barrow's narrative.   Those who are apt to find fables
everywhere in history, may learn here how exaggeration
and marvel may gather in course of time round a perfectly
authentic fact.

PLAGUES OF FIELD-VOLES (*Arvicola arvalis*) IN
ANCIENT AND MODERN TIMES

In the *Zoologist* for September 1892 there was an interesting
account of a plague of these destructive little animals, which
ravaged Thessaly in the spring of that year.   The account was

translated from the *Centralblatt für Bacteriologie*, and the writer was Dr. Loeffler of Greifswald, who had been invited by the Greek Government to attempt the extirpation of the pests by introducing among them a bacillus fatal to mice. Not long before this there had been a very serious plague of the same voles in the south of Scotland, when birds of prey arrived in large numbers and did much execution on them. In both cases the harvest, which promised to be very good, was not only threatened but seriously damaged.

These sudden plagues of mice were well known in the ancient world, especially in Greece. Aristotle (*Hist. Anim.* 580 B) says that ' such an inexpressible number of field-mice has sometimes appeared that very little food remained. Their destructive power is also so great that some small farmers, having on one day observed their corn ready for harvest, when they went the next day to cut it, found it all eaten. The manner of their disappearance also is unaccountable, though up to that time they could not be exterminated either by smoking or digging them out.' He adds that nothing can get the better of them but rain.

Whether he was right about the rain I do not know ; but the report of the Greek Government, quoted in the *Zoologist*, amply confirms the most striking feature of Aristotle's description. ' One evening a field was visited which was to be mown the next day : but when the labourers came to the field next morning they found nothing left to cut. The voles had destroyed the entire crop in a single night.'

A little later I drew attention to these facts in the *Classical Review*, and suggested that the cult of Apollo Smintheus, the Mouse Apollo, might be better explained as having some relation to such plagues, than as a relic of totemism, as Mr. Lang had shown himself disposed to look on it in his *Myth, Ritual, and Religion*. Mr. Lang wrote to me from Edinburgh that he would not ' go to the stake ' for the totemic explanation, and that the other might perhaps be the right one. A few days later I found in the *Daily News* a short but delicious article, in which he urged the farmers

of the Lowlands to set up the worship of Apollo Smintheus
without delay, in case they should again be attacked by the
voles.

> Armati terram exercent, semperque recentes
> Convectare iuvat praedas et vivere rapto.

I have always thought of Virgil's lines (*Aen.* vii. 748–9)
as giving us our best available picture of old Italian life in
the age of the first settlements made by invaders who afterwards became Latins, Umbrians, and Samnites. The picture
is reproduced in bk. ix. 607 ff. :

> At patiens operum parvoque adsueta iuventus
> aut rastris terram domat aut quatit oppida bello.
> omne aevum ferro teritur, versaque iuvencum
> terga fatigamus hasta.

In the former passage Virgil is speaking of the Aequi,
the very people who in Livy's earlier books descend so often
from their hills to raid the Latin territory in the plain below :
' Horrida praecipue cui gens adsuetaque multo Venatu
nemorum, duris Aequicola glebis.' In the ninth book he is
drawing a picture of the Rutuli, who stand in the poem for
the wilder tribes then inhabiting Latium itself. Where did
the poet get his knowledge of this uncomfortable kind of
life, which seems characteristic of tribes that still live largely
by hunting, but keep sheep and cattle for purposes of clothing,
and have begun to cultivate patches of ground cleared in
the forest, and perhaps to hide the produce in pits underground,
the prototypes, as I believe, of the Roman *mundus* of later
times ? Perhaps he knew of such tribes in the foothills of
the Alps, near his own Mantuan home ; or he and Livy may
both have known of traditions in Latium of the old days
when neither your cattle nor your corn was safe from the raids
of your neighbours. However that may be, Virgil's terse
and intensely graphic picture seems to appeal to the reader
instantly as being true to the life. I have recently stumbled
on an equally graphic picture of this very condition of life,

dating no further back than 1864. The author, Dr. Tristram, knew his Bible almost by heart, but had forgotten his Virgil, or he would have quoted the passages I have printed above.

After a first attempt to penetrate into the hill-country beyond Jordan, in which he and his friends were themselves raided and robbed, the party hired a strong Arab escort and tried again successfully. The Bedouin tribes in this land of Gilead were, and still seem to be, in exactly the state described by Virgil, hunting, cattle-keeping, and cultivating small patches, which may at any moment be raided by a hostile tribe. On approaching a certain hill-village, the party created a panic among the inhabitants, who took them for enemies out for plunder. ' Cows were driven away in all directions, men snatched up guns and stood on the defensive. When the mistake had been discovered and the travellers passed on, the men, with their reaping-hooks and plough-shares, but of course with their guns slung on their shoulders, were hurrying back to their peaceful occupations in the fields. What a country to live in, with a plough in one hand and a firelock in the other ! ' In other parts of his book (*The Land of Israel*, 1866) Dr. Tristram has also described the underground pits in which these tribes bury the produce of their fields for safety (e. g. p. 108).

I have long been of opinion that it is exactly this condition of life which was represented in central Italy by the cult of Mars, who has so often puzzled investigators as being at once a numen connected with agriculture, and a deity of war, as we know him in historical times in the Roman State-worship. ' A spirit who dwells on the outskirts of civilization, and can with profit be propitiated both for help against the enemies beyond, and for the protection of the crops and cattle within, the boundaries of human activity.' [1]

---

[1] *Religious Experience of the Roman People* pp. 133 ff.

THE DISAPPEARANCE OF THE EARLIEST LATIN POETRY : A MODERN PARALLEL

The following note is part of the result of a conversation with a Rhodes scholar about the famous Ballad theory of Niebuhr, of which we seldom hear now except in connexion with Macaulay's *Lays*. Niebuhr, of course, let his imagination carry him too far, and believed in the existence of a Roman national epos as the foundation of the ' history ' of the regal period. He thus laid himself open to trenchant criticism, e. g. that of Schwegler in the first volume of his *Roman History*, which wiped out his theory, and rather unluckily diverted attention from the texts on which it was based. Recent criticism seems rather to look on these as proving not indeed a national epos, but the practice in the early republican period of singing at meals and funerals the praises of famous men to the accompaniment of the *tibia*. H. Nettleship accepted this conclusion,[1] E. Meyer raises no difficulty about it,[2] and Païs has adduced parallels to the practice among other peoples.[3]   And, indeed, whoever reads these once famous passages will find it hard to deny that they must represent a sound tradition of an actual Roman practice. But what these songs were really like, we know no more than we do what the music was like which accompanied them ; for words and music have alike utterly vanished.

It may be as well to quote these in full, as otherwise my suggestion of a modern parallel would be less intelligible.

Cic. *Tusc.* iv. 2. 3 ' Gravissimus auctor in Originibus dixit Cato morem apud maiores hunc epularum fuisse ut deinceps qui accubarent canerent ad tibiam clarorum virorum laudes atque virtutes.   Ex quo perspicuum est, et cantus tum fuisse rescriptos vocum sonis et carmina.'

Cic. *Brutus*, 75 ' Atque utinam exstarent illa carmina, quae multis saeculis ante suam aetatem in epulis esse cantitata a singulis convivis de clarorum virorum laudibus, in Originibus scriptum reliquit Cato ! '

---

[1] *Essays in Latin Literature*, p. 58.   [2] *Gesch. des Altertums*, ii. 2. 397.
[3] *Storia di Roma*, i. 9, note.

Cic. *de Orat.* iii. 51. 197 ' Nihil est tam cognatum mentibus nostris quam numeri atque voces . . . quorum illa summa vis carminibus est aptior et cantibus, non neglecta, ut mihi videtur, a Numa, rege doctissimo, maioribusque nostris, ut epularum sollemnium fides ac tibiae, Saliorumque versus indicant.'

Valerius Maximus, ii. 1. 10 ' Maiores natu in conviviis ad tibias egregia superiorum opera carmine comprehensa pangebant, quo ad ea imitanda iuventutem alacriorem redderent.'

Varro, *ap. Nonius,* p. 77 (Lindsay, i. 107) ' In conviviis pueri modesti ut cantarent carmina antiqua, in quibus laudes erant maiorum, et assa voce (i. e. without accompaniment) et cum tibicine ' (*de Vita Pop. Rom.* lib. ii).

Now the complete disappearance of this poetry was made use of as one of the most damaging criticisms of Niebuhr's theory ; Schwegler, for instance, asks why no commentator of the age of Roman learning cared to unearth them for his purposes. Niebuhr himself ascribed this disappearance mainly to the influence of Ennius, i. e. of a foreigner whose genius simply overwhelmed the old Italian poetry and gave the Romans something better to think about. And this is indeed the only explanation possible. Ennius came in on the crest of the wave of Greek tendency, at a time of momentous change in the modes of thought and habits of the Romans. Greece, in fact, invaded Italy with a great general, Ennius, at the head of her victorious host. It has occurred to me that we may find an instructive parallel to this sudden disappearance of a native art in the history of our own country.

In the first half of the eighteenth century, Germany and Italy invaded musical England in the person of Handel, a German by birth and an Italian by training. The result was that our own ancient national music almost entirely vanished from the minds of Englishmen. It could not, indeed, wholly vanish from the world, for it was in manuscript or in print, and some of it survived in our cathedral services. The obliteration was less complete than with the old Latin songs. But none the less Handel was the Ennius of our musical history. So effectually did he and his great German successors wipe out the memory of the English music of the fifteenth and sixteenth centuries, that not even the all-pervading German research of to-day has ever reached it. The Germans know as little of it as the Greeks knew of the old Latin poetry ; like the learned scholars of the Roman Empire they remain unconscious of a fine field of inquiry. On this point I may refer to Dr. Ernest Walker's excellent *History of Music in England* (Oxford, 1907).

The parallel may be pushed even further. For at least a century after Ennius Rome produced no great poet. When at last Roman poetry suddenly became great, it was because men of real genius had so thoroughly absorbed all that the Greeks had to teach them, that they were now free to assert their own poetical individuality, to express their own national traditions in their own way. They were not hampered by their Greek training, but rather aided by it, in expressing themselves. So in English music ; for a century after Handel's death there was no really great English composer, and it is only in the last half-century that two or three have been able to express their own individuality in spite of the overwhelming influence of German music. Doubtless this process of gaining freedom will increase in strength, for the Germans can now no longer persuade themselves and the world that the secrets of the musical art are their own peculiar possession.

ROMAN *LEGES DATAE* AND ENGLISH ENCLOSURE AWARDS

To the Roman political mind it seemed natural and necessary that every *municipium*, every town, that is, included in the Roman body politic in any sense or degree,[1] should have a document, a charter, in the Roman speech a *lex*, as the legal basis of its municipal existence, fixing its constitution and other details. The Roman legal instinct required such documents, and did not look on them as mere ' scraps of paper ' ; for every province, for example, it demanded a *lex*

---

[1] I use the word in the widest sense, in which throughout Roman history a *municipium* could mean any town having the whole or a part of the Roman *civitas*.

provinciae, for every temple a *lex templi*, regulating the rights, customs, revenues, &c., of the institution. How were these charters obtained ? The *lex templi* was the legal work of the college of pontifices ; but the charter of a province or a *municipium* had its legal basis in an Act of the Legislature, which in each case appointed a commissioner or commissioners, to frame the necessary document. This document, being imposed or bestowed on the town, was called a *lex data*, in contrast to the *lex rogata* of the Comitia from which it derived its legal authority. Of such *leges datae*, as every student knows, we have several specimens preserved more or less completely, but among them only one relating to an Italian town—a fragment of the *lex data* of Tarentum, discovered in 1895.

While studying the history of enclosures in England, and in particular the Enclosure award of my own village history, I have often been struck by the close analogy between the *lex data* of a Roman *municipium* and the Enclosure award of an English parish. Like the *lex data*, the Enclosure award had its legal basis in an Act of the Legislature ; and it was imposed (or bestowed) on the parish by commissioners (one or more) appointed under that Act. Thus in England as at Rome, we find examples of the regulation of local institutions by commissions deriving their legal authority from Acts of the Legislature. Let me explain this a little more fully.

An Enclosure is a rearrangement of the land of a parish in respect of ownership, whether of individuals or corporations, and in respect of rights, such as those of common pasture or fuelling. Before the eighteenth century it was often effected by the owner or owners of land without recourse to Parliament ; but in the eighteenth and nineteenth centuries it was deemed necessary to give it legal sanction by the legislative process. An Act, private indeed, but fully open to criticism and defeat, empowered commissioners to go to the parish in question, and after due inquiry, and under oath to act impartially, to effect the necessary changes.[1] The result, when completed

---

[1] See Gonner, *Common Land and Enclosure*, pp. 56 ff., and chap. iii ;

by the commissioners, was an award binding on the parish, a charter from which there was no escape except by further legislation. The resemblance to a *lex data* will be obvious to every student of Roman history.

The work of the commissioners was naturally found to increase in complexity with the increase and variety of the parishes to be enclosed ; but ' so far as the general structure of these private Acts is concerned, and by consequence of the awards resulting from them, a fairly constant form seems to have been attained by the end of the reign of George II ' (1760).[1] It is probable that Roman commissioners also developed a ' forma communis ', as Mommsen called it,[2] without the immediate aid of any general law regulating the aims and procedure that should govern the action of commissioners. Such a tendency to uniformity was in England no doubt the result, as Professor Gonner suggests,[3] of the practice of sending each bill to a committee, which again led to certain standing orders of the House of Commons on the subject. Yet beyond doubt there was much variety of practice, arising from the soil, history, usages, &c., of the parishes to be enclosed. Towards the end of the eighteenth century, after thousands of enclosures had been effected by these awards, we find a growing desire to have a *general Act* which should secure such uniformity as had been already attained, and facilitate and improve the work in each case. After some previous attempts, such a general Act was passed in 1801. Before we return to Italy, let me give a brief indication of the nature of this general Act.

It is described as consolidating in one Act certain provisions usually inserted in private Enclosure Acts.[4] For example, it took some forty clauses commonly found in these, and

Hammond, *The Village Labourer*, chap. iii ; Prothero, *English Farming Past and Present*, pp. 249 ff.

[1] Gonner, op. cit., p. 65.

[2] See Legras, *La Table latine d'Héraclée*, pp. 268 ff.

[3] op. cit., p. 65.

[4] The best account is given by Gonner, op. cit., pp. 62 ff. ; cf. Hammond, op. cit., p. 77.

provided for their incorporation in future bills. It also introduced a few new features; e. g. it allowed affidavits to be taken as evidence, and relieved witnesses from coming to London to make oath before parliamentary committees; and it instructed commissioners to have special regard to the convenience of small holders of land. No change in the methods of enclosure was introduced; the commissioners and their ' leges datae ' went on as before. But their work was simplified, and their tendency to uniformity increased, by the insertion in this general Act of principles of action which experience had already approved.

Let us now return to Italy, and see whether this last phase in the history of enclosing in England has any bearing on that of municipal legislation at Rome. It is curious that there is a lively dispute at the present time as to whether there ever was or could have been a *general law* regulating the action of commissioners appointed to draw up *leges datae* for *municipia*.[1] I must very briefly explain how this dispute has arisen.

It is of course in the period immediately following the enfranchisement of Italy, 89 and following years, that we should most naturally expect to hear of municipal *leges datae*. Almost all Italian communities which had formerly been ' allies ' of Rome (*civitates foederatae*) now became *municipia*, lost their *foedera*, which had so far supplied the legal basis for their relation to Rome, and needed fresh charters to justify and regulate their civic existence. Whether in these years of confusion and civil war, or even for many years after the death of Sulla, this need was sufficiently supplied, is a disputed question into which I need not enter here. I will only express my own opinion, after careful study of the controversy, that it was only supplied gradually and sporadically. I see no reason why a town should not have continued to use its old constitution, together with its new rights of *civitas*, while

---

[1] See Reid, *Municipalities of the Roman Empire*, p. 147; Mommsen in his Commentary on the *lex data* of Tarentum, *Ephemeris Epigraphica*, ix. 1; and Hardy in *J. R. S.*, 1914, pp. 96 ff., criticizing H. Legras, op. cit., pp. 233 ff.

in expectation of a charter that might be long delayed. It is as well to remember that such work as the ' constituting '[1] of *municipia* would hardly be sought for by distinguished Romans, who were busy making war or making money in this period ; and that the wars and proscriptions had greatly thinned the ranks of persons qualified for such delicate legal operations.

The difficulty of answering this question as to the constituting of *municipia* in this period has led to the dispute among the learned to which I alluded just now. The question is this : Was there, apart from single *leges datae* for individual *municipia*, any general law intended to affect *municipia* in general, to lay down principles on which commissioners should act in each case, so as to secure at least a certain amount of uniformity ? And is the document known to us as the *lex Iulia municipalis*, or at least the latter part of it, which deals with certain municipal institutions in general terms, such a general law ? Formerly, and in fact until 1903, it was assumed by most inquirers that Mommsen was right in claiming the document as a general municipal law ; but in that year, in commenting on the newly discovered fragment of the *lex data* of Tarentum,[2] he entirely recanted this opinion ; and ever since then there has been a growing tendency to deny that such a general law was necessary or even possible. The whole question will be found reasoned out with exactness and discrimination by Dr. Hardy in his recent criticism of the revolutionary work of a French scholar on the so-called *lex Iulia municipalis*. Dr. Hardy has come to the conclusion that there was such a general law, and that it was intended ' to fix the *forma communis* to bind the commissioners in respect to principles, and to afford them guidance though naturally with greater laxity, in matters of detail ' (p. 100). He also conjectures that the *lex Iulia municipalis* ' was not the first formulation of a general municipal law, but a revision

---

[1] The word was *constituere*, as in Caesar, *Bell. Civ.* i. 15, of Cingulum, quod oppidum Labienus constituerat '.

[2] See above, p. 176 note 1.

and re-enactment of earlier laws, together with certain new provisions, of which two are preserved on the Table of Heraclea ' ; and that the date of that law was probably 45 B. C. (p. 108).

It seems to me that the evidence of our English method of dealing with certain local problems, which beyond doubt closely resembles that of the Roman in curiously similar circumstances, strongly confirms Dr. Hardy's conclusions. If there was nothing impossible or even unlikely in the enactment in England of a general law of regulation, even after the process which it was intended to regulate had been going on for some time, I do not see why such a law should have been unlikely or impossible for Roman lawyers and statesmen.[1]

THE GREAT SERPENT OF THE RIVER BAGRADAS

While turning over Niebuhr's *Lectures on the Punic Wars*, I came on a tale which had never yet attracted my attention. The modern historian does not trouble himself with portents, monsters, miracles, and such fairy tales ; he has more important things to attend to. Yet I have always found it interesting and sometimes useful, to turn over the pages of Julius Obsequens's *Record of Portents*, for it tells us something of the mind of a people, and occasionally something of the natural history of the Mediterranean. For example, the great plague of locusts in 125 B. C. I have shown by analogy to be essentially true, and not without historical significance.

Niebuhr, who let himself talk in his lectures about anything that interested him, did not scruple to tell his hearers at Bonn the tale of the great serpent of the River Bagradas (Mejerda), though he fancied that it was an invention of the poet Naevius, who wrote in verse the history of the first Punic War. It has reached us through the epitomist of Livy's lost books, who could not forbear to mention it as an integral part of the

For a Prussian general municipal law, to which the constitutions of individual cities were required to conform, see Niebuhr's *Life and Letters*, III. xxxix.

eighteenth book, just as in book sixty he selected the locusts as likely to interest people who had not time to read the full text of Livy. His way of introducing it is amusing, and might suggest that the serpent was an even more formidable enemy than the Carthaginians. ' Atilius Regulus in Africa serpentem portentosae magnitudinis cum magna clade militum occidit, et cum aliquod proeliis bene aduersus Carthaginienses pugnasset . . .' &c.

To get a fair idea of what Livy really wrote about this marvel we must go on some four centuries to Orosius,[1] as we did with the locusts ; for these things happened in Africa, to which province Orosius belonged, and that excellent Christian was not only fond of marvels but fond of connecting them with his own country. He shall speak for himself.

Regulus, bellum Carthaginiense sortitus, iter cum exercitu faciens haud procul a flumine Bagrada castra constituit : ubi cum plurimos militum aquandi necessitate ad flumen descendentes serpens mirae magnitudinis devoraret, Regulus ad expugnandum bestiam cum exercitu profectus est. Sed nihil in tergo eius proficientibus iaculis atque omni telorum ictu inrito, quae per horrendam sqamarum cratem quasi per obliquam scutorum testudinem labebantur mirumque in modum, ne corpus laederent, ipso corpore pellebantur, cum insuper magnam multitudinem morsu comminui, impetu proteri, halitu etiam pestifero examinari uideret, ballistas deferri imperavit, per quas murale saxum spinae eius incussum conpagem totius corporis soluit. (At this point Orosius digresses to inform his readers of the way in which snakes move along the ground, which account, strange to say, is correct in the main. He goes on to tell us that the creature was mortally wounded by a stone from a ballista, and then killed with javelins.) Corium autem eius Romam devectum, quod fuisse centum viginti pedum spatio ferunt, aliquamdiu cunctis miraculo fuit. (*Hist.* iv. 8.)

That the monster had to be killed by having siege machinery brought to bear on him, does not seem to me incredible ; but we may reduce the number of Roman soldiers whom he devoured to one or two. The length of the beast, 120 ft., may be reduced by one-half or more, to come within the

---

[1] Valerius Maximus (i. 8. 19) also tells the story from Livy. Silius Italicus has an amusingly absurd account of it : vi. 146 ff.

range of reality, as we shall see directly. Niebuhr remarks
that the length is exactly that number of feet which so often
occurs in Roman institutions, namely a multiple of 10 and 12.
He is thinking, I suppose, of the threefold division of the legion
of the second century B. C., into bodies of 1,200 each. But
Pliny, who had been attracted by the story, quite accepts
the 120 ft., and adds that the skin and jaws were preserved
in a temple at Rome ' usque ad bellum Numantinum '
(*Nat. Hist.* viii. 37). This seems to me to help us in believing
the main outline of the tale ; for skin and jaws would be
exactly the parts which it would be natural to preserve, if
the creature were really a serpent, and not e. g. a gigantic
crocodile. I could wish that Pliny had told us what temple
was honoured with these remains. There were no museums
in those days, and if such a gift were given to a temple it must
have been as a religious offering ; the only one to which
such an offering would seem appropriate was that of Aescula-
pius in the Tiber Island. It was handy to a ship arriving from
Africa, and the offering may have been thought useful for
completing the conquest of the Carthaginian territory.
Regulus, when the incident occurred, was in the full swing
of his first success, and had not yet achieved the fame that
arose from his defeat and capture. Why the skin remained
in the temple till the Numantine war and no longer I cannot
divine ; but it may be that snakes became unpopular at that
time, for in Julius Obsequens I find that the unlucky Mancinus
was warned against going to Spain by a snake coming on board
his ship at Genoa (ch. 24, ed. Jahn).

Supposing that there is a bottom of fact in the story, what
could this monster have been ? A crocodile it assuredly was
not, for the crocodile was well enough known in the Mediterranean world. I leave it to experts to decide this question :
only remarking that water serpents in great rivers do even
now reach a very large size. Bates in his *Naturalist on the
Amazons* (p. 215, ed. 5) heard of specimens of the anaconda
which measured forty-two feet ; and adds that the natives
of the Amazons country universally believe in the existence
of a monster water-serpent, said to be many score fathoms

in length, which appears successively in different parts of
the river. ' They call it the Mai d'agoa—the mother, or spirit,
of the water. This fable was doubtless suggested by the
occasional appearance of serpents of unusual size.' Aristotle
knew of great serpents in Africa (*Hist. An.* viii. 27. 6), which
attacked ships as they sailed along the coast. On the whole
there is sufficient evidence, I think, to make it possible that
this was the survivor of a species even then all but extinct.

VERGILIANA

THE SWANS IN *AENEID* I. 390 ff.

Namque tibi reduces socios classemque relatam
nuntio et in tutum versis Aquilonibus actam,
ni frustra augurium vani docuere parentes.
aspice bis senos laetantis agmine cycnos,
aetheria quos lapsa plaga Iovis ales aperto
turbabat caelo ; nunc terras ordine longo
aut capere aut captas iam despectare videntur :
ut reduces illi ludunt stridentibus alis
et coetu cinxere polum cantusque dedere,
haud aliter puppesque tuae pubesque tuorum
aut portum tenet aut pleno subit ostia velo.

THIS is not a simile but an omen ; we need not look for
too exact a parallelism between swans and ships. This is
one thing to remember in reading the passage ; another is
that neither swans nor ships had at the moment reached
their destination, though they are on the point of doing so.
This is perfectly clear in the case of the swans, who at the
moment of vision are ' laetantes agmine ', and also by the
rather puzzling line 398 (' et coetu cinxere polum cantusque
dedere '), which if interpreted by the preceding line (' ut
reduces illi ludunt stridentibus alis ') can only mean that
they have recovered their formation and after circling round
the sky, they have decided where to alight and are about to
do so. To me it is quite clear that all the birds are still flying ;
and if so, there is only one meaning for ' capere terras ', the
one in which Servius saw no difficulty, viz. ' take in with
their minds ', as in *Georg.* ii. 230 ' ante locum capies oculis '.
Our word ' spot ', which will soon become classical, exactly

gives the meaning. In vain Mr. Page dogmatically insists that *capere* cannot mean this, and must mean that the leading swans have alighted on the earth ; he at once gets into hopeless confusion. Swans have a leader, as Virgil knew (xii. 250), and when the leader has fixed the point to make for, they can already look down on it as they draw nearer. ' Terras ordine longo aut capere aut captas iam despectare videntur.' No need to alter *despectare* ; the MSS. GMR, of which G goes back to the fourth century, are sufficient evidence.

Now for the ships. Like the swans, they have not yet reached land ; they are ' making ' the port. *Portum tenet* need not mean that they have entered the harbour, but as in v. 159 ' iamque propinquabant scopulo metamque tenebant ', where, as the *meta* was on the *scopulum*, it is plain that the boat was only *about* to reach it (cf. xii. 754). And this is made certain by the words that follow, ' aut pleno subit ostia velo '. The sails are still unfurled, i. e. of the ships that are not in the van ; they cannot therefore have even *almost* reached the harbour ; but they are approaching it quickly, as the swans still flying look down on the land.

portum tenet. Virgil uses *tenere* much as a Somerset friend of mine uses the word ' hold '. He loves to plan a long country walk to end in catching a train, with no time to spare ; and he always says we ' hold the train ', even a mile or two away from it, if we have still enough time left to get to the station.—R. S. C.

THE HARBOUR IN *AENEID* III. 533–6

Portus ab euroo fluctu curvatus in arcum,
obiectae salsa spumant aspergine cautes,
ipse latet : gemino dimittunt brachia muro
turriti scopuli refugitque ab litore templum.

Here Mr. Page makes difficulties where there are none. Has he ever been to Lulworth Cove in Dorset ? If so, he will have seen the very scene Virgil describes. There the sea has broken through a rampart of Portland rock at one point only, and has washed away in a wide curve the softer deposits of sand and chalk within that rampart. On each side of the

narrow entrance the rocks of harder material stand firm—
' obiectae salsa spumant aspergine cautes ', and ' gemino
dimittunt brachia muro turriti scopuli ', while the cove
within is quiet (' ipse latet '). Even the temple is there ;
for withdrawn a little way up the low cliff to the west of
the cove is the remnant of the ancient abbey of Bindon,
which stood here till it was moved to Wool. I do not know
whether Virgil is describing a scene which he knew personally ;
but at any rate he is describing one which is perfectly natural,
and needs no elaborate explanation, no forcing of simple
language.

NOTE ON DIDO AND AENEAS

The tendency in modern times has been to throw the
whole blame upon Aeneas ; very strong language has been
used, e.g. by Fox, Matthew Arnold, and many others. To
the chorus of execration Dr. Glover is an exception ; and this
is simply because he is less affected by the ideas of the nineteenth century, and understands Roman feeling better than
most. Moreover, he understands the character of Aeneas
as a whole, and is not so wholly absorbed in the passion of
the fourth book as to lose his balance in judging of the question.

Aeneas is throughout the poem, and to its very end, the
impersonation of family life and affection, and of the other
ties which bind civilized men together, friendship, hospitality,
good faith, and justice. This is why at the very end of the
poem all that was best in the pure and wholesome Italian
tradition of family life and social relationship is placed in
striking contrast with the wantonness of an individual
warrior without scruple and without mercy. But this is no
doubt what the modern reader does not readily see, because
such impersonations are not personally attractive. I suppose
that David is a much more popular Bible hero than Moses,
who is the impersonation of a Jewish ideal, just because David
is a human being of warm feelings and frequent failings.
I am not of course comparing Moses and Aeneas ; I only
mean that it takes both knowledge and insight to see the
human traits in either of them ; they are too serene and quiet

for the casual reader to catch at a glance. These traits in Aeneas are mostly to be found in the last six books, which are not nearly so well known as the earlier ones. But I doubt if we can do full justice to Aeneas without a real knowledge of them, and I hope that in my recently published little volumes I may have contributed something to that end.

Aeneas was a married man and a father when Troy was captured, though he was not the head of a family; it would be as well if every one were to go back to the second book (559 ff.) before beginning the fourth. There he tells Dido how at the death of Priam the probable ruin of his own happy family life suddenly flashed on his mind :

> At me tum primum saevus circumstetit horror.
> obstipui ; subiit cari genitoris imago,
> ut regem aequaevum crudeli vulnere vidi
> vitam exhalantem ; subiit deserta Creusa
> et direpta domus et parvi casus Iuli.

This terrible prospect so maddens him that a wild desire for once gets the better of him to slay the woman who is the cause of all the trouble.[1] When he leaves the burning city with his father on his back, his little son grasping his hand, his wife following, the disappearance of Creusa drives him back in search of her at the risk of his life. This he tells to Dido. I need not quote what follows, for Virgil has put all his heart into it, and I would advise all who wish to form an opinion about the Dido story to begin by laying it to heart. I will only draw attention to the lines (781 ff.) in which the promise is given him of a new and royal family life in Italy, on the banks of the Tiber.[2]

His father Anchises, who up to his death continued to

---

[1] I have not the smallest doubt that this passage (567 ff.) is really Virgil's, and that the first editors cut it out simply because of the apparent violation of Pietas which the slaying of a woman would have implied.

[2] It is sometimes asked, why should the new city be at Rome rather than in Africa ? The answer is that all foundations of cities were matters of religion ; and that in this case the oracles had so directed. If it be answered, Why trouble about the oracles ? all I can say is that the foundation of colonies without the oracle was in Greek history unthinkable ; and Cicero had reminded the Romans of this (de Div. i. 1. 3). We cannot be just to Virgil if we forget such things as this.

govern the family group, was the next to leave him. Let us remember that the visit to Carthage happens just when this loss has come upon him. He is certainly meant to appear at the first somewhat helpless ; he loses heart at the storm (i. 92 ff.), and then, landing in Africa, falls unwittingly a victim to the superb charms of Dido—charms used with consummate skill. I might go on to show his recovery after that fall, and the alteration of his character in the later books ; but this I have already done in the eighteenth chapter of my *Religious Experience of the Romans*, to which I may refer the reader. Suffice it to say here that courage combined with gentleness, tenderness combined with justice, are shown again and again in his relations both with friends and enemies ; with his own boy, with Pallas entrusted to his care by his father Evander, and even by the death of Lausus, the son of his most ferocious enemy, which brings all the feelings of a father welling up in his mind.

Let us turn to Dido. We know that Virgil altered the story of Dido to suit his own purpose, and the change should tell us what that purpose was. In the traditional form, the queen, ' who had resolved to remain a widow after the murder of her husband Sychaeus, was pressed, not without threats, by a neighbouring prince, Iarbas, to become his wife. Her own subjects urged her to comply, but she, professing that she was going to perform some rite which should absolve her from her vows, erected a great pile of wood near her palace, which she kindled, and then threw herself into the flames '.[1]

Now Virgil makes Dido fall violently in love with Aeneas ; when she has induced him to fulfil her passionate desire, he is warned by Jupiter to forsake her and make for Italy. This leads to a frenzied outburst on the part of the queen, which ends in her suicide while Aeneas sails away. To me it is quite clear that Virgil altered the story in order to contrast the fury of ungovernable love, love of the animal type, with the settled order, affection, and obedience, of the Roman family life. Let me explain this.

Up to the departure of Aeneas the true nature of Dido's

[1] Nettleship, *Vergil*, p. 58.

passion is not revealed, yet it is clear that there is something wrong about it. She had vowed never to marry again ; but already at the end of book i the arts of Venus and Cupid have begun to destroy her resolution (i. 715–22), and she cannot sate her passion for her guest. When the hero's tales are finished, at the beginning of book iv, her sister Anna leads her on to believe that he may be kept at Carthage (iv. 51), that the ghost of Sychaeus would not mind (34), and so on ; and that sacrifices to the gods may legitimatize a union with Aeneas (' pacem per aras exquirunt '). Now mark the poet's comment :

> Heu vatum ignarae mentes ! quid vota *furentem*
> quid delubra iuvant ? est mollis flamma medullas
> interea et tacitum vivit sub pectore vulnus.

(iv. 65 ff.)

The point is in the word ' furentem '. Dido was possessed by a spirit of madness (' heu furiis incensa feror ', 376), which was quite incompatible with serious marriage. This is ' human passion bent on its own fulfilment in contempt of the gods, and ending, as it can only end, in infatuation and ruin '.[1]

This madness is of course increased tenfold when she discovers that the object of it is deserting her. The great scenes in which she gives vent to her indignation—scenes which have won the pity of the world—are in reality meant to exhibit a spirit and temper entirely out of place in Roman family life. And she knew perfectly well that she was sinning. The terrible lines (450–73) in which the poet has described her dreams, prove that she knew she was breaking a vow, sinning against *pudor*.

The modern reader asks, Why should she not have settled down with Aeneas—why should they not have reigned at Carthage together ? The usual answer given is that the fates had decreed otherwise, and that the great deity of the future Rome was determined to save Aeneas for Italian civilization. But this would not, if I am not mistaken, have been the whole of Virgil's answer. He would have said that Dido's character,

---

[1] Nettleship, *Essays in Latin Literature*, p. 125.

as he conceived it, was utterly incompatible with Italian ideals. She does not understand the combination of virtues which made up the ideal Roman matron. She has lost all power of self-restraint ; not *coniugium*, but *Amor*, is her aim ; ' improbe Amor, quid non mortalia pectora cogis ? ' Yet in the background of her mind there is always the thought of her Sychaeus (460 ff.), and when she meets Aeneas in the shades, it is to the company of Sychaeus that she turns for comfort.

> Tandem corripuit sese atque inimica refugit
> in nemus umbriferum, coniunx ubi pristinus illi
> respondet curis aequatque Sychaeus amorem.
>
> (vi. 472 ff.)

Virgil had good reason to draw this terrible picture of an infatuated woman. In his own day Cleopatra had poisoned the mind of one, if not two, great Romans, and the escape of Augustus from her charms was a matter of enormous importance in the history of Rome, as all his contemporaries knew. Nettleship believed that he was following the idea of certain Greek tragedies where the conflict of individual inclination with the divine will is represented (pp. 124 ff.). But the passion of ungovernable love, even without the treatment of it in tragedy, must have been before the poet's mind ever since he studied Lucretius, or wrote his own third Georgic. It was common to man and the animals ; not so the ordered life of the family, which to the Roman of the older and nobler type was as an institution from heaven. This explains why Venus is represented as bringing the madness about through the agency of Cupid (bk. i. 657 ff.) : she knows that such love is incompatible with the life to which Aeneas looks forward, and that Jupiter will take care that he is not led by it to give up the hope of Italy.

There are one or two subsidiary questions on which it may be as well to say a word. For example : Was Aeneas himself in love with Dido ? Of this there is not a trace till after the fatal meeting in the cave. It is then expressed in the passage beginning ' At pius Aeneas ', which has been so obnoxious to some critics. 'Multa gemens magnoque animum labefactus

amore, Iussa tamen divum exsequitur classemque revisit.'
His emotion is also visible in lines 448–9 : ' magno persentit
pectore curas : Mens immota manet, lacrimae volvuntur
inanes.' But he was only half won. ' As Caesar was half won
by Cleopatra, Aeneas is half won by Dido ', writes Nettleship.
I was quite wrong when I wrote of his ' passionate love for
Dido ' in *Religious Experience*, p. 416.

Then again, what are we to say of the part of the gods in
all this, more especially that of Juno and Venus ? I confess
that it is to me one of the least attractive features in the
poem. There is no sort of pleasure in reading of plot and
counterplot ; and we cannot bring our modern minds to
think of them as standing for right and wrong designs of
Powers over whom man's free will has no control. But so
much as this may be said : Juno stands all through the
Aeneid for the Power working against Rome, and on behalf
of Rome's most deadly enemy. Her plan is a treacherous
one ; she does not mean real marriage of a strict Roman
type. ' Conubio iungam stabili propriamque dicabo,' (126) like
99 ff., is not said of Roman marriage, and so Dido takes it :
' coniugium vocat, hoc praetexit nomine culpam ' (172). The
counterplot of Venus is the strangest thing of all. She sent
Cupid to make Dido fall in love with Aeneas—not the respectful
love of Roman marriage, but the animal love of a ' furens '.
If she can succeed, Aeneas is saved ; because this wild love,
as I have said, is incompatible with true marriage ; and
Aeneas is not the man to enslave himself to it, or to renounce
the joys of sober family comfort that he has known so well.
It will drive him away ; Dido knew this, and Anna expressed
it clearly for her in iv. 51. Anna sees the condition of her
sister's mind, and the necessity of detaining Aeneas by every
art in her power. They succeeded in driving him away, as
Venus intended, and this explains his precipitation. Not
a moment was to be lost. But the escape was a narrow one.
He was already beginning his functions as co-founder of
Carthage when the messenger of Jupiter found and roused
him with that stirring speech that sounds once again the great
fugue subject of the *Aeneid*.

NOTE ON *AENEID* V. 5–6. *AMORE POLLUTO*

Interea medium Aeneas iam classe tenebat
certus iter fluctusque atros Aquilone secabat
moenia respiciens, quae iam infelicis Elissae
conlucent flammis. quae tantum accenderit ignem
causa latet ; duri magno sed amore dolores
polluto, notumque furens quid femina possit,
triste per augurium Teucrorum pectora ducunt.

Polluto is usually taken as meaning spoilt or ruined by
Aeneas's desertion; *amor* being ' sacred ', as Mr. Page says. But
was *amor* sacred in any Roman sense ? Far from it. Mackail
translates ' trampled ', which seems to me far from the mark.
Servius has ' laeso '. But these interpreters do not seem to
notice that Virgil is speaking of the effect of the fire on the mind
of the Trojans, who would be far from attributing the ' pol-
lutio ' to their loved leader. To me it seems more likely that
Virgil is here reflecting his own view of the mischief, viz.
that Dido's love was, or had become, poisoned by her own
madness ; [1] hence the words that follow, ' furens quid femina
possit ', which cannot be separated in meaning from those
which precede them.

The mischief was in Dido's own heart ; with true oriental
ungovernableness she had given full way to her passion, and
deserted, in spite of *pudor*, her vows of loyalty to Sychaeus's
memory. Even at the end of bk. i we find that ' vulnus alit
venis et caeco carpitur igni '. She becomes madly careless
of her name and fame. ' Heu furiis incensa feror ' (376),
and when Virgil uses the word *furiae* he always means some
sort of violent disorder of the mind (e. g. xii. 101, 946). She
sees horrible omens, dreams dreadful dreams ; she pretends
magic and is half in earnest about it.

The whole course of her love had gone wrong ; and chiefly
of her own doing. This is in the poet's mind ; he has used
all his resources to draw a woman whose real nature was

---

[1] Weise, *Language and Character of the Roman People*, Eng. trans., p. 24 ;
' amor was to the Roman a malady, a consuming fire, a fatal wound.' In
the *laudatio Turiae* (see ante, p. 126 ff.) the word is never used ; the love of
husband and wife is *pietas, concordia, constantia*, &c.

that of Medea, or Clodia, or Cleopatra ; women whose nature was utterly incompatible with all Roman ideals of family and social life. True, Aeneas was himself to blame, but in my opinion more sinned against than sinning.

AENEID V. 197 (Cf. *IL.* XXIII. 408)

hoc vincite, cives,
et prohibete *nefas*.

The commentators from Servius downwards have understood the word *nefas* in this line to mean disgrace or shame, with the exception of Henry, who very properly observes that they all seem determined to emasculate Virgil, that is, to make him mean something commonplace when he really means more. Certainly *nefas* does not mean shame or disgrace simply, but must always have a religious allusion implied in it. Here the religious allusion can be easily detected. These games were as much funeral games as if Anchises had just died ; they therefore had an unmistakably religious character ; [1] this is perfectly clear in the account given of them in lines 72 ff. Secondly, the prizes are of a religious character, e. g. the sacred tripods. Thirdly, the prayer and vow of Cloanthus, and its reception by the deities of the sea, add to the religious atmosphere. Lastly, the one competitor who failed was rewarded by Aeneas with a kind of consolation prize, of which the object was, I think, to avoid, not shame or disgrace, so much as a failure in religious duty. In the competition of shooting Aeneas is careful to give every competitor a prize.

Notice how one is reminded of the connexion with Anchises consistently throughout. Aeneas is ' satus Anchisa ' in 244 and 424 ; ' Anchisiades ' in 407 ; in 536 the prize is a bowl which belonged to Anchises ; 550, ' ducat avo turmas '. I may also note the curious appeal to God's will in 465 ff.

---

[1] This religious character, if not entirely absent, is hardly perceptible in Homer, *Il.* xxiii ; which to a modern reader may seem the more natural of the two accounts. In Virgil it is plainly shown by the *coronae* (lines 72 ff. and Serv. *ad loc.*) ; and also by the *tuba* (113 and Serv.), for the use of which in funerals see Marquardt, *Privatleben*, p. 341.

AENEID IX. 15

Dixit, et in caelum paribus se sustulit alis
ingentemque fuga secuit sub nubibus arcum.

The second line, as so often, explains the first ; or rather,
helps it out. Iris opened her wings and soared heavenwards,
taking her way along the great bow under the clouds.
Mr. Mackail as usual sees into the poet's meaning ; ' flashed
under the clouds in a long flying bow.' Iris *was* the rainbow,
and as she progressed the bow shone out ; this must be why
Servius explains *secuit* by *duxit*. By getting rid of the notion
of cleaving or cutting we get a far more beautiful picture.
So in x. 107 ' quam quisque secat spem ', where the idea
is that a man goes along with his hope, not simply follows it.
H. Nettleship, in his *Essays in Latin Literature*, p. 370, in
a note of great interest, concludes that there is a fair amount
of evidence for a Latin word *seco*, which meant originally
' to go ', ' to go after ', or ' to follow ' ; or as I should put
it on Virgilian evidence, ' to go along with '. Servius quotes
vi. 899 ' ille viam secat ad naves ', which seems to me to be
an exact parallel to our passage ; meaning not that he
followed a road, but that he went on his way. I am not
sure that in viii. 96 ' viridesque secant placido aequore silvas ',
the real meaning is not of the same kind.

Our poet is faithful to nature, as usual, and manages to
combine nature with myth very pleasantly. Turnus, gazing
up from the earth, sees the cloud quickly vanish, and Iris
and her bow with it ; then the bright sky appeared, brighter
in contrast with the cloud. In the clear sky he sees strange
things—the stars by daylight, or perhaps by the earliest light
of dawn, as Etruscan wise men had seen them : ' Vulsiniis
prima luce flamma caelo emicare visa : cum in unum coisset,
os flammae ferrugineum ostendit, caelum visum discedere,
e cuius hiatu vertices flammae apparuerunt.' [1] Without doubt
Virgil knew Cicero, *de Div.* i. 42. 97 ' caelum discessisse visum
est atque in eo animadversi globi.' What these apparitions

---

[1] *Julius Obsequens, Prodigiorum liber*, ed. Jahn, ch. 52 ; a book not without
its occasional usefulness.

were, globi vertices flammae, palantes stellae ', or whether
' they were anything but the dreams of an Etruscan, we cannot
tell.   None the less the picture is a beautiful one, and its effect
on the solitary Turnus is as striking :

> sic effatus ad undam
> processit summoque hausit de gurgite lymphas
> multa deos orans, oneravitque aethera votis.

Lines 30 ff. :

> Ceu septem surgens sedatis amnibus altus
> Per tacitum Ganges, aut pingui flumine Nilus
> Cum refluit campis et iam se condidit alveo.

This fine simile is Virgil's own ; but he is applying his
knowledge of the Padus to rivers he had not seen.   Mantua
was just the place where the main tributaries of the Po
(excluding the Adige) combine to form a great silent stream ;
but why he did not use his own river I cannot guess.   Fullness
and silence are the two points of the simile ; the troops
collecting on the open field swell in numbers and slacken
in pace, silently advancing, as the Ganges collects its great
tributaries, and now ' too full for sound or foam ' flows with
the gathered force of silent waters.   Can any other language
find such words to express a majestic idea ? *surgens*—of
volume, not overflow—*sedatis, altus, per tacitum* !

This is another proof of Virgil's way of looking at a river ;
he thinks of it as a whole, tributaries and all.   The seven
tributaries of the Ganges may safely be left to the commentators.

AENEID IX. 79

Prisca fides facto, sed fama perennis. This is almost the only
real fairy story told by Virgil himself ; those in the third
book are told by Aeneas, and the Cacus story in bk. viii by
Evander.   By a fairy story I mean one of those Mediterranean
marvels, usually about the sea, storms, birds and so on, such
as abound in the early books of the *Odyssey*.   Heinze fancied
that Virgil invented this one of the ships turned into
nymphs;[1] but I cannot agree with him.   This is a transforma-

---

[1] *Virgil's epische Technik*, p. 298.

tion story like that of the birds of Diomede, and stands quite apart from the ordinary run of divine miracles ; and from most of the metamorphoses in Ovid. The nearest approach to it in Homer is the change of a ship into a rock by Poseidon at the bidding of Zeus, *Od.* xiii. 140 ff., no doubt suggested by the shape of a particular rock. The tale took Virgil's fancy ; what its ancient original was we cannot guess, nor did it matter for him. The difficulty was to introduce it ; for he was not writing a fairy poem, but one of great seriousness. He does it very happily ; he appeals to the spirit of poetry, the Musae ; let them tell it. And then, before he begins, come the half apologetic words, ' prisca fides facto sed fama perennis '. He carefully avoids saying that his own age believes in such wonders ; but they love a good story still, whether they believe it or no. The words are a beautiful example of the Latin genius for condensed expression, and also of the fullness of meaning in Latin words. But *prisca* has been rather troublesome to the learned, from Servius downwards.

The ' sed ' gives the clue to the shade of meaning wanted in *prisca*. Henry's ' old-fashioned ' will do very well, for it is not the story which is *prisca*, but the belief in it. ' Old-fashioned folks may still believe it, but we all like to listen to it.' [1]

AENEID IX. 214

Solita aut si qua id fortuna vetabit. Henry proposed *saltem* for *solita*, but we must accept the manuscript reading, which after all makes quite a good sense. Servius's note shows that a difficulty was felt about it, no doubt because in his day (and long before) most of the slain in battle were recovered and buried on the field, and the bodies of all chiefs would be identified. But Virgil is no doubt right in assuming that in ancient times the usual fate of a slain man was to be lost, and to remain unburied.

---

[1] In the *prisca fides* of vi. 878 (Marcellus) the adjective has something of the same meaning ; righteousness like that of his ancestors.

The idea of the cenotaph, which Virgil here introduces, is found also in iii. 304 and vi. 505. Cenotaphs were not common at Rome, so far as I know; probably for the reason given above. The most famous instance is that of the young Caesars, grandsons of Augustus, who were worshipped with a regular ritual at their cenotaphs at Pisa, though their bodies were in the Mausoleum at Rome.[1] But, as Marquardt[2] says, it was quite in keeping with the Roman idea of the *monumentum*, as distinguished from the Etruscan practice of burial in a house sealed up for ever, or only opened for new inmates. The desire not to be forgotten, which was urgent under the Empire in the gilds, is common to both Greeks and Romans, but is not expressed in Etruscan burial.

THE EPISODE OF NISUS AND EURYALUS: WHY INTRODUCED HERE?

I suggest four motives: (i) The desire to put off typical fighting of the Homeric kind; Virgil knew that it could not be treated again with the same felicity, and it was not after his own heart.[3] (ii) His love of boys just growing up,[4] an *amor pius*, as with this pair (296), love of young manly beauty, and the happy relation between elder and younger. (iii) A wish to imitate and surpass the Doloneia of Homer, in which he was beyond doubt successful. (iv) There was here a chance to bring Ascanius forward; see on xii. 87 ff. Being too young to fight, he might have fallen out of these last books. His part here is admirably conceived; it is dignified, affectionate, and yet quite boyish; e.g. his astonishing promises of rewards (263 ff.), which so puzzled Gossrau that he thought the poet must have been slumbering, are simply the result of boyish enthusiasm. See below on 252 ff.

---

[1] *C. I. L.* xi. 1421; Dessau, *Inscr. Select.* i. 140.
[2] *Privatleben*, p. 355, note.
[3] See *Aeneas at the Site of Rome*, p. 1. [4] *Death of Turnus*, p. 90.

AENEID IX. 252 ff.

Aletes, annis gravis atque animi maturus, says to the youths
about to start on their perilous journey :

> Quae vobis, quae digna, viri, pro laudibus istis
> praemia posse rear solvi ? pulcherrima primum
> di moresque dabunt vestri : tum cetera reddet
> actutum pius Aeneas atque integer aevi
> Ascanius meriti tanti non immemor unquam.

A passage of great importance for the mind of Virgil and his
idea of the Roman mind at its best. Conington refers to
Servius, Servius to Cic. *Phil.* ii. 44 [1] ('satis in ipsa conscientia
pulcherrimi facti fructus'), but neither of them seems to feel
the ethical force of the words, or of the appeal to 'mens
conscia recti' (i. 604). No earthly reward is called for in the
first place—such things are purely secondary. 'Pulcherrima
primum Di moresque dabunt vestri.' This is the true Roman
spirit of the good old times, and it is the spirit too of men like
Scipio Aemilianus, Cato the elder, the Gracchi, and many more,
before the days of unnatural ambition for triumphs and
supplicationes. *Di moresque* were the two pivots of old Roman
social life, and a faithful *pietas* toward god and good custom
needed no reward. Rare indeed, compared with ours of to-day,
were rewards for Roman soldiers, who were fighting for the
divine inhabitants of their city, and for the good traditions
of the human ones. Read Gellius, v. 6 (*de coronis militaribus*),
and especially the quotation from Masurius Sabinus in sec.
13 ff., and from Cato in sec. 25. Note that these words
(252 ff.) are spoken by one who is 'annis gravis atque animi
maturus', and that the readiness of Ascanius to promise
praemia, which so puzzled the rather wooden-headed Gossrau,
is by way of contrast, as the enthusiasm of a boy, who seizes
on the chance given him by Aletes ('immo ego vos, excipit
Ascanius '), for the moment forgetting the *di moresque*.

---

[1] Add *Phil.* i. 9 ; *de Rep.* vi. 8 'sapientibus conscientia ipsa factorum
egregiorum amplissimum virtutis est praemium'. This is, however, the
Stoic idea of *virtus*, which is like that of the old Romans, but not related
to it.

AENEID IX. 275 ff.

Ascanius has just been promising Nisus an astonishing number of good things (*praemia*) if he returns safely. Then he turns to Euryalus :

> Te vero, mea quem spatiis propioribus aetas
> insequitur, venerande puer, iam pectore toto
> accipio et comitem casus complector in omnes.
> nulla meis sine te quaeretur gloria rebus :
> seu pacem seu bella geram, tibi maxima rerum
> verborumque fides.

What does Virgil mean by *venerande puer* ? If he wrote the *Culex*, he had used the same expression of a boy who can, in my opinion, hardly be other than Octavius, afterwards Augustus.[1] There the boy is also *sanctus* (26 and 37) ; and *sanctus* might be used of any *praetextatus*, for well-born children were all in some sense ' holy ' till they took the *toga virilis*. But *venerandus* is a still stronger word, and in Virgil always (except here) implies worship. As applied to Octavius in the *Culex* it can hardly have a reference to divine descent, for Octavius was not yet Octavianus ; but it may mean reverence for a superior in birth and quality, though not in age. Here it is used by a princely boy of one who is not much older than himself and below him in rank, but one whom his enthusiastic affection has made his model and leader. Euryalus is to be his adviser and counsellor in the days to come when he will reign over the new city. For Nisus he feels as a prince to one of his best chieftains ; but towards Euryalus he feels as a younger to an elder boy, and the combined affection and reverence produce the word *venerande*. The whole passage to 313 shows a depth of feeling rarely equalled in poetry.

AENEID IX. 435

These three exquisite lines, says Mr. Page, ' are borrowed partly from *Il*. 8. 306, partly from Catullus, 11. 22 (cf. 62. 39 ff.) '. If the reader will look out these passages, instead of taking them for granted, he will see that the essential beauty of the

---

[1] *Culex*, 25 ; *Classical Review*, 1914, p. 119.

Virgilian simile is not borrowed from either of them. In
Homer the victim, Gorgythion, is a chance one, and our pity
is not specially roused for him among a hundred others.
In Catullus the thought is a lovely one, but comes at the end
of an unpleasant poem. Virgil's lines are inspired by the
fact that it is a beautiful boy, *integer aevi*, ' with all his life
before him ', who is the subject of the comparison. Euryalus
has been before us all through the story; we can almost
love him as Virgil loved him, as Ascanius loved him; and the
simile touches us keenly, we care not whence it comes. What
was simply a charming thought in the older poets has become
a perfect bloom, full of beauty, colour, and feeling.

A word about the poppy. Whether Homer's plant was
really a poppy I cannot say, but Virgil's undoubtedly was.
It is an interesting fact that our own common scarlet poppy
hangs its head only *before* the bloom unfolds itself, in order
to protect its most valuable organs from the rain. When
old enough to resist the showers it holds up the head and the
bloom begins to appear. If our poppy was that of Virgil,
or if other species have the same habit, perhaps he had noted
the fact without fully understanding it.

AENEID IX. 641 ff.

Apollo sees Ascanius from a cloud, and addresses him in
words which the boy cannot hear : ' Macte nova virtute,
puer, sic itur ad astra '; then descends to earth in the form
of Butes, and speaks to him in person. Servius asks, why
Apollo ? and the answer he gives shows that such an unusual
event as an appearance of Apollo not only needed an explanation, but did not get a very satisfactory one. It is, says
Servius, because Ascanius had killed Remulus with an
arrow ! What is the real reason, one naturally asks ?

This is almost the only occasion in the *Aeneid* when Apollo
is seen personally ; he is *alluded to* as a prophet half a dozen
times. In xi. 785 Aruns prays to him as the deity of Soracte,
and he answers the prayer. Nowhere else is he prominent,
unless it be for an instant on the shield of Aeneas (viii. 704),
and this is very good proof that Augustus had not asked

the poet to make much of his favourite deity in the *Aeneid*.

Here he is introduced as a prophetic deity, beyond doubt. There are three distinct prophetic allusions : (1) ' dis genite et geniture deos ' ; (2) the closing of the temple of Janus, as in i. 294 ; (3) the assurance that Troy is not to be the centre of the future empire. All these are references to Augustus in the years when the *Aeneid* was being written.

' Macte nova virtute ' is exactly the Irish ' more power to you '. *Rel. Exp.*, pp. 182 ff. For ' sic itur ad astra ' see *The Death of Turnus*, p. 70.

AENEID IX. 731

Continuo nova lux oculis effulsit et arma
horrendum sonuere, tremunt in vertice cristae
sanguineae, clipeoque micantia fulmina mittunt.

mittunt *PR* : mittit *M.* Clipei *P.* On the whole the line as written above has the best manuscript support. But Conington and Mr. Page read *mittit.*

Let us remember what is happening. Turnus has penetrated into the new city, and has escaped notice, till suddenly ' nova lux effulsit, &c.', and the essential ' frightfulness ' of Turnus becomes conspicuous. In the Gathering of the Clans we had this frightfulness fully described ; it consisted of two objects, the crest on the helmet breathing flame, and the smooth shield with its artistic reliefs. These are the two points in his equipment on which Virgil insists. So in x. 270 ff. with the armour of Aeneas ' stans celsa in puppi ' as he approaches the land ; ' ardet apex capiti cristique a vertice flamma Funditur et vastos umbo vomit aureus ignis.' It seems to me impossible to take the shield in the passage I am discussing as an enemy's (so my friend Professor Conway *in litt.*) ; it must be that of Turnus, as every one will allow who compares the two other passages. If it be that of Turnus, what do the four words mean, ' clipeoque micantia fulmina mittunt ' ?

I take *cristae* as subject to *mittunt* ; the blood-red crest flickers with motion of the warrior's head, and lights up the shield—passes on its lightning to the shield. Professor

Conway says that the shield, held on the left arm, could not
catch the flashing crest. If that is a fatal objection—I do
not myself think it is—we are reduced to taking *mittunt*
in a neuter sense, which does not recommend itself to me at all.
The armour is not that of ordinary human make; as in
x. 270, its illumination is superhuman; and I see no reason
why crest and shield should not combine to flash their light.

AENEID X. 1–117

This curious scene of the celestial senate, and the bitter
speeches of Venus and Juno, followed by the strange decision
of Jupiter, seem unnatural to the modern reader, though
Virgil is but following Homer in the fourth and eighth books
of the *Iliad*. Servius indeed says (comment on line 104)
that Lucilius in his first book did the same thing, and that
' totus hic locus ', by which I think he means the whole scene,
was taken over from that poet. But Servius is apt to speak
rashly of Virgil's ' imitations ', and it is almost inconceivable
that our poet should have been thinking of what must have
been a travesty, with intent to scoff, of Homer's sittings of
the divine council.

But why does he introduce the scene at all? Merely to
find opportunity for that skill in rhetoric in which Macrobius
thought him quite as much distinguished as in poetical
expression? No doubt this motive was present; it is difficult
for us to realize how strong was the demand for oratory,
whether in prose or verse, among the Roman educated classes
of that day. There was also, I think, the desire to postpone
further fighting yet awhile, as uncongenial to the poet himself,
and monotonous if indulged in. Perhaps yet another motive
is that he wished to pause and bring the rights of the whole
struggle before the minds of his readers at a critical moment;
for of the two speakers Juno is obviously meant to seem on
the wrong side in her bitterness against the Trojans.

However this may be, it is perhaps worth while to examine
the whole scene as evidence of one characteristic of Virgil's
poetic mind. Johnson complained of *Paradise Lost* that it
comprises neither human actions nor human manners. ' The

man and woman who act and suffer are in a state which no other man and woman can ever know. The reader finds no transaction in which he can be engaged ; beholds no condition in which he can by any effort of imagination place himself. . . . Milton knew human nature only in the gross, and had never studied the shades of character nor the combinations of concurring or the perplexity of contending passions ' (Preface to Shakespeare). This is certainly not true of Virgil ; so far from it, that even in the council of the gods he finds room for Roman and Italian actions and manners, passions and rhetoric. So it is throughout the poem ; it is *character* in which Virgil rejoices, and in which he rejoices more and more to the very end of his poem. His characters are drawn on a grand scale, more especially that of Aeneas, but from time to time we find those delightful details which make them living and human for those who are not blind. These characters are governed by a supervising destiny, yet there is always to be seen in them that free action of the will which was a Roman's inheritance. And as I have noticed elsewhere, these characters, or some of them, are not *static* but grow and change ; Aeneas of the last books, a consummate warrior, is not the hesitating Aeneas of the earlier books, and his son grows in wisdom and stature all through the poem.

It was then the natural instinct of Virgil to think of human beings, their moods and passions, not only in dealing with men but with gods. Whether this has any advantage for the reader I will not attempt to determine.

Jupiter's attitude at the end of this episode has often been described as weak and vacillating, e. g. by Professor McInnes.[1] To my mind this is not only a great mistake, but quite impossible. The whole passage seems to me meant to show the god's tremendous power as compared with that of all other gods ; a truly Roman idea. Venus enlarges on it at the beginning of her speech, and in line 100 he is ' pater omnipotens, rerum cui prima potestas ' ; as he begins to speak there is universal silence, and he ends with that awful oath by the Styx on which I have commented in *The Death of*

---

[1] *Classical Review*, 1910, p. 169, where other alleged instances are given.

Turnus, pp. 141 ff. A few words on the relation of Jupiter and the other gods to the Fates may be useful here. After reading everything I can find on the subject I have come to a fairly definite conclusion ; but it should be clearly understood that Virgil is not wholly consistent throughout the poem, as was inevitable for a poet who had to adapt a decaying system of polytheism to the philosophical needs of his story.

I find that Virgil shared the view of almost all the thinking men of his day that there was a great driving force at work in the world, which was responsible for the rise and growth of Rome ; and that his word for this is usually *fata*, which however expresses it rather as it was interpreted to men by oracles and signs than as a thing in itself. It is in fact the Stoic idea of Destiny, and might be thought of as the will or plan of the Soul of the universe. Man was subject to it, but none the less his will was free ; a view which was natural and traditional with all educated Romans. But what of the gods, who are after all only a superior sort of men ? Were they subject to it ? Undoubtedly the deities in the *Aeneid* could not effectually oppose it, though they might hamper and delay. Juno and Venus for example had different views of what it ought to be, the one taking the side of Carthage, the other of Rome, and quarrelling between themselves they ask a decision of Jupiter. Jupiter clearly says, ' Enough of this fooling '. But now comes the crucial question ; was Jupiter himself capable of making a decision outside the driving force of destiny ? Beyond all doubt he stands far above the other gods, partly owing to his kinship with the Zeus of Homer, partly perhaps to his Roman inheritance as a heaven god ; but whatever the cause, no other deity has anything like the power over human life which he has. Can we, however, say either that he can overrule destiny, or that his will is identical with destiny ?

On the whole I think the answer must be No. If we read carefully his great speech in bk. i. 257 ff., though it is by no means perfectly clear, I think that the general result is that Jupiter is rather the high priest (so to speak) of destiny than identical with it ; as also in i. 375–6 he rather consults it than controls it. True, he sometimes uses language which seems to put him in the place of destiny, as in i. 278 ; but that should not be a serious difficulty. A prophet may not unnaturally speak as if the events he foretells were of his own making. In the passage before us he seems to claim the power of interfering with destiny, but will not exercise it. His last words mean ' destiny will find its own way ' (not, will *find out a way*) ' without any help or interference from me '. The two goddesses have power enough to hamper the action of destiny, and Jupiter refuses to check them by deciding for one or the other. The evolution of things will work out most satisfactorily if the squabbles of goddesses be left to take their own course. This is really, as Servius saw, equivalent to a decision in favour of Aeneas and Rome ; and the reason of it is that Juno must be allowed to have her turn with Carthage in a struggle for world-power. Had Jupiter decided to suppress Juno altogether, there could have been no Punic Wars ; and that he could have suppressed her I can have no doubt.

In the difficult lines 107–12, it is best, I think, to follow Henry, who puts a full stop at the end of line 108, and encloses the first three words of 111 in a parenthesis.

AENEID X. 287 ff.

> Interea Aeneas socios de puppibus altis
> pontibus exponit. multi servare recursus
> languentis pelagi et brevibus se credere saltu,
> per remos alii. speculatus litora Tarchon
> qua vada non spirant nec fracta remurmurat unda
> sed mare inoffensum crescenti adlabitur aestu. . . .

Landing by *pontes* was the orthodox way, but it took time ; and many, not caring to wait their turn, jumped into the shallow water as the wave retired, or slid down the oars. This last mode of landing amuses Mr. Page ; but he has forgotten the length and size of the oars of a ship of Virgil's day—ten to thirteen feet—rather too long either for use as a walking-stick or (as Heyne fancied) a leaping-pole.

In the next line *spirant* is such an expressive and beautiful

word, and is so fully borne out by words that follow, ' nec
fracta remurmurat unda ', that it is a pity to find *sperat*
in our Oxford text. True, there is good manuscript authority
for *sperat* ; but then the copyists would have found *spirant*
rather beyond them. Henry's note is here excellent (Mr. Page
follows him without acknowledgement) ; quoting Lucr. vi. 890,
of a spring bubbling up in the sea and crinkling the surface,
and Seneca, *Thyestes*, 755, of the heaving of the arteries in
a man. But Virgil himself decides the reading : *Georg.* i. 327
' fervetque fretis spirantibus aequor '. Here Keightley notes :
' By *spirantibus* is meant the foaming and boiling up of water
when driven against land or rocks.' Here I think it rather
means the slight disturbance of the surface caused by a rock
or stone below it ; such a disturbance as is well known to
fishermen, suggesting that a trout is lurking in the lee of
a stone below the surface. The next line, the last I have
quoted above, is, in contrast with the foregoing ones, one of
Virgil's most expressive and beautiful ones.

AENEID X. 356 ff.

Magno discordes aethere venti
praelia ceu tollunt animis et viribus aequis ;
non ipsi inter se, non nubila, non mare cedit ;
anceps pugna diu, stant obnixa omnia contra.

These curious lines are almost unnoticed by the commentators. I suppose they are not troubled as I am to discover
what aerial phenomenon the poet is really thinking of. He
does not seem to be imitating *Il.* xvi. 765, where Eurus and
Notos are at strife in a mountain ravine, breaking the trees,
nor can I find the original among the storms of Lucretius.
The contending armies make no way, either of them ; ' expel-
lere tendunt Nunc hi nunc illi ; haeret pede pes densusque
viro vir '. When does such a balance of forces occur in
nature ? A passage in Sir A. Geikie's *Love of Nature among the
Romans*, p. 214, has suggested to me that the poet may have
been thinking of the solemn quietude that sometimes precedes
a thunderstorm, a phenomenon which he must often have
noticed in Italy. It sometimes occurs in this country ; see

e. g. an account of the extraordinary storm of August 9, 1843, described by the Rev. J. Jordan in his *History of Enstone*, p. 401 : ' Sitting in the house I endeavoured, by opening windows and doors, to obtain a draft, but the air was stagnant. . . . The storm rose very slowly and majestically, and *directly in the teeth of the wind, which, though imperceptible in the slightest degree,* was indicated by the weathercock to be in the east, while the storm came from WNW.' ' Anceps pugna diu, stant obnixa omnia contra.' The introduction of the sea in 358 is puzzling ; it is an imaginative touch added to the familiar phenomena.

AENEID X. 362 ff.

The geography here is not very clear, and has unfortunately been confused by Boissier, who imagined that the Arcadian and Etruscan cavalry here mentioned had come by land from Agylla, crossing the Tiber. Of that I see no sign ; they had come with their horses on board ship (see 181, where Astur, ' equo fidens ', was on board), and landing rather farther down the coast than the rest, were pushing up one of the rocky ravines or defiles that lead from the sea into the hilly region. Pallas was with them, or watching them, and he saw that they had dismounted on account of the rough track, and were suddenly attacked in front. In giving way they must make for the sea ; hence his words ' ecce maris magni claudit nos obice pontus, Deest iam terra fugae : pelagus Troiamne petamus ? ' The sea was behind them ; the new city Troia but a little to their left rear. ' Don't go back ; you have only the sea behind you ; you must cut your way to the camp through the enemy in front of you.' There remains the difficulty that they were near the Tiber, since in 420 ff. Pallas addressed the river-god ; but as Pallas did actually bring them victoriously through the foe, they would be close to the river, and in touch with the new city.

AENEID X. 537 ff.

This is to me one of the strangest passages in the *Aeneid*. A priest of Apollo and Diana (' Phoebi Triviaeque sacerdos ')

is fighting on the Italian side against Aeneas and Fate, for
the two deities whom, but two years after Virgil's death,
Horace had to treat as the chief deities of the *Carmen saeculare*,
at Augustus's bidding. Aeneas sacrifices this priest, ' lapsum-
que superstans *Immolat* ingentique umbra tegit ' ; and
a trophy of his spoils is dedicated to Mars under his ancient
cult-title of Gradivus, of which the meaning is lost. If we
read *insignibus albis* with Probus, Virgil may have been
thinking of the white dress of Greek priests (art. Sacerdos in
Dict. of Antiquities, 572 B) ; no Roman priest wore white.
But I think we should keep the *armis* of the manuscripts.
If so, and as the *arma* were made into a trophy, the fact that
he was fighting may have been fatal to him, priest though he
was. Or it may be that an enemy priest had no claim to be
spared on the field of battle. In xi. 768 ff. Chloreus is ' sacer
Cybelo olimque sacerdos ', i. e. at Troy ; but he is not killed
by Camilla. Cf. vi. 484 : ' Cereri sacrum Polyboeten.'

Ingenti umbra tegit : Henry is clear that it was Aeneas's
body that threw the shadow. I think so too ; but the idea
of death may be also implied.

It is obvious that Aeneas's wrath is terrible when the
battle-fever is on him ; his speech 557 ff. is almost too much
for us. ' Onerabit membra sepulcro ' reminds us of Byron's
' On thee shall weigh no ponderous tomb '.

AENEID XI. 5

Ingentem quercum decisis undique ramis
Constituit tumulo fulgentiaque induit arma,
Mezenti ducis exuvias, tibi, magne, tropaeum
Bellipotens.

The description of the trophy follows. Servius says :
' Constituit tumulo, in colle : quia tropaea non figebantur
nisi in eminentioribus locis. Sallustius de Pompeio : Devictis
Hispanis tropaea in Pyreneis iugis constituit. Ex quo more
in urbibus tropaea figebantur in arcubus exaedificatis ' (i. e.
when the arch was completed they put the trophy on the top).
Does this statement of Servius answer to the fact so far as we
know it ?

The evidence is slender, but the point is interesting as bearing on the origin of the triumphal arch. The list of such arches begins with Augustus, but we need not suppose that there was nothing of the kind before his time ; the principle that trophies must be erected in conspicuous positions might lead to something in the nature of an arch before it was introduced into the city by Augustus. We know of three arches erected in Augustus's time, one at his triple triumph in 29 B.C., one in 20, when he had recovered the standards of Crassus, and one after the recovery by Tiberius of the standards lost by Varus. Only the second of these is known in any detail ; a denarius of 19 B. C. (Cohen, *Monnaies impériales*, nos. 82–4) has Augustus on a *quadriga* on the top of an arch, with Parthians presenting him with a military ensign and an eagle ; no bas-reliefs adorned this arch so far as we can see, and the *quadriga* on the top with Augustus may have been an innovation in place of a trophy. In the provinces triumphal arches sometimes had among their ornaments sculptured trophies, as at Orange. ' Arcus cum tropaeis ' is the expression of Suetonius (*Claudius* 1) for one erected to Drusus the elder on the via Appia ; and Ἀψίς τροπαιοφόρος occurs in Dio Cassius, xlix. 15 ; li. 19, &c. If we had more representations of these earlier triumphal arches, we might be able to confirm Servius's statement ; as it is we must be content with guessing.

My information as to these arches is derived from Courbaud, *Le Bas-relief romain*, p. 116, who discusses the date of the arch of Orange on p. 331 ff. He believes it to be of the time of Tiberius, and to reflect the style of the Pergamean sculptures. See also the same work, p. 373. He thinks that the architrave was an addition to the arch ; but I am not sure that the process was not exactly the reverse, and that the Porta triumphalis, originally a *iugum* perhaps, was not the origin of the triumphal arch, combining with the notion that a trophy must be *elevated*. Courbaud allows that triumphal arches properly speaking did not exist in Greece ; would it have occurred to the Romans to imitate the Greeks in this particular form ? I doubt it.

NOTE ON VIRGIL, *AENEID* XI. 160

' Vivendo vici mea fata '

In a paper in the *Classical Quarterly* for January 1917, by Miss L. E. Matthaei, on the Fates in Virgil, there is a passage which so completely puzzled me that I fear I wasted some time over it ; for I find after six months that it baffles me as much as ever. I am greatly indebted to the article in many ways, and have constantly had recourse to it ; but I now see clearly, what I suspected at the first reading, that Miss Matthaei has put more undigested philosophy into Virgil's mind than ever was there when he was writing the *Aeneid*, and has made too little allowance for the feeling and language of a poet.

On p. 12, commenting on *Aen*. xi. 160, in the lament of Evander for his slain son (' Vivendo vici mea fata '), Miss Matthaei says that there is in ' this very odd expression ' a contrast ' very dimly expressed between what life is and what it should be ', and fate is made to stand for what it should be, its best possibilities. With this she contrasts x. 154, where the Etruscan people is said to be *libera fati*, because they have accepted the leadership of Aeneas, as they were directed to do by a *haruspex* (vii. 499) ; they were free, that is, in the sense in which a man was free of a vow when he had performed it. Then comparing the two passages, she finds that in the one ' fate is what life ought to be contrasted with what life is ' ; while in the second ' fate is what life is contrasted with what it ought to be '. Well may she ask what stable notion can be rescued from such a contradiction ! It convinced her that she now had her finger on the whole gist of the Virgilian problem of the fates. ' I believe that Virgil inherited a gloomy and pessimistic definition of fate, as of a malignant pursuer of men, a power to be feared and placated, but without moral inspiration or elevation of any kind. . . . But the Romans had always struggled against this miserable doctrine, and foremost among them is Virgil. The consequence is that he is always swaying between the thought of a moral world and the thought of a sad and unjust world.'

This attitude of mind is of course common to all who give any sort of serious thought to the changes and chances of this mortal life ; but Miss Matthaei goes on to develop her view that Virgil was a pessimist in spite of his better instincts, and the *Aeneid* a pessimistic poem, in which fate makes mockery of humble human effort. This is a view which I cannot possibly share, after an intimate acquaintance with our poet for over half a century ; and I doubt whether Miss Matthaei would have reached such a conclusion if she had not begun by mistaking the meaning of the word *fata* in the expression ' Vivendo vici mea fata '. What the meaning really is is made quite clear by Dr. Henry in one of his best notes. *Fata* is not here used in any metaphysical sense, but simply as we use the word ' lot ', both the Latin and the English words being used for the span of life, though originally denoting the idea of a method by which the future might be foretold. All that Evander means is that he has reached beyond the ordinary span of human life, his wife and son having gone before him ; just as in xii. 395, we find *proferre fata* used of seeking to prolong a man's life. And all the other passage means is that the Etruscans have obeyed the utterance of the soothsayer who bade them look for a foreign leader. In both cases there is a reminiscence of Virgil's favourite Euripides.[1] Henry quotes *Alcestis*, 939 :

> ἐγὼ δ᾽, ὃν οὐ χρῆ ζῆν, παρεὶς τὸ μόρσιμον,
> λυπρὸν διάξω βίοτον· ἄρτι μανθάνω.

and 694 :

> σὺ γοῦν ἀναιδῶς διεμάχου τὸ μὴ θανεῖν,
> καὶ ζῇς παρελθὼν τὴν πεπρωμένην τύχην,
> ταύτην κατακτάς.

Conington quotes for ' libera fati ' Eur. *Phoen.* 999 :

> οἱ μὲν θεσφάτων ἐλεύθεροι
> κοὐκ εἰς ἀνάγκην δαιμόνων ἀφιγμένοι.

Lastly, there is no mystical meaning in the phrase *vincere fata* ; it may, as Henry thought, be a reminiscence of Plautus

---

[1] For the close affinity between Virgil and Euripides see Dr. Glover's *Virgil*, pp. 53 ff.

Epid. ii. 1, 6 ' eam (i. e. uxorem) vivendo vincere ', of a man surviving his wife.

The study of fate in the *Aeneid* is of course a difficult and fascinating problem, and of recent years has been well handled by Professor Conway (*Proc. Class. Assoc.*, October 1906), and by Professor McInnes (*Classical Review*, 1910, pp. 169 ff.). But we must not make difficulties where in reality there are none. Miss Matthaei has raised such a difficulty by bringing together two passages which have nothing whatever to do with each other, and discerning in each of them a dim mystical meaning which, to the best of my belief, Virgil never meant to be discerned there. Starting from this misapprehension, she overlaid her otherwise very useful discussion with a good deal of nebulousness. In my humble opinion we shall always get into difficulties if we look for anything in the nature of a philosophical system in the *Aeneid*. We have no evidence that Virgil had made a special study of philosophy, though we know that he meant to do so when he had completed revising his poem. He had studied philosophy as he had studied poetry and mythology, astrology and medicine. True, if the fifth poem of the *Catalepton* be his, he had at one moment a passion for Epicurism, and boyishly threatened to abandon poetry for it ; but to this plan he certainly did not adhere. Beyond question he passed through various moods while the *Aeneid* was being written, with the result that those who will can always find contradictions in his view of life and destiny ; but in drawing conclusions from such contradictions we must beware of getting involved in a labyrinth of speculation about his ways of thinking.

NOTES ON HORACE
ODES, III. 1–6

ALL German scholars are fond of Horace ; and Mommsen, happening to refresh his memory of the Odes in his old age, made the *Römeroden* (as the Germans call the famous six) the subject of a Festrede to the Berlin Academy, in which he tried to interpret them historically.[1] Since then Professor von Domaszewski of Heidelberg has attempted a further interpretation of the same kind,[2] which however falls far short of Mommsen's paper in general interest, and shows imperfect acquaintance with Horace and Horatian criticism. He starts with the assumption that these six poems were written at one time and with one object, and that the object was to illustrate the inscription on the shield of gold set up in Augustus's honour in the year 27 B. C. by Senate and People.[3] This inscription testified to the *virtus, clementia, iustitia,* and *pietas,* of the Princeps ; and Domaszewski sees in these odes (except the first, of which he says nothing) a sermon or sermons on these Augustan virtues ; viz. 2 on Virtus, 3 on Iustitia, 4 on Clementia, 5 on Virtus again, and 6 on Pietas.

It is easy to be attracted by speculations like these, especially on a first reading ; I have felt their blandishment myself. In any case they need very careful testing, and do not often get it. In the following notes I hope to show that I have some good reason for distrusting them.

ODE I

Odi profanum vulgus et arceo, &c. This first stanza seems to be meant as an introduction to all the six odes, and so, I believe, it is generally understood. But it is by no means

[1] *Reden und Aufsätze,* i. 168 ff. The occasion was the birthday of the ex-Kaiser Wilhelm II.
[2] *Rhein. Mus.* lix. 302 ff. ; reprinted in the author's *Abhandlungen zur röm. Religion,* pp. 111 ff.
[3] *Mon. Anc.* c. 34 (Mommsen, *Res Gestae Div. Aug.,* p. 103)

certain that the six were all written at one time ; I myself
find this difficult to believe.[1] It may be that this curious
little preface was placed where it is when the six odes were
collected. This first one might begin quite naturally and after
Horace's familiar manner with the fifth line.

What is the object and meaning of this preface ? Wickham
and others have thought that the figure is of initiation into
mysteries ; but they mean Greek mysteries, and there is
nothing peculiarly Greek in these lines. *Profanum* is a characteristic word of Roman worship, meaning what is outside
of a temple and its ritual. *Profanum vulgus* does not mean
the uninitiated, but all who have no right in sacred law to
be present at the temple worship, e. g. strangers, slaves,
in some temples men or women respectively, and in all
temples those who had not performed the requisite ablutions.[2]
Thus we must think of the mongrel un-Roman nature of the
greater part of the city population, in order to realize Horace's
thought fully. In contrast with this *profanum vulgus* are the
virgines and *pueri*, nobly born and nurtured, *patrimi et
matrimi*,[3] *ingenui*, pure in body, pure in mind, who take part
in the temple service, and are here conceived as about to learn
the odes and the music to which they are to be set. This,
I feel sure, was Horace's primary meaning.[4] *Virgines puerique*
are always for Horace the two choirs of children, as in *Odes*
i. 21, where they pray Apollo to avert war and famine, and
in iv. 6. 31, and the *Carmen Saeculare*, which last Horace
himself taught his choirs at a later time.[5] And thus I think
he means not so much that he is going to give general moral
lessons to the new generation, as that he is going to turn his
art to new account as *Musarum sacerdos*—which title supplies
the key to the tone of all these odes. ' I have things to say
which I wish to consecrate as priest of poetry, *vates sacer*,

[1] See H. Nettleship, *Essays in Latin Literature*, pp. 160 ff.
[2] *Religious Experience of the Roman People*, pp. 30 ff.
[3] See *Journal of Roman Studies*, 1916, p. 187.
[4] In a note on p. 313 of his *Sappho and Simonides* (in which he has included
a chapter on Horace) Wilamowitz-Moellendorf also takes this view.
[5] Add *Odes*, iv. 1. 25 ff. ; iv. 11. 10.

O 2

and to teach to a few highly-born and highly-nurtured young
pupils.' There may be something more than metaphor in
the lines ; it looks to me as if he had always wished to hear
his odes sung. However that may be, he expressed the same
thought long afterwards in *Epist*. ii. 1. 126 ff., a passage
which I quote in full that it may be fully considered :

> Os tenerum pueri balbumque poeta figurat,
> torquet ab obscenis iam nunc sermonibus aurem,
> mox etiam pectus praeceptis format amicis,
> asperitatis et invidiae corrector et irae :
> recte facta refert, orientia tempora notis
> instruit exemplis, inopem solatur et aegrum.
> castis cum pueris ignara puella mariti
> disceret unde preces, vatem ni Musa dedisset ?
> poscit opem chorus et praesentia numina sentit,
> caelestis implorat aquas docta prece blandus,
> avertit morbos, metuenda pericula pellit,
> impetrat et pacem et locupletem frugibus annum.
> carmine di superi placantur, carmine Manes.

In this charming passage Horace brings to perfect utterance
an idea of the value of poetry which, if I am not mistaken,
had occasionally been present to his mind ever since he wrote
Epodes vii. and xvi.

In the second stanza Mommsen fancied that when writing
' reges in ipsos imperium est Iovis ' Horace had Augustus
in his mind. The fact was that the historian had Augustus
in his mind, and read him into Horace's language. It often
seems to be assumed that Augustus is the leading figure in
these odes, but the more I meditate on them the less I think
so. To do full justice to Horace we must be careful not to
exaggerate the prominence of Augustus in his poems. Horace
was always disposed to be independent, and until these first
three books of the *Odes* were published there is no evidence
that he was intimate with Augustus himself, or in any sense
in his service.[1] I prefer to think that these six poems were

---

[1] Nettleship, op. cit., p. 164. This is certainly the conclusion to be drawn
from Suetonius's account of Horace's life (*Suetonius*, ed. C. L. Roth, p. 297).
Wilamowitz, op. cit., p. 313, says that these odes were ' am wenigsten bestellte
Ware ', i. e. by no means written to order.

not, like the *Carmen Saeculare* later on, directly inspired by
Augustus, but were rather the result of a serious mood that
came upon the poet at times, when he allowed himself to
think about the shortcomings of his age.   This mood had
possessed him when he wrote the seventh and sixteenth
Epodes and the fourteenth ode of bk. i ; and when he felt
it come upon him again in writing these six odes and the
twenty-fourth of this book (' Intactis opulentior '), the mood
was Augustan only by accident.   Once or twice a point of
Augustan policy is alluded to or criticized, but the spirit
of the poetry is free and genuine throughout.

The real subject of this first ode is the limitation of all
human effort, and the need of accommodating our ambitions
to this law of human nature.   Mommsen saw in it that
Epicurean Quietism of which Horace is reckoned an exponent.
But as with Virgil, who had in his youth Epicurean leanings,
the true Roman Stoicism is never far off.   ' Aequa lege
Necessitas sortitur insignes et imos.'   The practical philosophy
of that day was an amalgam.   *Necessitas* seems to be here
rather the Determinism of the Stoics, the Fates of the *Aeneid*
(cf. iii. 376, for the metaphor of the lot), than the Necessity
of Lucretius, from which there is an escape through the
declination of the atoms.

ODE II

Mommsen thought that this ode was a song for the new
army which Augustus was beginning to build up during these
years. · So too he fancied that the last eight lines, about the
virtue of silence, had special reference to the new Imperial
officials, most of them freedmen who were not only efficient
but trustworthy.   But it is much better to read the poem in
a broader sense, and as Horatian in origin rather than Augustan.
Let us take it as a poem on the old Roman virtues, as a whole
in itself, not as a make-up of various political allusions.   Let
us remember, for example, that silence in matters of State,
like hardiness in recruits, was an old Roman characteristic,
as is well shown by Cato's charming story of the boy who

refused to divulge to his mother and her friends what he had heard in the Senate House.[1] It has been suggested [2] that there was a special reference here to Cornelius Gallus, who in the year 26 B.C. fell into disgrace with Augustus ; but the crime of Gallus was not specially the betrayal of secrets. There is no need to drag in Augustus at every point in the poem. Fides and Virtus, it is as well to remember, were always closely connected in the Roman mind ; as in *Odes*, iv. 9. 40, where Horace seems to be recalling to his memory the one we are discussing.

It seems hardly worth while to refute another fancy of Domaszewski, to which he was led by the *dira cupido* of discovering references to Augustus. ' Virtus repulsae nescia sordidae Intaminatis fulget honoribus ', &c., he says, contains an allusion to the successive consulships of Augustus from 27 to 23 B.C.! Can any one doubt, unless he be a German professor, that *virtus* is here used in its true sense of manly vigour and valour, and that the poet is contrasting it with the anxious meanness of the candidate for office ? There is no gap in sense between the fourth and fifth stanzas ; the one follows the other quite naturally. Horace might be thinking of the story of Coriolanus. There is the same thought in the ode quoted just now (iv. 9. 39), ' consul non unius anni '.

This true *virtus*, the poet goes on, secures a man immortality, ' recludens immeritis mori caelum '. It can have nothing to do with the rabble of the city and its chatter ; a thought quite in keeping with the introductory stanza of the first ode, which, as I said, gives the tone to the whole collection. Horace was at one time fond of strolling about the Forum, and knew well what its vulgarity and gossip were. Now he preferred his Sabine farm, where he could indulge his genius for right and rational thinking, and meditate

---

[1] Cato's story is preserved by A. Gellius, i. 23. I have told it in a little book on Rome in the Home University Library, p. 63.

[2] Domaszewski, op. cit., p. 114, who with professorial assurance states his conjecture as if it were a fact. The late Dr. Verrall thought of the conspiracy of Murena, which was detected in 22 B.C., too late a date for any of these six odes (*Studies in Horace*, p. 69).

on the poet's power to teach, and to immortalize his pupils.
Loose thinking and loose talking make the god of good faith
angry. Is not this the sense of the last three stanzas ? and if
so, does not the whole ode make a beautiful and wholesome
appeal to the Roman people ?

There is however a difficult question to answer here. When
Horace sings of ' Virtus recludens immeritis mori caelum ',
what kind of an immortality is he really thinking of ? Is it
only a literary immortality, as Wickham tells us in his note ?
There is much to be said for this view ; and especially his
language in iv. 9, which seems to have a close connexion with
these odes.

> Vixere fortes ante Agamemnona
> multi : sed omnes illacrimabiles
>   urgentur ignotique longa
>   nocte, carent quia vate sacro.

To be forgotten, if you have done well in this life, was at all
times for the Roman a horrible thought, as we know from the
ius imaginum and the *monumenta*, such as those of the Scipios.
The same feeling was extremely strong under the Empire
among the middle classes ; hence the innumerable burial
gilds. That a man should be utterly neglected and forgotten
after death, seems to have been the shadow ever hanging over
his life. We may doubt whether the hope of spiritual immortality had, as a rule, anything to do with this anxiety. It
was rather an inherited instinct than a faith or creed that
moved these poor people. So with the soldier of whom
Horace is here thinking. But here, as in *Aen.* xii. 234 and
ix. 641, there may also be an allusion to the widely-spread
belief that a life of good deeds secured the rise of the
soul to some vaguely conceived heaven after death, of which
the earliest indication is in Cicero's *Somnium Scipionis*.[1]
There is an interesting chapter on this subject in Cumont's
Astrology and Religion, pp. 167 ff.

Saepe Diespiter neglectus incesto addidit integrum. In

---

[1] *de Rep.* vi. 15, *ad fin.* ' iustitiam cole et pietatem ; quae cum sit magna
in parentibus et propinquis, tum in patria maxima est : ea vita via est in
caelum '.

Roman Ideas of Deity, p. 152, I observed that in spite of their appeal to righteousness, there is little in these six earnest odes of an appeal to religion in its support. We find it in the sixth ode, but elsewhere only in the passage just quoted, where *neglectus* must mean that the worship of the great god was little heeded. But what does Horace mean by worship ? This is always a difficulty when we think of the relation of an individual Roman to his gods. I will say something more of it when I come to the sixth ode. Here we can only compare the thirty-fourth ode of bk. i ('Parcus deorum cultor et infrequens '), in which there is some community of thought with this one, as is shown by the use of the old name-form Diespiter in both of them.[1] Is he thinking of the neglect of attendance at temples ? There were of course no regular services which a man could attend, and we may suppose that in Horace's younger days all interest in such things was vanishing. But some feeling there must have been, in the years when these odes were written, when temples were being rebuilt and old religious ceremonies revived, that a man should throw in his lot with the new public spirit of prayer and thanksgiving ; how exactly this was to be done it is not easy to conjecture.

ODE III

This is the least satisfactory of the six odes, in spite of its famous beginning. It does not make its object clear at once, or even when we have read it through. Are we to suppose with Domaszewski that its theme is Justitia, taking our cue from the inscription on the shield mentioned above ?[2] The answer is that there is little about Justitia in the ode ; and with such a truly Roman subject before him, Horace would hardly have let himself be run away with, in Pindaric fashion,

---

[1] In both odes there is probably an allusion to the doctrines of Roman Stoicism about Jupiter. Almost from the very beginning of Stoicism the school had seized on Zeus to convey, under the guise of a personality and a name, some idea of the Reason in the universe. When Horace was abandoning Epicureanism, its place was taken in harmony with the tendency of the time, by that form of Stoicism which could include the gods. See the last chapter of my *Social Life at Rome*.   [2] p. 210.

by mythology, only to scramble back from it for a moment at line 49. The only subject that seems to bind the whole ode together is *constancy of purpose* ; [1] the emphasis given to this in the second stanza seems to show that the words *tenax propositi* are really the text of the discourse, and that the point is not the righteousness of the righteous man (*iustus*), but his constancy in right doing in spite of all opposition and all calamities. We may take the speech of Juno as a lesson in this virtue, with special application to a question deeply interesting at that time to the Roman world.

This is the question of transferring the capital from Italy to the eastern Mediterranean, whether to Byzantium as Mommsen suggested,[2] or to Alexandria, or to the plains of Troy. Owing to the want of contemporary history and correspondence, we are almost entirely in the dark about popular feeling in Rome when these odes were written ; we have to guess it mainly from the poetry of the day, which may be a pretty sure guide, but one certainly difficult of interpretation. We must date this ode in the year 27 or somewhat later, since the name Augustus is found in it, which was assumed in January of that year. There must just at this time have been a feeling, as we know there was at the end of the life of Julius,[3] that a change of capital was possible or even imminent ; once again attention had been specially directed to the East for two or more years, and for long past it had been felt that the eastern half of the Empire was now of much greater moment in many ways than the western. The ' Pan-Romans ' of that day would like to be rid of the old republican associations of the city, and at the same time to be nearer the centre of the Empire. Pompey's conquests, as well as his great imperial powers, had wrought a great change, both

---

[1] The effect is spoilt if we try to make Augustus the *iustus et propositi tenax*, words which, as the whole poem shows, are not to be attached to any particular individual, though they have a particular application of another kind.

[2] op. cit., p. 175. In Suet. *Iul.* 79 Alexandria may mean either Troas or the Egyptian city ; more likely, I think, the latter. For Alexandria Troas see Dr. Leaf's *Troy*, pp. 47 and 118 ff.

[3] Suet. *Iul.* 79.

political and geographical, and it was now realized more forcibly than ever before that for intellect, philosophy, even religion, Rome would have to draw upon the East, not as yet from the comparatively uncivilized West, nor even from Africa.[1] The bilingual educated class was at this time showing a distinct tendency to drift from Rome towards the pleasant cities of the Asiatic coast, as the reader of Horace's odes will have noticed in the seventh ode of the first book.[2]

It does not, of course, follow that Augustus had any such plan in his mind ; but there are strong indications that the Romans suspected it. Apart from this ode, of which the evidence seems to me very strong, we have lately been shown by Dr. Walter Leaf that the fourteenth ode of bk. i may best be interpreted in this way ;[3] and at the end of the twelfth book of the *Aeneid*,[4] which must have been written later on, the insistence on the final abandonment of things Trojan is too marked to be missed :

> sit Latium, sint Albani per saecula reges,
> sit Romana potens Itala virtute propago :
> *occidit, occideritque sinas cum nomine Troia.*

It is quite possible that the beauty and fervour of the eighth book of the *Aeneid*, of which the theme is ' Aeneas at the site of Rome ', may have been inspired by the fear of losing the capital ; and I seem to see the same feeling in the third stanza of the fifth ode of this third book.[5] The grand speech which Livy put into the mouth of Camillus at the end of his

---

[1] In Strabo's survey of the Empire, the eastern half, including Greece, occupies some two-thirds of the whole work.

[2] ' Laudabunt alii claram Rhodon aut Mytilenen, Aut Epheson ', &c. Cf. *Epist.* i. 11. 1 ff. It was Mommsen, I think, who first drew attention to this feature of the age.

[3] In *Journal of Philology*, 1918, xxxiv. 283 ff., Dr. Leaf gives this ode a double meaning ; but both meanings are revealed only by recognizing the popular feeling alluded to above.

[4] *Aen.* xii. 826 ff.

[5] See below, p. 224. Professor Conway was the first to notice this allusion in *Aen.* xii, in National Home Reading Union (*Special Courses Magazine*, p. 194).

fifth book, also probably written in these years, urging the
people not to move from their own glorious site to that of
the captured Veii, was surely inspired by the same motive.
I have a strong feeling, of which I have more to say directly,
that there is more than an accidental analogy between these
chapters of Livy and the Odes I am discussing. I think
that Horace and Livy must have known each other and compared ideas. There is no doubt that Livy was writing his first
decade while the first three books of the Odes were being
put together ; and two literary Italians must have known
something of each other at Rome.

Horace puts his opposition to the dreaded plan into the
mouth of Juno, and connects it with the constancy of purpose
shown by the heroes of old, and now (as he cleverly assumes)
to be shown by Augustus. ' Hold fast ', he says, ' to the
immortal seven hills ', as Aeneas held fast to the pursuit of
Italy, and having found Rome, was to leave it for ever to
the care of his descendants. When we see clearly that this
is the real subject of the poem, we can understand why the
poet suddenly turned his ode on to a new system of rails at
the fifteenth line : ' Hold fast to Rome, for it was on that
condition that Romulus was immortalized.' The shift is
rather a violent one ; more so than in the Regulus ode,
line 15—there is no jar there. In Pindar's odes there are
transitions equally abrupt, but in the supple Greek language
we feel the abruptness far less.[1]

In lines 11–12 of this ode (' quos inter Augustus recumbens
Purpureo bibet ore nectar ') I am disposed to see, with
Nettleship, an allusion to the Pantheon of Agrippa which was
built or building this same year. Dio tells us[2] that it was
intended for the glory of the Julian family, and that among
the statues of gods in the *cella* were those of Mars and Venus,
the reputed founders of the family ; and that there were
statues of Augustus and Agrippa in the *pronaus*. I prefer in
any case the better attested *bibet*, and think it may be a

---

[1] A good specimen of Pindar's skill in transition is *Olymp*. iii. 9–16.
[2] Dio, liii. 27. Nettleship, *Essays in Latin Literature*, p. 162.

forecast, before the completion of the building, of the position Augustus was to have there. At the same time it is quite possible that Horace, like Virgil in the introduction to the first *Georgic*, was here influenced by the doctrine of ' Catasterism ',[1] then beginning to be prevalent in Rome—the belief that men for their great services to mankind are transferred at death to the heaven as constellations. It was no doubt believed that Hercules and other demi-gods reached immortality in that way, as Horace says ; and when Tacitus sneered at Tiberius for insisting that he was *mortalis*, he upbraided him for failing to follow in the footsteps of these great ones of old.[2] How far either Horace, Virgil, or Tacitus, really held this view it is impossible to say ; but they certainly reflected a widely held belief.

Purpureo ore no doubt means that the face was bright, shining, as that of a god ; the colour appropriate to the ever young immortals. Cf. *Aen.* xi. 818, where it represents the colour of a living man as opposed to the pallor of death : ' Labitur exsanguis, labuntur frigida leto Lumina, purpureus quondam color ora reliquit.' So too in *Ecl.* ix. 40, Virgil calls the spring *purpureum*—full of glowing life.

> 49 ff.   Aurum irrepertum et sic melius situm,
>   cum terra celat, spernere fortior
>   quam cogere humanos in usus
>   omne sacrum rapiente dextra.

No doubt there is an allusion here to the Stoic paradox that riches are not a good, and that the precious metals had better have been left untouched. But the word *sacrum*, indirectly applied to the gold, has suggested to me that Horace may also have had in his mind the story of the gold in the Capitoline temple of Jupiter. Livy tells us that Camillus had the gold of the Gauls and the temple treasures buried under the *sella Iovis*, and thus made *sacrum*—made over to the god as his property.[3]

---

[1] See Cumont, *Astrology and Religion*, p. 176. Dr. D'Alton, in his useful book *Horace and his Age*, p. 230, has an adequate account of Catasterism.

[2] Tac. *Ann.* iv. 38.

[3] Liv. v. 50. 6 ' Aurum quod Gallis ereptum erat quodque ex aliis templis inter trepidationem in Iovis cellam conlatum cum in quae referri

Now this hoard of gold was robbed by some one, formerly
supposed to be Crassus, in the year 55 B.C., just before the
departure of Crassus for Syria, where he perished.　I am
strongly inclined to think that there is more than an accidental
resemblance between this ode (and also the fifth) and the
concluding chapters of Livy's fifth book, and it may be that
the poet had this story in his mind.

As regards the last stanza of the poem, my own feeling is
that Horace made a mistake in adding it to the speech of Juno.
He seems never to have quite shaken off the feeling that even
the Alcaic metre was not necessarily suggestive of serious
thoughts ; cf. the end of *Odes*, ii. 1.　But the superb ending
of Ode v of this book shows that he knew how the metre
could assume a severe beauty both of thought and expression.
Possibly this last stanza was put in as an afterthought, to
connect this ode with the next, which is of a lighter tone.

ODE IV

If in reading this ode, which is much more charming and
skilful than the last, we keep out of view, so far as is possible,
the obsession of Augustus of which I have spoken above,
I think we shall find without difficulty the real subject of
the poem.　This is not Augustus, but Horace himself and his
art.　The best commentary on it is the passage which I have
quoted above from the first Epistle of the second book, in
which he expresses his conviction of the good work that can
be done by poetry in the civilized world, and especially (as
he insists in this ode) in the new era now beginning.　' I,
Horace, have been destined for this work from my infancy,
preserved by divine influence in all personal perils.　I can
cheer and refresh the mind of Augustus when he returns from
war ; for the kind of brute force that he has had to overcome

oporteret confusa memoria esset, sacrum omne iudicatum et sub Iovis
sella poni iussum.'　Plin. *N. H.* xxxiii. 14 mentions the robbery in the
third consulship of Pompeius (this should be the second consulship if
Crassus was concerned in it), but the name of Crassus is not mentioned in
the Teubner text of Pliny, nor in Nonius (Lindsay, p. 338, quoting Varro).
Augustus deposited a large sum in the same place ; Suet. *Aug.* 30.

has been at all times paralysed by the civilizing power of poetry.' This surely is the drift of the ode ; the reference to Augustus is not the essential object of it, but a happy illustration suitable to the times (cf. Tibullus, ii. 5. 9).

Domaszewski's treatment of this ode [1] is a good illustration of a German professor's method—the same method that has been so diligently applied of late to German propaganda. Assuming that Augustus is the central figure of these odes, and that the inscription on the shield is the clue to interpret them, he has to find one that can be said to embody the *clementia* of Augustus. This is the only one that will in the least answer his purpose, and in Teutonic forceful manner it is made to do so. The *lene consilium* of line 41 is all that he can find ; and that expression, taken in connexion with the *recreatis* of the line before it, seems to me to be exactly suited to the new phase of Augustus's policy, without any special reference to the sparing of his enemies. ' The power of poesy is wholesome, gentle, hallowed, gracious, and Augustus and his armies, reposing in comfort after their many trials, shall feel this power if I have any skill to use it.' Did the professor ever try to put himself in the position of Horace when writing an ode on the *clementia* of Augustus ? Did it never occur to him that for Horace to claim for his poetry the credit of such *clementia* might be looked upon as an impertinence ?

In the first stanza, whatever may be the meaning of lines 3 and 4, it is worth while to remember that the tibia was the peculiarly Roman instrument ; and Horace may use it here for that reason, to express the Roman character of his singing, while alluding in the words that follow to the Greek additions in musical accompaniment which had been introduced in plays and dances.[2]

---

[1] *Abhandlungen*, p. 116. He quotes Augustus's own words in the *Mon. Ancyr.* (iii. 22 and i. 13–15), remarking on the ' Anklang '. The latter of these passages, which emphasizes the policy of *clementia*, is certainly worth quoting here, but it was of course written long after the ode, and must not be allowed to warp our idea of the poem as a whole.

[2] See Friedländer in Marquardt (*Staatsv.* iii. 545), and Cic. *Legg.* ii. 13. 39 ; *Ars Poet.* 202 ff.

In line 6, for *pius* unusually applied to a place, cf. *Culex* 39 ' et tibi sede pia maneat locus '. It is hard to translate, for ' holy ' (Mr. Page's word) does not exactly hit it ; it has, I think, a suggestion of kindliness, as so often in the *Aeneid*. We may think of Milton's lines in *Lycidas* :

> Where other groves and other streams along
> With nectar pure his oozy locks he laves,
> And hears the unexpressive nuptial song
> In *the blest kingdoms meek of joy and love*.

Line 10. Why should we reject ' limina Pulliae ', which, though not recognized by Acron and Porphyrion, is the reading of two of the best extant manuscripts ? The name Pullius is not uncommon in inscriptions : see Dessau, index to *Inscrr. Lat. Selectae*. Mommsen accepted Pulliae : op. cit., p. 177, note.

Line 20. I agree with Mr. Page that *animosus* may here very well mean ' inspired ', i. e. with poetic feeling, a child of the Muses.

ODE V

There is no doubt about the strength of the feeling at Rome that the disgrace of Carrhae should be wiped out and Roman credit in the East restored. It was in itself a terrible disaster, and its effects were far-reaching both for the Roman government and the men of business. Julius had intended to conquer Parthia, Antony had tried and failed ; the duty now passed to Augustus, and that this was keenly felt is shown by many allusions in these three books of the odes.[1] It seems, however, that it was now beginning to be known that Augustus would proceed not by invasion and conquest, but by diplomacy ; and this ode is good evidence that it was thought that he would ransom the 20,000 Romans who were held captive in Parthia. It was indeed true that he realized the danger of attempting too much in the East, and preferred a policy of negotiation, which suited him best, and eventually met with complete success. Horace seems to have known of this policy, and whether or no he approved it, he made protest against any

e. g. i. 2. 22 and 49.

ransoming of prisoners. In this he seems to have been successful ; when the captured *signa* were restored by the Parthians
in the year 23,[1] we hear nothing of such ransom.

Such a magnificent protest as this ode must have been
inspired by some real or supposed danger of dishonour, and
the poem stands by itself among the six as voicing a general
feeling which Augustus found himself unable to resist. It is
by no means, as Domaszewski thought, a hymn in honour
of Virtus or Honos or both.

The latter part of this grand ode calls for no comment from
me, but I find difficulties at the beginning. The connexion
of the first stanza with the rest of the poem is sufficiently
explained by the commentators, but they do not seem to me
to have given quite its full meaning to the expression *praesens
deus* considered in relation to the religious thought of the
age. Augustus as *praesens deus* is contrasted with Jupiter
in the sky, and the contrast curiously illustrates the need of
a more intimate and helpful spiritual power than the old
polytheism could supply even in its finest form. The Man-god
is in evidence all through this period of history, and the desire
to believe in him was genuine. Jupiter of the Capitol had not
been able or willing to defend Rome in the East, and the
past tense *credidimus* seems almost to suggest that the people
were losing faith in him, or could not think of him as *praesens*.
But here was a real *praesens deus*, a deity known to all,
mighty to save. *Praesens* used of a deity seems to express
one's sense of his power and willingness to help ; as in *Ode*,
i. 35. 2 (of Fortuna) ' praesens vel imo tollere de gradu ', &c. ;
and *Epist.* ii. 1. 134 ' praesentia numina sentit '—a very
Roman passage.[2] Thus the contrast between Jupiter and

[1] *Mon. Anc.* c. 29 ; Velleius, ii. 91 ; Suet. *Aug.* 21. Propertius, iv. 6.
79 ff. refers to a *foedus* made with the Parthian : ' hic referat sero confessum
foedere Parthum : " Reddat signa Remi, mox dabit ipse sua." ' Dio alone
mentions prisoners (liv. 8), but as restored without ransom.

[2] Cf. Virg. *Ecl.* i. 41 ; *Aen.* ix. 404 ; xii. 245 (this last is peculiar as meaning
powerful for *harm*) ; Cic. *Cat.* ii. 9. 19. There is a curious passage in Vegetius
about the *nomen Augusti* : ' imperator cum Augusti nomen accepit, *tanquam
praesenti et corporali deo* fidelis est praestanda devotio ' (Veg. ii. 5, quoted
by Pelham, *Essays*, p. 110)

Augustus is one between the distant and often dangerous Heaven-deity, and the hallowed and gracious presence of a human being endowed with grace divine.

In lines 8–12 the traditional reading *armis* is made certain by the *anciliorum* in line 10—a fact which Bentley did not notice when he supported the conjecture *arvis*. The captive Roman carries the arms of his master, forgetting the arms of Mars, the emblems of Roman warlike *virtus*; *anciliorum* thus gains in meaning, and should certainly be followed by *et*. *Nominis* is usually explained as the name of Rome; surely it is the prisoner's own name, the bestowal and the form of which made him a free Roman, member of a family and *gens*.[1] In Parthia he would be given a new name, just as slaves at Rome lost their original names. *Ancilia, nomen, toga*, are all three chosen with skill and point.

I have already suggested that in lines 11 and 12 there may be an allusion to the necessity of keeping Rome as the centre of the Empire; I may now add that the words *urbe Roma* following immediately on *incolumi Iove*[2] seem to reflect the *dea Roma* of provincial worship. Lastly, we may note with Professor Pelham (*Essays*, p. 97, note) that the Italians, Marsus et Apulus, are here spoken of as being bound to feel the inspiration of Roman cults and customs, in full accordance with the policy of Augustus.

The story of Regulus is embalmed for ever in this beautiful ode, and no one who reads it here need trouble himself about the truth or falsity of it. If, as the historians one after another maintain, it is an invention, of which the object was to cover

[1] See Marquardt, *Privatleben der Römer*, p. 8.
[2] There are allusions in the speech of Camillus quoted above to the cult of Jupiter on the Capitol, in language that might almost suggest that Livy had read this ode or that Horace had read Livy's manuscript (liii. *ad fin.*, ' nos Capitolio, *arce incolumi*, stantibus templis deorum, aedificare incensa piget ? ') The *ancilia* are twice mentioned; liv. *ad fin.*, lii. 7, where also the *aeternae Vestae ignes* will be found. Add the rebuilding of temples, l. 2, and the strong appeal to the religious sense all through the speech, and as in the *praefatio* of Livy, some consciousness of sin (lii. 7 ff.), violation of *ius gentium*, and *negligentia deorum*; and it becomes tempting to believe that Livy and Horace had in some way or other compared notes.

some piece of Roman treachery and cruelty, I can only say
in astonishment, What a marvellous effort of the imagination !
Who invented all these wonderful stories that took possession
of the Roman mind ?   Assuredly not Greeks ; they are genuine
fruits of a Roman imagination of which the critics have little
to say.

But I am by no means certain that in this instance the critics
are wholly right.   True, Polybius says nothing of the story ;
and Diodorus tells in its place another story of the savage
cruelty of Roman women to Carthaginian captives, which
to me seems absolutely incredible.   On the other hand,
Cicero speaks of it as ascertained fact, compared with Greek
legends : ' omittamus et fabulas et externa : ad rem factam
nostraque veniamus ' (*de Off.* iii. 99), and tells the story with
such explicitness that he makes Regulus refuse ' sententiam
dicere ' in the senate on the ground that he was not a senator,
being bound *iureiurando hostium*, i. e. by the oath imposed
on him at Carthage—a characteristic Roman touch.   The
sacredness of the oath is a topic that runs all through
Roman history, and Cicero pursues it here with curious
insistence.   If the story was an invention, it is more likely
that its object was to illustrate this conviction of the Roman
mind, than to cover an abominable and most un-Roman
crime.[1]

Doubtless Horace knew Cicero's account ; indeed it is
possible that he remembered it when he wrote this ode.
' Cuius cum valuisset auctoritas, captivi retenti sunt ; ipse
Carthaginem rediit, neque eum caritas patriae retinuit, nec
suorum. Neque vero ignorabat se ad crudelissimum hostem
et ad exquisita supplicia proficisci : sed iusiurandum con-
servandum putabat ' (sec. 100).

ODE VI

If the fifth is the most beautiful and touching of these odes,
this one is the most truly in earnest. Horace was a man of
changing moods, and here he writes in the same mood of serious

---

[1] *Roman Ideas of Deity*, p. 41.

depression as in the sixteenth epode, and in Ode 24 of this
book. The depression is not of a hopeless kind, but it is worth
noticing that there is no mention in any of the three poems
of an individual ' saviour ' ; Augustus does not appear in
them. This one seems to be more directly addressed to the
rising and hopeful generation ; at least, I infer this from the
word *immeritus* in the first line, which is in strange contrast
with the last line of the poem, but yet seems to suggest that
when he began the ode Horace was thinking of the young
and innocent, the *virgines puerique*, who had the duty set them
of doing justice to the worship of the gods.

Yet the exposition of weakness in the State, and the remedy
suggested, are those of Augustus as we know him. In his
hands the remedial policy was begun on his return from the
East, the policy, that is, of restoring the ancient religion and
morals of the State ; and Mommsen, followed by Nettleship,[1]
ascribes this ode and the twenty-fourth to that year 28.
I rather prefer to think that both these odes were written
before the return of Augustus,[2] and were suggested not by
any declared policy, but by facts which were obvious to every
observing mind. In the 24th ode this seems to be indicated
by the twenty-fifth and following lines, which are obviously
an appeal to Caesar, though stated in general terms.[3] It is
not impossible that Ode 24 may have been written before
Actium ; the similarity of its language to that of Epode 16
has been noticed, and as that epode is almost certainly one
of Horace's earliest poems, the inference seems to be that
Ode 24 was not very far removed from it. If that were so,
there may be something in Wickham's suggestion that Ode 24
supplied some at least of the subjects of these first six odes.

This ode, and especially its last lines, breathe exactly the
spirit of Livy's Preface to his History, as has often been
noticed. We have no certain ground for fixing the date of
that Preface, but if he wrote it when starting on his great

[1] Mommsen, op. cit., p. 181 ; Nettleship, *Essays*, p. 160.
[2] But this one, if *Aethiops* in line 14 is rightly explained of Egypt, cannot
be earlier than Actium.
[3] ' O quisquis volet impias Caedes et rabiem tollere civicam ', ff.

work, of which there can be little doubt, it can hardly be much later than 28 B. C.[1] It is undoubtedly a pessimistic utterance, and the extreme beauty of its language seems to show that the writer was deeply in earnest. I would say the same of the three poems of Horace, the 16th epode and the 6th and 24th odes of this book ; for a poet, and especially a Latin poet, is at his best, as Cicero was in prose, when writing from his heart. I should say indeed that all the six with which I have been dealing, are genuine inspirations not directly prompted by any great personage or published policy.

Lastly, a word as to the restoration of temples and the neglect of the cult of the gods. Here again we have a return of the old feeling, never entirely worn out, that the gods who had once taken up their abode in the city as divine inhabitants of it, could only be retained there by sacrifice and prayer. If that is denied them, they cease to care for the community that so neglects them. This is not the Stoic feeling of 2. 29, where Jupiter is the great deity of good faith and righteousness, but the genuine old conviction that the protecting deities of Rome are linked to the eternal site of Rome by the homes which Rome has built for them, and that nowhere else would they be of any use to the Roman world. This is the feeling that Livy so admirably puts into the mouth of Camillus at the end of his fifth book ; and that expressed by Varro too, when he says that he feared the gods would simply perish by *negligentia* (Aug. *Civ. Dei*, vi. 2).

Thus Horace naturally puts the necessity of restoring temples and cults in the forefront of this great ode, before he goes on to the moral evils of the day. So does Livy in his account of Camillus's doings after the departure of the Gauls.[2] ' Omnium primum, ut erat diligentissimus religionum cultor, quae ad deos immortales pertinebant rettulit et senatus-consultum facit ; fana omnia, quoad ea hostis possedisset, restituerentur terminarentur expiarenturque, expiatioque eorum in libris per duumviros quaereretur.' The position of Camillus at the moment, let us note, was almost exactly

[1] See Schanz, *Gesch. der röm. Litt.* iii. 421. [2] v. 50. 1.

that of Augustus ; he had saved the city, and had been hailed
by the soldiers as ' Romulus, parens patriae, conditorque
alter urbis '. But Camillus himself attributes his success to
the gods ; ' tam evidens numen hac tempestate rebus adfuit
Romanis ut omnem negligentiam divini cultus exemptam
hominibus putem '.   That is, in Horace's words, ' dis te
minorem quod geris imperas '. ' Look ', says Camillus, ' at
the good and bad fortune of these recent years, and you will
find that when you obeyed the gods all went well with you,
and all went ill when you neglected them '. This is precisely
the feeling of the first four stanzas of the ode.   Then the poet
turns to moral evils, leaving it uncertain whether he means
us to infer that they too are the result of neglect of the gods ;
in this he is perfectly consistent with himself, with Livy, and
with Roman authors generally. The Roman did not understand that his gods could make him morally good, nor did he
pray to them with that object ; but he fully understood that
by neglecting the gods he brought calamity on himself, and
that to do so was therefore sin. The sense of sin apparent
in this ode must therefore be taken in both a religious
and a moral sense.

B. G. NIEBUHR, 1776–1830 : A SKETCH

It is remarkable that both Niebuhr and Mommsen, the
two great chieftains of Roman historiography in the last
century, were natives of what Germans call the Duchies,
the much disputed territory of Schleswig-Holstein.   They
were not typical Germans ; they were quick and sensitive,
and had a peculiar strain of romance in them, quite different
from the sentimentalism of the Teuton of the interior.   They
belonged to the same stock as our Nelson, who, though
coming from our east country, was both in genius and
temperament the very opposite of the typical Englishman.
But though born in what was then Denmark, both Niebuhr

and Mommsen emphatically called themselves Germans. The Mommsen brothers fought on the German side against Denmark in 1848. When in 1806 Niebuhr was offered a post in the Prussian Government, after having spent all his previous life in what was then Denmark, he did not feel that he was exchanging his Fatherland for a foreign State, in the usual sense of the term. 'He was wholly German in his nationality—of German descent, and brought up in a German province ; all the ties of race bound him to Germany and not to Denmark. And among the German states, Prussia was the one which most engaged his sympathies and hopes. He looked to her as the head of Protestant Germany—the nation which was the most thoroughly German in spirit, and offered the brightest prospects to the future political and intellectual development of the German People.'[1]

Let us note at once that Niebuhr knew Prussia in her saddest time, the time of her downfall and despair, which brought out all the finest qualities of her race. She had not yet learnt, in spite of the great Frederic's teaching, to look upon herself as dominating the rest of Germany, and in the years in which Niebuhr served her faithfully she had a hard struggle for existence as a State. Thus it was that Niebuhr, though he admired Prussia and even loved her, thought of himself as a German rather than a Prussian. We constantly find him using the phrase ' we Germans ', which has become so intolerably familiar to us in recent years. He did not, however, use it to show the world that a German was made of finer clay than any one else, though as we may see later, he had a dim consciousness of the assumption, especially when living in Italy.

It is also remarkable that neither Niebuhr nor Mommsen went through the mill of German education as we know it now ; they were home-bred until almost of age for the University. But here the likeness ends. The Mommsens were sons of a country parson ; Niebuhr's father was a man of European fame, the Arabian traveller Carsten Niebuhr,

---

[1] *Life and Letters of Niebuhr*, i. 165.

and he was an only son. Mommsen had an iron constitution ;
Niebuhr was weakly, nervous, excitable, and apt to overwork
himself. When he left his home for the University of Kiel
his mental exertions seem to us appalling. The desire to
know all that could then be known was strong in him. To
specialize on any subject was utterly foreign to his nature ;
he did indeed prefer history to any other study, but it was
history in the widest and most practical sense, and it was
only by degrees that Roman history came to claim his best
powers. 'My head swims when I survey what I have yet to
learn—philosophy, mathematics, physics, chemistry, natural
history. Then, too, I must perfect myself in history, German,
and French, and study Roman law, and the political constitutions of Europe as far as I can, and increase my knowledge
of antiquities ; and all this must be done within five years
at most—so far as a foundation can be laid in that time ;
for truly it will not allow me to accomplish more than that
with regard to most of these things, and it would be hard
indeed if I could not find time and opportunity afterwards
to complete the superstructure. *I must* know all these
things, but how I shall learn them, Heaven knows ! That
I shall require them, as a learned man, or in any position
I may occupy, I am fully convinced.' So he wrote to his
father soon after arriving at Kiel.

Fortunately this thirst for universal knowledge was tempered
in Niebuhr by a turn of mind far more practical than theo-
retical ; this it was that kept him from becoming a typically
dryasdust German professor.[1] His father's influence backed
up this natural propensity ; he did not wish his son to be
a professor but a man of affairs. Quite early in life Niebuhr
began to interest himself in finance, and also in land tenures,
which he had good opportunity of studying in his native

---

[1] Of the professor of classics in general he writes (i. 83) : 'The lot of the
philologist working among his books is wearisome indeed. He is ever
treading on the brink of pedantry, a yawning chasm, in which, if we were
laughing on the subject, we might say he would be buried in dust and dead
leaves if he made a false step.' There is much more to the same effect in
this very interesting letter of September 6, 1797.

province of Ditmarsh,[1] and such subjects continued to occupy his mind to the end of his life, and were turned to good account in his dealings with Roman history. Before he came to that subject there had been much learning devoted to it, much investigation of texts, and some little criticism ; [2] but no one had brought a knowledge of modern usage to bear on ancient problems, or found his field of research suddenly illuminated by a recognition that human nature is essentially the same at all times and places, and that much may be learnt about Greece and Rome from one who understands the social life and economy of the modern State. We may compare him with a German of a later day, who like himself was not bred a professor, Wilhelm Mannhardt. Mannhardt was the first to discover that light may be thrown on problems of ancient belief and practice by investigating the folk-lore of our common people, and the impetus at once given by the discovery to the whole study of religious origins was truly astonishing. True, both Niebuhr and Mannhardt sometimes overshot their mark, and arrived at doubtful conclusions with undue confidence ; but they were both pioneers, making roads in a difficult country, and their names are never likely to be utterly forgotten.

Niebuhr broke off his University career to become private secretary to the Danish Minister of Finance. This was in January 1796 ; in June 1798, at the age of 22, he travelled to England, and spent more than a year in London and Edinburgh. He was all his life an indefatigable letter-writer, and his letters from our shores to his father and his friend Moltke throw much light on his character and disposition. We see him in these letters an excellent and devoted son and friend, honest, eager, affectionate, pure in life and thought. But

[1] There are frequent allusions to Ditmarsh in vol. i of the *History*; e. g. pp. 305, 307 ; ii. 31.

[2] The beginnings of criticism are mentioned in the preface to the first volume of the *History* (ed. 1826). The Frenchman Beaufort was the most important of the critics (see e. g. i. 548 ; ii. 551). But the *spirit* of criticism in Niebuhr's early life is best seen in the work of F. A. Wolf on Homer; and to some extent also in Heyne. See Pattison's essay on Wolf, in his *Essays*, i. 390.

they also show his faults and limitations ; he was too sensitive, too self-conscious, too critical, to enjoy himself thoroughly amongst strangers. He expected much, and criticized severely, without sufficient knowledge or experience of life. He was ready, within a day or two of his arrival in London, to generalize about the English character, which in some important points he never really learnt to understand. One whose thoughts were so constantly turned on himself could not but be conscious of these defects, and he was perhaps his own sharpest critic. But in England he was too much disappointed to see that the disappointment was largely his own fault. He had excellent introductions, and all noted travellers were glad to see him for his father's sake ; Sir Joseph Banks, who had been round the world with Captain Cook, took him to a Royal Society dinner, and apparently he could talk English and understand it well enough to be at his ease on such an occasion. This was surely rather a remarkable honour for a youth of his age ; but he expected philosophy and science, and did not find them there. The conversation, he writes, was below the every-day conversation of learned men in Germany. He could not understand that men of science might avoid talking ' shop ' at such gatherings and prefer to enjoy themselves like ordinary human beings.

In Scotland, as one might expect, he fared somewhat better. He attended lectures at Edinburgh on philosophy and science, and was fairly satisfied with them. He had a geological walk to Salisbury Crags with Professor Playfair.[1] But neither in London nor Edinburgh did he succeed in getting to know any man of letters of real note, and he seems to have thought that English poetry was then at a very low ebb. This perhaps was natural, for it was not likely that he should discover Wordsworth, Coleridge, and Southey, who were then but little known, and he was too early for the great poets that were to come. It is however singular that so far as I can

[1] He met Playfair again in Rome long afterwards, and speaks of him with affection.

discover he does not mention Burke, who had just died, and whose combination of statesmanship and literature should naturally have attracted him. It is a melancholy fact that nowhere in these letters does he express any genuine admiration either for man or book.

But it is probable that Niebuhr learnt more in this country than we might guess from his letters. He noticed the activity and industry of the people ; ' everybody here is in action ; idleness and half-done work are certainly less common than with us ; practical ability is more general, a false show of knowledge rarer ; the word of a man may be depended upon, and I believe the better sort trouble themselves little about the opinion of others '. It was indeed a strenuous time of war, when we were gradually becoming conscious of the military ambition and far-reaching schemes of Bonaparte. To the end of his life these practical qualities drew him to England, and he valued her more highly than any European country but his own. France he could not love, for the Revolution had filled him and his with horror, and the French people were in his eyes a permanent danger to Germany and Europe. The Italians he utterly despised, as we shall presently see. In England alone he found a practical genius and a love of truth which claimed his constant admiration, in spite of occasional moods of criticism. But of that vein of romanticism in the British character which was to come out so strongly before the end of his own life he knew nothing. He seems to have thought of Pope as our great poet of the eighteenth century, and, like so many foreigners, never penetrated beneath the rationally ordered surface of the English mind.

When Niebuhr returned to Denmark in 1801, he married a lady to whom he had long been engaged, and settled down in Copenhagen a happy man, with two posts in the Government, one of finance and one of trade, sufficient to keep him busy and affluent. For six years he continued to hold these posts, or others of the same financial nature, and his experience thus gained made him a recognized authority on the subject.

It is interesting to find him, more than twenty years later,
fully acquainted with the British budget of the day, and anti-
cipating in the strongest possible manner the necessity of
imposing a permanent income tax, or property tax as he calls
it, and thus reconstituting the whole method of our finance.
In 1801 Denmark and her fleet became a powerful menace to
British sea-power, and thus also to the liberties of Europe,
of which that sea-power was the most vital safeguard. Both
Denmark and Prussia were playing a very doubtful game
in these years, and (to use Nelson's language) it was necessary
to crush a most formidable and unprovoked coalition against
Great Britain—that is, the union of the fleets of Denmark
and Russia to put the Baltic and its trade into the hands
of Napoleon. The battle of Copenhagen, regrettable in every
way but equally unavoidable, took place while Niebuhr was
in the city, and his letters describing it have real historical
importance. The American Admiral Mahan, in his *Life of
Nelson*, fully justifies the conduct of Great Britain and her
hero in this emergency, and Niebuhr himself continued to
think of Nelson with admiration, and deplored his death at
Trafalgar. At the time the Danes were of course very sore; but
the danger to Europe from the north vanished with the
battle.

A new danger in the south made it clear to Niebuhr and the
Danes that Great Britain was right in this matter. After
the peace of Amiens in 1802 Napoleon was not long in forming
new schemes of conquest. The war began again ; Austria
was crushed quickly and decisively, Prussia was induced
to remain ignominiously neutral, and Napoleon became
practically dictator of the whole of Europe. Too late, and with
a thoroughly rotten military system, Prussia ventured herself
single-handed against the tyrant, and was utterly defeated
at the battles of Jena and Auerstädt in October 1806. Ten
days before the battles, Niebuhr had joined the Prussian
Government as Minister of Finance, in accordance with an
invitation which he had received some months before from
the great minister Stein. He therefore became instantly

involved in the general confusion and chaos which had over-taken Prussia at this darkest hour of her fortunes. I need not enter into the miseries of the time that followed. It is enough to say that all Niebuhr's studies were hopelessly interrupted, and the Roman history, which had been in his mind at odd times for the last six years, as one may see from his letters, was now of necessity abandoned.

But better times were coming. For two or three years he was employed by the Prussian Government, in conjunction with Stein, in the attempt to set Prussia on her feet again. It was at this time that the first great social reforms, such for instance as the emancipation of the serfs, were successfully carried out, and the financial part of these reforms was placed in Niebuhr's hands. But with this part of his work I am not concerned here. Suffice it to say that he helped to lay the foundation of that new Prussia which rose in 1813 against the despotism of Napoleon in Europe ; but that with the fall of Stein, who had to leave his post when Napoleon discovered what he was doing, Niebuhr also left the Government. There seems no doubt that as a colleague he was difficult to work with, owing to his passionate temper and other faults, which in private life may make a man all the more lovable to his friends, but in positions of responsibility unfit him for per-manent good work. In Niebuhr's case too there was always a hankering after those studies which were really the most congenial part of his work in life. Thus it was that in 1810, when the new university of Berlin was opened, and the best men in Germany were being sought for as professors, Niebuhr became one of these, and for another three years was able to utilize the material he had so long been collecting on the early Roman history to give two series of lectures, which eventually became the first two volumes of his famous *History*.

The reception of these lectures was all that he could wish. They were attended not only by students but by professors, and professors of the type of Savigny, whose name is even now a great one in the history of Roman legal studies. It

happens that Savigny has given some account of the success
of these lectures in an essay on Niebuhr contributed to the
German edition of the *Life*.[1] He tells us that Niebuhr, who in
spite of his experience of affairs was still a young man, had
as yet earned no fame as a writer, and thus his reputation
as a scholar was limited to his personal acquaintance. Niebuhr
told Savigny that he only expected to have a few students. But
besides a large audience of students, the lectures were attended
by members of the Academy, professors of the University,
public men and officers of all grades, who spread the fame of
the lectures, and thus continually attracted fresh hearers.
Savigny adds an interesting note about the mode of his
delivery. 'He had written down his lecture *verbatim*, and
read it off before his hearers. This proceeding, which usually
injures the liveliness of the impression, had in his case the
most animated and powerful effect. His hearers felt as if
transported into ancient times, when the public reading of
new works supplied the place of our printed books, and there
was a less extended circulation, but they made a warmer and
more personal impression.' The effect of this great success,
says the same writer, reacted on Niebuhr's susceptible nature,
and filled him with fresh inspiration, and the daily intercourse
with other men of learning made this time one of the happiest
in a chequered life. He now at once began to convert these
lectures into a book, and the first volume of his *Roman
History* was published at the end of 1811. A second series of
lectures immediately followed, and underwent the same process of conversion. The third volume was long delayed and
never actually finished ; of this volume I will say something
later on.

It is not easy, as one turns over the opening chapters of
that first volume, to imagine how enthusiasm can have been
roused by the ethnology of ancient Italy, a subject which
could not at that time be scientifically treated. But I know
from personal experience that if a lecturer is himself interested
in a subject, he cannot help passing on his interest to an

[1] vol. i of the English edition, p. 307.

intelligent audience.[1] I can well understand how Niebuhr
carried his audience with him, watching them as he went on,
determined that they should not go to sleep. His very
egoism had its value here. He did not trouble much about
what other scholars had written, but went straight to the heart
of the matter himself, forming his own views, nursing them
with a mother's affection, watching them grow, and at last
becoming so certain of their truth that he would claim an
almost divine inspiration for them. Let us take an example
of this in his memorable ballad theory, as it was called. This
was probably quite new to his audience, though it had to
some extent been anticipated, as he eventually found, by
Perizonius in the seventeenth century.

Niebuhr expressed it thus : ' It was the custom at banquets
for the praises of great men to be sung to the flute ; a fact
known to Cicero only through Cato, who seems to have spoken
of it as a usage no longer existing. The guests themselves
sang in turn ; so it was expected that the lays, being the
common property of the nation, should be known to every
free citizen. According to Varro, who calls them old, they
were sung by modest boys, sometimes to the flute, sometimes without music. The peculiar function of the Camenae
was to sing the praises of the ancients, and among
the rest those of the kings. For republican Rome never
stripped herself of the recollection of her kings ; in the
best times of her freedom their memory was revered and
celebrated.' [2]

Niebuhr here uses the comparative method, not without
justification. He refers to the similar lays of other semi-
cultured peoples, and even to the well-known essay of Addison

---

[1] At the end of a Gifford lecture at Edinburgh on what I thought must be
a most uninteresting subject, I promised them something better next time.
A gentleman, as he passed out, came to my desk and said, ' You need not
be afraid of being uninteresting, sir, as long as you are so much interested
yourself '.

[2] *Hist. of Rome*, i. 254. The passages which prove the existence of these
' lays ' are Cic. *Brutus*, 62 and 75 ; *Tusc.* 4. 3 ; *de Legibus*, ii. 62 ; Varro
ap. Nonium, p. 76 (p. 107, ed. Lindsay) ; Val. Max. ii. 1. 10. See above,
p. 171.

on the ballad of Chevy-chase.[1] Thus he gets a foundation
for the history of the kings, claiming that the legends as we
have them in Livy and other writers originally existed in
a poetical form, and though by no means to be accepted as
history, yet represented what the Romans of a later day, and,
according to Niebuhr, the plebeian or popular element,
believed to be a record of what actually happened. They
were meagre, he thought, until they reached the time of the
first Tarquin ; then, reading Livy's delightful narrative into
his theory, he found a great epic poem ' which in power
and brilliance of imagination leaves everything produced by
the Romans in later times far behind it '.[2]

There cannot be a doubt that he was here quite right as
to the facts of the ballad-singing. The often quoted passages
make it absolutely certain that these lays or *carmina* did exist,
nor is there any doubt that they were written in the Saturnian
metre, the native measure of Italy for song and dance. This
metre was used in the third century B. C. by Livius, Naevius,
and other poets, and as Nettleship has said,[3] it is impossible
that there should not have been an earlier literature as the
foundation of such considerable poems. Why that earlier
literature should have entirely disappeared has puzzled many
scholars, and made others doubtful as to its existence ; but
it is not more mysterious than the disappearance of our
older English music, as I have suggested in another paper,
under the influence of Handel and the German school.

But Niebuhr's enthusiasm carried him too far ; he came to
believe that he knew much more about these poems than was
possible to an ordinary mind ; he knew where one lay ended
and another began, and gradually allowed himself to think
of them almost as if he had read them himself.[4] No wonder

---

[1] A more complete list of such lays will be found in Pais, *Storia di Roma*,
i, p. 22, note 1.

[2] i. 259 ; cf. p. 495, note.   [3] *Essays in Latin Literature*, p. 57.

[4] See i. 510. The following passage is interesting (ii. 14) : ' When an
inquirer, after gazing for years with ever-renewed undeviating steadfastness,
sees the history of mistaken, misrepresented, and forgotten events, rise
out of mists and darkness, and assume substance and shape, as the scarcely
visible aerial form of the nymph in the Slavonic tale takes the body of an

that he was severely criticized both in his lifetime and after-wards ; and by degrees it came to be recognized that the problem of the kings of Rome must be attacked from other directions, from the side of religion, law, and archaeology. So the once famous theory soon sank into oblivion ; but the conviction that there really was some kind of a ballad history of the famous stories of the kings still holds good, and is still the starting-point for all investigations of Roman literature. It survives in this country in the preface to Macaulay's *Lays*, and in those delightful *Lays* themselves.

For Niebuhr's real historical value we must look in another direction, to the economical and political questions of early Roman history. These are matters into which I cannot enter here, but it may be as well to take as an example the agrarian problem, which lies at the root of the social life of Rome. It is hard for us to understand the full depth of darkness in which, before Niebuhr, the student moved and groped when trying to find his way among agrarian difficulties. When Niebuhr himself first touches the question, he too seems to be still groping ; but as we read on we find that he has formed a perfectly right conception of the essential facts. He looked at them not merely from the point of view of Sigonius and the older Latin scholars, but as one experienced in the land tenures of Denmark and Prussia, and in the problems which in his own lifetime they suggested to the statesman.[1] He fully recognized the distinction between garden ground or allot-ments as private property held in absolute ownership (*here-dium*), and pasture land for cattle and sheep held in common by the cultivating community. In other words he was the

earthly maiden beneath the yearning gaze of love—when by unwearied and conscientious examination he is continually gaining a clearer insight into the connexion of all its parts, and discerns that immediate expression of reality which emanates from life—he has a right to demand from others, who merely throw their looks by the way on the region where he lives and has taken up his home, that they should not deny the correctness of his views, because they discern nothing of the kind.' That the historical eye can discern shapes in the darkness I know well ; but how far they answer to the reality is another matter—and the vital one.

[1] For some idea of these in Prussia see Seeley's *Life of Stein*, i. 430 ff.

first to reach perfectly clear and sound ideas of the essential difference between *ager publicus* and *ager privatus* ; and as he pursued his studies he also came to recognize in its various forms and tenures the nature of those public lands which occasioned the long series of agrarian laws, and the way in which they were dealt with by the State. In all this he was no doubt greatly helped and encouraged by his friend Savigny ; he it was perhaps who first saw the value of the writers on land measurement in dealing with this part of the problem. The very valuable edition of these writers of the Empire by Lachmann Rudorff and Mommsen appeared within eighteen years of Niebuhr's death, and may be reckoned as directly inspired by an appendix which he added to the second edition of his second volume, and which is specially and honourably referred to on the first page of their preface.

The first two volumes of the history may seem to us rather chaotic and bewildering ; but this is only because criticism was beginning, and beginning with doubtful methods and on uncertain foundations. Much progress was made in this respect before Mommsen began his history hardly more than twenty years later, and before Schwegler about the same time criticized the legends and the earliest history with masterly clearness and good sense. It is indeed remarkable how many of the special problems first pointed out by Niebuhr have been investigated by a succession of Germans who wrote with real knowledge and enthusiasm,[1] a combination which their descendants of the present day do not often achieve. In England too the Roman history was carried on with literary skill and judgement by Dr. Arnold, and with great acuteness of criticism by Sir George Cornewall Lewis.

It is not till we come to the third volume, written long afterwards and left unfinished, that we see Niebuhr's real idea of the art of writing history. There, from page 158 onwards,

---

[1] Among these may be mentioned O. Müller (Etruscan antiquities), Ambrosch (religious topography), Hartung and Preller (religious antiquities), Marquardt (the whole field of religious and social life), and many more of a later date than these.

we find ourselves lighted with highly intelligent criticism through the dark labyrinth of the Samnite and Etruscan Wars, and though we naturally feel that we are still groping, the landmarks that are distinctly visible begin to increase in number. When he came to the war with Pyrrhus, the more cosmopolitan nature of which entirely suited his bent, he wrote still more freely, sometimes almost with eloquence. He had followed the military events of his own time with his usual enthusiasm ; he thoroughly understood both strategy and tactics, and was master of his authorities, which were here purely literary ; so now he could let himself go, and it is amusing to find him once or twice introducing speeches after the manner of Livy, in which to embody his comments on the military and political situation. Had he lived to write the history of the Punic wars, we should certainly have found him at his best. The notes of lectures which he afterwards delivered at Bonn on the whole range of Roman history are unluckily too imperfect to do more than help us to understand that he had, beyond all his contemporaries and most of his successors, that gift which is the real secret of history as an art—the power to realize what men were thinking and doing at the time about which his mind is occupied. ' He strove to attain such a conception of ancient institutions, that their mutual dependence, their application, their practical working seemed to be preserved, in all their living activity, to his eyes.' [1]

In 1813 Niebuhr returned to public life, and among other duties paid a second visit for financial purposes to Holland. He had also been with the Prussian army, and witnessed from a distance the unfortunate battle of Bautzen ; and the strain of Napoleon's prolonged and unexpected resistance after the retreat from Russia, together with his wife's ill-health, produced a nervous prostration, which doubtless made him very difficult as a colleague. An unlucky quarrel with Stein was mainly the result of a misunderstanding produced by

---

[1] *Life and Letters*, ii. 435, from an essay on Niebuhr as a historian by his friend Professor Loebell of Bonn.

this condition of health. One who knew both said that though both were irritable, Niebuhr was the worse of the two ; but there is no doubt that Stein was both rude and haughty,[1] and Niebuhr writes bitterly that it was impossible for an ordinary man in Germany to get on with such an aristocrat. But I need not go here into this painful episode in Niebuhr's life, which deprived Germany of the services of one of her ablest men for the rest of his life. It will be found fully and on the whole fairly narrated in Seeley's life of Stein (iii. 148 ff.), where there is perhaps a slight bias, but only a slight one, in favour of the author's hero.

About the time of Waterloo his wife died, and it became in every way desirable to get him away from Berlin. But within a year he had married again, and again very happily, and was thus provided with an affectionate companion for the post he now accepted of Ambassador from Prussia to the Vatican. He had never yet been in Italy, and the prospect must have seemed most attractive. They set off in July 1816, accompanied by Professor Brandis of Bonn as Secretary of Legation. Niebuhr made it his business to visit all libraries within his reach, to inspect all manuscripts, and especially to look out for palimpsests, in the hope of discovering something that had been entirely hidden from the eyes of the learned. It was thus that in the library of Verona Cathedral he made the great discovery of his life. He shall tell it in his own words :

The cathedral of Verona possesses a library extremely rich in very old Latin parchments . . . The first thing that fell into my hands, on opening the chest containing the manuscripts, was a very thin little volume of extremely ancient single and double leaves of parchment, which, according to the title-page, were collected from among dirt and rubbish by the said Dionigi in 1758. Most of them are biblical fragments, from perhaps the sixth to the eleventh century, and a note, by the hand of their diligent collector, exhibits their contents. But almost instantly I espied among them two

---

[1] Stein, as a Freiherr, belonged to the nobility of the Empire ; Niebuhr was simply a *novus homo* like Cicero, whom he resembled also in other respects.

fragments of quite a different kind, whose nature he did not understand, and of which he has therefore omitted all notice. I have only copied this fragment that nothing might be overlooked.[1]

Within a year after this discovery the whole text of Gaius had been recovered from the palimpsest by two professors, sent at once by Niebuhr's request from the Prussian Academy, with all the apparatus necessary for an operation so difficult ; and in 1820 the first edition was published. Since that time the text has gradually been purified and corrected by the labours of many well qualified jurists and scholars. I need not here dwell on the immense value of this achievement not only to Roman law, but to Roman history in general. Whoever has once had Gaius in his hand, or even referred to him for information on some matter of Roman public or private law, will recognize at once what I mean. How it delighted Niebuhr we can well imagine. In 1818 he wrote to Savigny :

The proof-sheets of the Gaius have thrilled me like an electric spark. If Göschen[2] is not inclined to the revision at present, he need not be afraid to put it off for a time. In a good mood he can do it admirably, and it *must* be done admirably. Be sure to send me all the proof-sheets as they are printed. What does the postage signify ?

I said that the Embassy to Rome must have been a delightful prospect for Niebuhr. But alas, it turned out to be an exile of no less than seven years, in a foreign land where he found no congenial society, no means of comfortably and steadily pursuing his Roman researches, no safety of travel in Italian country districts. His letters are numerous and interesting, but they are full of bitter complaints—complaints hardly justified in a man who was only just forty, and should have been able to make himself at home in Italian, and to do something to infect Italian scholars, such as they were, with his own enthusiasm. But from the first he took a strong

[1] *Life*, ii. 52.

[2] Göschen was one of the two professors who went to Verona to prosecute Niebuhr's discovery.

dislike to the whole Italian nation which never wore off.
Strange to say, this extended even to Italian history, in which
from Justinian downwards he could see nothing at all to admire
or interest. To dislike and despise a whole nation is unnatural,
even in a German ; [1] and we can only account for it by the
miserable fate of Italy, for centuries the victim of foreigners
and chiefly of Germans, which at intervals seems to have
paralysed both her imagination and her intellect. Niebuhr
was aware of course of the misfortunes of Italy, yet he seems
to have been unable to make any sort of allowance for the
paralysis of the Italian mind. It is curious to find him writing
privately to a friend that the government of Napoleon had
been a real remedy for many evils, and that the restoration
of the Papal Government to which he was accredited was for
Rome the greatest calamity that could have happened.

There were some alleviations of this unnatural misery,
which was, it is easy to see, in part the result of constant
ill-health. A son was born to him there, in whose education,
even before he left Rome, he began to take infinite delight ;
and we are not surprised to find him suspecting that he was
taxing that tender brain too hardly. Other children followed,
and for the first time in his life he found relief from vexations
not only in correspondence, but in family life. In his household too he had the companionship of Brandis, who understood Niebuhr and his almost unmanly fits of depression.
Then there were manuscripts to decipher, though the Vatican
Library was at that time in chaos and confusion ; and the
fragments of Cicero's speeches for Fonteius and Rabirius
(published at Rome in 1820) were the immediate fruit of
his labours. In the discovery and publication of the precious
fragments of the *de Republica* he was anticipated by Cardinal
Mai, whom he suspected of incapability. Then there were
many German art-students in Rome, among others the

---

[1] ' The life of the Italian is little more than an animal one, and he is not
much better than an ape endowed with speech. There is nowhere a spark of
originality or truthfulness ' (ii. 147). He says that he had not seen one hand-
some face since his arrival ; and that they have no music, and only screeching
instead of singing.

historical painter Cornelius, reckoned in Germany as great ;
a Frenchman, the Comte de Serre, for whom he conceived
a great affection, and occasional English visitors of distinction
and ability.   Once he actually found a young Italian who
filled him with admiration, and should have made him doubt
whether there might not be others worth knowing ; this
was the poet Leopardi, whom he found living in penury in
a Roman garret.[1]   Lastly there were visits in summer to
Tivoli and Nemi, and finally a trip to Naples, which for six
years he had neglected to visit.   One might imagine that he
had much to make his exile tolerable ; but when a man
insists on being an exile, there is no real alleviation for him.
Cicero and Niebuhr were alike in this respect, though the one
pined for Italy, and the other detested it.   Niebuhr never
felt that call which has so often led the finest northern spirits,
such as Shelley and Byron,[2] Goethe, and Thorwaldsen, to the
land of sunshine and art.

At last, in 1823, he was allowed to return northwards,
though still uncertain whether he might not have to renew
his exile.   To see his friend Brandis he paid a visit to Bonn,
where the latter was professor, and finding the place congenial,
took up his residence there.   He was still occasionally called
to Berlin on government business, and to instruct the Crown
Prince, the elder brother of the first Emperor of Germany ;
but from this time to his death in 1830 he resided at Bonn
as professor, occupying himself with a new edition of the
first two volumes of his history, with writing a third volume
which he did not live to publish, and with giving those lectures
which filled three octavo volumes as reported by Leonard
Schmitz and other hearers.   On the whole this was the happiest

[1] *Life*, ii. 448.   He was long unconscious of the existence of the great
archaeologist Borghesi, who lived in northern Italy.   For this, like the honest
man he was, he expresses some shame.   See *Hist. of Rome*, ii. 563, note.   It
is clear that he too readily assumed that nothing of any value to a student
was to be had from Italians.   So with Fabretti (i. 204, note 572).

[2] These two poets were in Italy during the last two years of Niebuhr's
residence there, and Shelley was drowned in July 1822 ; but Niebuhr
had nothing in common with either of them, and apparently does not
mention them.

time of his life ; I think this can be discerned in these lectures, in which he was able to talk quite freely to an appreciative audience not only about Roman history, but about anything else that interested him at the moment. He now lectured, we are told, entirely without notes. Probably no lecturer has ever had such vast treasures of knowledge to draw upon, or used them with such satisfaction to himself and his audience. Few people read these volumes now, but they are well worth looking into. If any student should be induced by this paper to turn over their pages, let him remember, first that they are a rather doubtful amalgam of several reports, and are not to be guaranteed as the actual words of the speaker ; secondly, that if he finds strange literary criticisms, such as the unworthy depreciation of Virgil, or wild prognostics of the politics of his own day, he should remember that Niebuhr never expected that his lectures would be published in any form, and that he delivered his opinions sometimes with an almost wanton 'cocksureness' which we can only find rivalled in Macaulay's earlier writings.[1]

One word about Niebuhr's attitude to the politics of his own day. The continent was then split up between revolution and freedom on one side, reaction and arbitrary government on the other. To understand Niebuhr's position, we must remember that the Germans had naturally had enough of the French Revolution, and enough too of Napoleon, who had succeeded in destroying the hope of popular self-government which had at one time dawned on Europe. It seemed to have been proved that the people could not govern ; that it was happiest when directed in politics by a governing class, or a despot, and left in peace to attend to agriculture and petty local government. There was much then to be said for this view, which was in action only yesterday in Germany and Austria ; and there seems no doubt that this was the

---

[1] Here is an example : 'I know England as well as if I had been born there.' *Life*, ii. 256, letter to de Serre. 'I have asked myself what I should do in Mr. Canning's place, with his principles and character' ; and he adds that it was by such methods that he came to divine the projects of Napoleon and even the plans of his campaigns.

view of Niebuhr himself. Revolution was to him perdition ; he associated it with all that was bad and dangerous in political and social life. Yet both he and Stein were in their way liberals, seeking to get rid of abuses, bent on developing the talents and opportunities of their people ; but they profoundly distrusted the ability of that people to choose their own path of progress as the French had done, or to take any sort of active part in the government. Hardenberg, who was probably the ablest of the three, was entirely with them in this view. ' There must be a revolution in the good sense ', he argued, ' a revolution from above, in which the wisdom of the Government would foster the ennobling of humanity.' ' Your Majesty,' he told the King of Prussia, ' we must do from above what the French have done from below.' [1] For internal reforms this may have been the right course ; but it unluckily encouraged the German people in that habit of unthinking obedience in politics which is only at last (1919) being seriously disturbed. And worse still, it deprived them of all power of independent thought in foreign affairs ; it delivered them years later bound hand and foot into the power of Bismarck. Since then till now there has been no power of free criticism when they have been called on to make war, no sense that they were merely pawns in a game, compelled to fight by irresistible pressure from above, and justified in all they were doing by the united voice of a submissive professoriate.

Whether the remarkable man whose life I have been sketching would have approved of the Bismarckian policy which began its sinister influence on Prussia within twenty years after his death, I seriously doubt. I think that the root principle of freedom was too deeply fixed in his mind for that, in spite of his horror of revolution. In July 1830, when Charles X was deposed at Paris, he blamed the folly of that reactionary monarch quite as much as the violence of a revolutionary mob. At Bonn he was near enough to France to feel that ' the Revolution ' might any day overwhelm

[1] See the *Quarterly Review* for January 1919, p. 37.

him and his—that a French army might be on the Rhine before Germany was ready for it. He became so excited that he devoted a whole lecture to the subject, leaving ancient history to take care of itself, and prophesying the worst things for both countries. This excitement took him out one bitter night in the December of that year to a public reading-room, where the latest news was to be had ; and the warmth of the room and his own excitement so overheated him that on coming out into the cold air he took a severe chill, followed by an attack of pneumonia which ended his life at the early age of fifty-four.

In writing this brief sketch of Niebuhr's life and work, I have had to allude to certain faults of character which damaged him as a statesman, if not as a historian. Let me conclude it by dwelling for a moment on the finer side of his nature. He was invariably throughout life an absolutely straight and honourable man ; his life was perfectly pure and clean, and he could not put up with any man of bad personal character among his intimates and colleagues. It is more than probable that his unfortunate quarrel with Stein was largely owing to the very doubtful private character of the able Minister Hardenberg, whom Stein believed to be necessary to Prussia at that crisis in her fortunes. In religion Niebuhr was a staunch Protestant, but without a trace of fanaticism. As a critic of ancient history and historical documents, he could not but see that the same kind of criticism would before long be applied to the ancient Jewish history and also to the New Testament, and he was even tempted to set his own hand to this work, though he did not go on with it. From what he says himself we may be quite sure that it would not have affected his belief in the essentials of Christianity. Belief he defined as a conviction for which a man is ready to die ; and declared that he himself would readily lay his head on the block for the divinity of Jesus.

I will end with a story which illustrates at once his goodness of heart and his freedom from narrow religious prejudice.

During his journey to Rome he visited Speckbacher, one of the peasant heroes of the Tyrolese rebellion, and asked him whether he could do anything for him at Rome. Speckbacher replied that he would dearly like to have a rosary which had been blessed by the Pope. Almost the first business that Niebuhr transacted with the Pope was to tell him of this, with the result that a splendid rosary was sent to Speckbacher as a gift from His Holiness.

THEODOR MOMMSEN[1]: HIS LIFE AND WORK

I BELIEVE that there is a very general impression among those who have not been classically educated, that the study of Greek and Roman life and literature is now little more than a leisurely and luxurious amusement ; that it can have little or no bearing on the life and thought of the modern man. If there be such an impression, it is the very natural result of the revolt so long successfully going on against the too exclusively classical character of the education in our great schools, and I do not wish to complain of it now. My object this evening is to give you some slight sketch of a long life almost entirely devoted to classical study, and to leave you to judge from it whether in these days, which have seen, largely owing to the work of that life, a new era in classical study, there can be the least justification for such a notion. I have chosen Mommsen as the subject of this lecture, partly because he was by general consent the greatest figure in the region of classical learning that the nineteenth century

[1] This lecture, which is printed exactly as it was delivered in Oct. 1909, was put together, apart from personal recollections, with the help of Mommsen's *Speeches and Essays* (*Reden und Aufsätze*), published since his death with an admirable portrait ; short Memoirs by Professors Otto Hirschfeld, Wachsmuth, and C. Bardt ; the beautiful and touching funeral oration by Professor Harnack ; and a short notice by my late friend Dr. J. B. Carter, Director of the American School at Rome. The fragment of autobiography by Tycho Mommsen, to which I refer in the lecture, was published in the *Jahresbericht* for Classical Philology a few years ago.—W. W. F.

produced ; partly because the story of his life's work is an extraordinary one, one that may well be of value to the real student in any department of knowledge ; and again because his character was one of singular interest, and his personality the most striking that I myself have ever had the good fortune to meet.

Let me begin by introducing him to you as I first saw him in the autumn of 1886, when he came for a short visit to Oxford to examine certain manuscripts in the Bodleian Library. He came to dine in my college, and as he entered the room I think we should all of us have said, if we had not known who he was, ' Surely this is a great poet '. We saw a slight, spare, old man, approaching seventy, with long, iron-grey hair, worn hanging over the shoulders in the old fashion of German professors, with a wide, firmly-set yet mobile mouth, thin aquiline nose, and the most piercingly brilliant black eyes that I have ever seen in a human being. He wore strong glasses, yet they did not in the least diminish the gleam of those eyes, which I can see at this moment, and which no one can forget who has ever seen them. But as I sat next him at dinner, I soon found that there was no reason to be afraid of him or his eyes. He talked, partly in English, partly in German, without the least constraint, and he enjoyed his dinner thoroughly. Now and then he flashed out with just a touch of that scornful opiniativeness which was one of his characteristics—perhaps one of his few weaknesses. I was asking his opinion of some other German scholars, and he answered in words which perhaps would not suit us so well now : ' You English think that everything that is German is good ; it is not so at all.' Our Rector attacked him on the subject of a famous depreciation of Euripides, which he had inserted in his *Roman History* thirty years earlier. ' If I were to write that passage again now,' he said, ' I should put it still more strongly.' He did not smoke, but later in the evening he came up to my rooms, and wrote his name in my copy of his *History*—an autograph which I shall always treasure.

Two or three years later he came to Oxford again, and I passed a whole evening with him and a very small party, which gave us a better opportunity of discovering what manner of man he was. It was in the days of the Home Rule question, and I ventured to ask his opinion about Irish affairs. As he had always been a strong Liberal in his own country, I was rather astonished to find him condemning Gladstone and his Irish land legislation in language which I will not now repeat ; but it gave me a glimpse of a strange, passionate nature, which never loved or hated men or things by halves, and was too apt to judge of them from feeling and prejudice. He was an ardent soul, and what he felt he felt strongly ; and it was quite in keeping with this that in fiction he loved best what was romantic and nervous. He had been reading *Jane Eyre* on his way from Berlin, and spoke of it with enthusiasm. The next day I met him coming out of a bookshop just as I was going in ; and I asked the bookseller what Professor Mommsen had been buying. They told me that he had been asking for *Ellis Bell's* novel, but as it did not occur to them that he meant *Wuthering Heights*, he had gone away without getting what he wanted. Of course I bought the book, and took it to him at once as a present, which so delighted the old man that he made me write his name in it, and afterwards sent me from Berlin a valuable publication of his own on the *History of the Eastern Goths in the Roman Empire*.

His evenings at Oxford were thus passed socially, as often in his own home at Berlin, where he was always a *persona grata*, loving his friends with all his own ardour ; and, as one who knew him well has said, needing friendship more than anything in this life. But all his day was spent in persistent work. At Oxford he was found waiting at the Bodleian at seven in the morning, and indignant when he found that it did not open till nine. At Berlin he rose at five, and set to work on a cup of cold coffee. When it was time to go to the university or the great library, he took a book with him, like Macaulay ; and a friend has described to me how, when he was once in a tram at Berlin, the conductor pointed out to the passengers the grey-haired figure leaning against a lamp-post, absorbed in a book : ' That is the celebrated Professor Mommsen ; *he loses no time.*' In the tram he was still buried in his book, and it became the regular practice of the conductors to touch him on the shoulder when he arrived at his destination. He never took a holiday, so far as I can discover, nor did he cease working on a Sunday, but those wonderful eyes never failed him till within a few weeks of his death, and he lived to be nearly eighty-six. He never knew fatigue in his work, we are told by one who was intimate with him. He never over-worked himself ; he knew exactly what he could do, and never did less or more. Perhaps the work itself was one continual holiday to him—certainly it was what he most enjoyed, the thing for which he lived. His disappointments were few, and he hardly knew what illness was. The day before he died was the only one he was ever known to have spent entirely in bed. With the highest ideal ever before him, with an iron will which mastered easily all petty obstacles, with the utmost contempt for all half-work and dilettantism, he worked on incessantly for more than sixty years, and was still at work when a sudden stroke took him quietly and painlessly to rest, on November 1, 1903.

I shall hope before I have done to give you some idea of the real substance and value of this work ; for the moment I must ask you to believe with me that in quality as in quantity it was, taken all together, the most wonderful life's work done in the nineteenth century. The power of work, as Mommsen himself said, is the special prerogative of the German ; but the German is often mastered by his work, or loses himself in minute details. Mommsen stands supreme and alone in the mastery of the minutest detail, supreme and alone also in the possession of that rare synthetic insight which puts each detail in its proper place, and gives it its due in the interpretation of the whole. So much I must ask you to take for granted while I go on to give a brief sketch of his life.

He was born in 1817, in a country parsonage in Schleswig, which then belonged to Denmark ; but his parents were not of Danish blood. They came from Friesland, and were thus living as Germans, and among a German population, under a foreign Government. This fact, and the harsh conduct of the Danish Government towards its German subjects, became of great importance in Mommsen's later life, as we shall see, and made him, from his youth upwards, an enthusiastic exponent of the idea of German unity. He has himself left no record of his early years spent in the Danish parsonage, but I have been able to gather something from a recently published manuscript of his second brother Tycho.

Theodor was the eldest son ; the two others, Tycho and August, followed at intervals of about two years. All three became distinguished in the field of classical learning. Tycho lived to be a great head master, and an authority of great weight in Greek, German, and English literature. His name will always be associated with the study of Pindar, but he was also a Shakespearian scholar. He had a hand in that wonderful German translation of Shakespeare which is said to be almost as good as the original, and twice visited England, and came to Oxford and Stratford-on-Avon. The third brother, August, also made his mark, and his book on the Athenian religious festivals is still quoted. One naturally asks whether there was anything in the parents, or in the circle of their friends, to account for such ability and industry in all three boys ; but Tycho only tells us that his father was a gentle character, fond of literature, and his mother sensible and judicious in training her children ; that they lived almost entirely by themselves, playing freely in a large garden, and rarely mixing with other children. At home Theodor remained till he was seventeen ; but he cannot have wasted his time, for he was placed at once in the highest class when, in 1834, he went to school at Altona, with his next brother. At school they found themselves in a new and to them a very uncomfortable world, and here again they were thrown much on their own resources. Tycho tells us of

a ' scientific society ', i. e. a society for acquiring real knowledge of whatever kind, among the boys, and of friendly
ladies who had influence on them, but of the teaching and the
masters he says little or nothing.

The young Mommsens then were practically self-taught ;
at any rate they learnt of themselves the most essential of
all lessons, which in our public schools we do not always
learn, that if you want a thing done it is best to do it for yourself if possible, and to think out for yourself the best ways
and means of doing it. And here I may remark, that at no
period of his life was Mommsen a believer in highly systema-
tized training. When in 1876 he was chosen Rector of the
University of Berlin, he told his students in his inaugural
address, with even more than his usual emphatic note of
conviction, that the historical craft cannot be acquired by
teaching. The passage is a remarkable one, for it brings out
with astonishing emphasis his profound belief that history is
not merely a matter of dry and dull ' research ', but that it
deals with the actualities, the doings and sufferings, of human
beings ; that it can only be interpreted by experience of human
life ; and that the qualifications it demands are much the
same as those of the man of business or the lawyer. ' It
may be affirmed ', he asserts, ' that the historian is not trained
but born, not educated by others, but by himself. History
is the record of human life ; you cannot learn to realize the
life of the past but by experience of the present and by independent thought.'

Mommsen was twenty-one when he went to the University
of Kiel. His character must by that time have been matured,
and he was at once capable of enjoying and appreciating the
intellectual society he found there. Here at last he came in
contact with men who were more learned than himself, for
the staff was of first-rate quality, including many men whose
names are familiar to students in various regions of learning.
I shall only mention one of them, who became a lifelong
friend of Mommsen's—a mind after his own heart, because
it was not that of a mere pedant or bookworm, but richly

stored with knowledge of literature, art, and music. Otto
Jahn the scholar and archaeologist may in due time be
forgotten, but he will never be forgotten as the author of the
best of all musical biographies, the great *Life of Mozart*. As
I write, a portrait of the great composer looks down on me,
which I bought when Jahn's vast library was sold after his
early death in 1869.

At Kiel, Mommsen was a student of law, and law in a German
university means, or meant at that time, chiefly Roman law.
The subject which he chose for his dissertation for the degree
of Doctor was characteristic ; it was no abstract question of
legal science, but ' The Secretaries and Marshals of the Roman
Magistrates ', and he followed this up the same year with
another on the guilds and co-operative societies of Rome.
It was the actual administration of the law that was interesting
him ; he wanted to explore and to realize the actual working
of that great engine which the Romans brought to such
perfection, and have handed down to us as an imperishable
legacy. He once defined law as ' the interference of the State
in the interests and passions of humanity ' ; and this interference—the action of the State and its authorities in every
department of Roman life—was what he never ceased to
investigate for sixty years. The last twenty-five years of
his life were chiefly given to this work, and the last great
book he published was a marvellous treatise on *Roman
Criminal Law*. All that he wrote on this subject was new
and epoch-making, because here for the first time law was
treated from the point of view of actual human life, the play
of society and thought as acting on legal history, and the
influence again of legal ideas and practice on the daily life
of the individual. In a word, while the study of Roman law
made him into a historian, his historical instinct infused new
life and meaning into all that he wrote about law.

The next year, 1844, a piece of good luck came to him,
which may be said to have secured him for us as the historian
of Rome. He accepted what we should call a travelling
fellowship from the Danish Government, and undertook to

collect in Italy inscriptions bearing on the study of Roman law. The Greeks and Romans, I need not remind you, recorded their legal documents on stone or bronze, and as at that time even the most valuable of such documents had been either imperfectly edited, or never published at all, this was a piece of work of the greatest importance for legal science. Three years were spent by Mommsen entirely in Italy on this work. In company with other young Germans, and with his brother Tycho, he travelled all over Italy, not merely deciphering stony records with the most painful care, but learning all about the country, its geography, agriculture, and history ; and acquiring so perfect a knowledge of its language that for some years a great part of his published work was written in Italian. Ten years later it was into Italian that his *Roman History* was first translated, and thenceforward he was almost adored by the Italian people. It is told of him that during a later visit to Italy he was so worried at Reggio with deputations and festivities, that he fled for liberty across the straits to Messina. In 1870, when the war broke out between Germany and France, and the attitude of Italy was doubtful, he issued a kind of manifesto to the Italian people, which was received with profound respect.

It was during this long stay in Italy that Mommsen began to make plans for that vast undertaking which will doubtless be the most permanent portion of his long life's work—the collection of all the inscriptions of the Roman Empire, from Syria to Britain. He had gone to Italy to procure correct texts of *legal* inscriptions ; but it grew upon him that there could be no solid and scientific basis for the study of Roman life while the tens of thousands of those records, civil, military, religious, commercial, which the Roman people had left behind them, remained inaccessible to students, or only accessible in bad and doubtful copies. This idea had long been a matter of consideration to the Berlin Academy of Sciences, and Mommsen was sanguine enough to hope that they might procure the necessary means from the Prussian Government, and that Otto Jahn and himself might be entrusted with the conduct of the work. But these hopes were doomed for a time at least to be shattered. The Academy gave the chief editorship to an incompetent man, incapable of organization ; and after long and somewhat bitter negotiation Mommsen refused to have anything more to do with the work. All his natural obstinacy, strength of will, conviction of the rectitude of his own position, came out in this controversy, of which we are only now beginning to know the details. I must not weary you with them. Defeated for the moment, he was eventually victorious ; a few years later the incompetent man was set aside, and he entered on a work of organization and generalship which has never been equalled, and probably never will be equalled, in the region of classical learning.

But in the meantime other clouds were gathering. The French Revolution of 1848 set the whole of Europe in a blaze. Every oppressed people rose against their oppressors, and among these the people of Schleswig-Holstein rose against the Danish Government. The three brothers threw themselves heart and soul into the cause ; the two younger took up arms, while Theodor used the weapons of journalism. There has lately been reprinted an article from his pen describing a battle in which his friends were victorious. From such work as this he was luckily rescued by a call to Leipzig as Professor of Law. But even at Leipzig he was not to find rest. The times were still disturbed, and he could never hold his tongue or his pen when his feelings were deeply moved. He was prosecuted for seditious language, and though acquitted, he, with Otto Jahn and another great scholar, had to resign their posts. Mommsen fled to Switzerland, took work at Zurich, and occupied himself with collecting the Roman inscriptions of the Alpine region, doing the work so thoroughly that it has never needed another hand, except for incorporation in the great scheme which he was eventually to carry out. At last, in 1854, he was called to a Professorship at Breslau, and four years later he migrated to Berlin, where he continued to live and work till his death.

It was in these years, the early 'fifties, that he wrote at
hot speed, and completed in four years, an extraordinary
feat, his famous *History of Rome to the Death of Caesar*. This
wonderful work, which was meant for the general reading
public, like the histories of Gibbon or Macaulay, took the
world by storm. It has been called the greatest feat of German
literature in the middle of the nineteenth century. Literature
it certainly was—a consummate specimen of the historical
art ; I use the word *art* intentionally, for Mommsen himself
has elsewhere insisted that the writing of history is not
a special business or trade, but essentially an *art*. The rest
of his sixty years' work he gave almost entirely to the formation of a scientific basis for Roman history. In these three
years only, 1854–6, did he let himself go in telling with all
the ardour of his fiery soul the wonderful story of Rome—in
telling it as it was never told before, and probably never will
be told again. The force of his convictions was equalled by
the strength of his language ; the audacity of some of his
judgements of men and institutions almost paralysed criticism,
and we have only begun in recent years to shake ourselves
free from the spell he laid upon us. The work was meant
only to give a readable account of results so far obtained,
without notes or references ; in reality it revealed to Europe
a new historical genius of the first order, who combined the
profound knowledge of the best type of German professor
with an extraordinary insight into the play of social and
political forces, and an almost dangerous gift of historical
imagination, which did indeed occasionally mislead him. But
even if he went astray in judging of individuals, of Pompey
and Caesar, of Cicero or Cato, we can only too easily forgive
him, for we must all form our own opinion of such characters,
as we do of Henry VIII or William Pitt, of Frederick the
Great or of Bismarck. But these are small matters compared
with the lesson taught to Europe of the government, the
economy, the family life and morality, the religion, the
literature, and the law of the great empire which preceded
the slow growth of our modern states. It was soon translated

into Italian, French, English, and Russian, and its author, though he was still under forty when he completed it, was recognized at once as among the great men of his time. Even now, more than fifty years later, it is still the indispensable text-book for Roman history. Yet Mommsen never recast it, never really continued it. He returned to the work which he believed to be the necessary preliminary to its continuation, to that collection of the material for the history of the empire of which he had dreamed in Italy, and the fourth volume of his *History* never came into existence. A fifth appeared many years later ; but for the story of Augustus and his successors he substituted the editorship of the *Corpus Inscriptionum* which was at last offered him while he was writing the *History*, and to which he now began to devote the best and ripest years of his life.

This new work showed him as something more than a great historian—as a great organizer, I might almost say a great general. Supposing that it were proposed to search out, decipher, and collect into one great treasure-house all those innumerable manorial documents from which in England we have of late begun to learn so much of the daily life, the economy, and the law of our English forefathers, what a gigantic task it would be, and what high qualifications would be called for in the man who should preside over it ! These records are scattered over every county, and in every county there would have to be a committee and staff of competent men, in due subordination to a governing centre in London, say at the British Museum. But even this would be a small campaign compared with that in which Mommsen was now appointed the generalissimo of the forces. For that campaign had to be organized over the whole of southern and central Europe, including Britain, over the north of Africa, over Asia Minor, Syria, and Egypt. Wherever the Romans and their subjects had left their records on stone, trained men had to be sent to discover and decipher ; and it was with the general an absolute condition of service that each of his lieutenants should if possible actually *see* each stone with his own eyes, or if the inscription were only preserved in copies made at some earlier time, as often happened, that they should see the original manuscript of such copies if possible. All this was necessary because, strange as it may seem, there were in existence an immense number of so-called inscriptions which turned out to be simply forgeries, the result of the foolish desire of old collectors to add to the volume and interest of their collections. All these false inscriptions have now been collected and printed apart from the real ones, so that there can never be in future any mistake about them.

Of course the brunt of the work lay in Italy, where about 36,000 inscriptions were collected, and a great part of them edited by Mommsen himself, with the help of trusty lieutenants on the spot. The British ones were perhaps the least troublesome of any. Forgeries there were none here, the number to be found was not so great, and they had been fairly well preserved in local museums and private houses. The German scholar who carried out the campaign in this country had a comparatively easy time ; yet he had to inspect and edit no fewer than 1,500 inscriptions, which fill the thinnest of all the huge volumes of the *Corpus*.[1]

Mommsen's generalship lasted for twenty-five years, and he lived to see the great work practically complete, in forty huge volumes, so far as was possible at the time. His great historical talents, his imaginative genius, his gift of style, were all deliberately set aside, that he might direct and carry out an undertaking the fruits of which he could hardly expect to live to reap. And by universal consent his direction was admirable ; he chose his staff, engaged their loyalty, controlled their work with tact and constant help and encouragement ; and allowed no sheets to go to press without passing them under his own eye. And lastly, by the force of his will and his marvellous power of inspiring others with his own enthusiasm.

[1] Since this lecture was written the work of preparing a new edition of vol. vii of the *Corpus* has been in the hands of Prof. Haverfield of Oxford, whose recent death is an irreparable loss to British scholarship.

he secured the continual support of the Prussian Government for this as for so many other undertakings.

You must not, however, suppose that during these twenty-five years he was so absorbed in this work that he took no part in the stirring events which in these very same years made Prussia into the leading state of Germany, and Germany into a united nation. He scorned the notion that a scholar whose work lies in the past should shut himself away from the life of the present. ' How miserable ', he once said, ' how miserable and small is the world in the eyes of a man who sees in it only Greek or Latin authors, or mathematical problems ! ' The little war of Austria and Prussia against Denmark in 1865 which made us in England so indignant, he regarded as the means of freeing his own people in Schleswig-Holstein from a foreign yoke ; and already he began to see the near approach of that unification of Germany, which a few years later roused in him the deepest enthusiasm, expressed in more than one speech of real feeling and eloquence. I know nothing finer in its way than the speech delivered before the University of Berlin in 1875, in commemoration of its members who had fallen in the great national war of 1870. Nor do I know any better way of getting to understand the profound national enthusiasm which took possession of the whole German people at that time, than by studying his speeches and addresses of those years. These were most of them delivered before the University or the Academy of Berlin ; but he was now a member of the Prussian House of Representatives, and kept his seat as member for Halle for many years. Unluckily for him, he was a strong Liberal, and .intensely disliked Bismarck's aristocratic domestic policy. With his usual audacity he attacked the man of blood and iron, and once went so far as to speak of some part of his policy as ' a swindle '—which was a crime not to be forgiven. Bismarck prosecuted him, and he only escaped by a final acquittal in the Court of Appeal. He did not remain long in Parliament after this, and the only Parliamentary speeches of his which have been reprinted since his death are two earnest appeals to the Government on behalf of the Berlin Museum and Library, which were sorely in want of funds : both of these appeals were successful. Would that we had in Britain at this moment a Mommsen who could inspire our Parliament with an enthusiasm for the cause of learning and science, and a Government ready and able to act upon the inspiration ! During the last evening I spent with him at Oxford we fell to talking about the neglect of these things by the British Government, and the way in which we have to depend on private enterprise for nearly all great scientific undertakings. He spoke with such warmth that we suggested he should write a letter to the *Times* while he was still in England ; but the next morning he said that he could not do it—that it would be an unwarrantable interference of a foreigner in our affairs.

I have now nearly finished the story of his life. At the age of seventy he had done a magnificent life's work, and might well rest on his oars. He had a large family, a son-in-law who is now the greatest Greek scholar in Europe, devoted friends not only in Germany but throughout Europe, sufficient means, and a secured reputation as the first of European men of learning. But not for one moment did he cease working, unless it was to translate some Italian poetry or to write an essay on Shakespeare. ' To rest on one's laurels ', he once said, speaking of the German nation after its great victories, ' is to rest uncomfortably.' He lost a great part of his library by a fire, but the universities of Europe did all they could to supply its place, and he worked on without a murmur. Now he began to make use of the material that had been accumulated in the *Corpus Inscriptionum*, and the first result of this was the fifth volume of his *History of Rome*, which contained a survey of the organization, government, popula-tion, and economy of all the provinces of the Roman Empire. In our youth we used to think of Gibbon's great History as almost a final authority in all that relates to the history of the Roman Empire ; but Gibbon had no *Corpus Inscrip-tionum* to work on, and had hardly an inkling of the wealth of interesting knowledge with which such a collection could illuminate his narratives of emperors and their wars. Mommsen's work was practically a new revelation of the life of the empire, readable by every ordinary man—the first-fruits, I might almost say, of a new learning.

Then he turned to the legal studies of his youth, always with his old conception of law as a matter of human life and experience, not as an abstract philosophical study, and completed what he himself once said was the crown of all his work—the three great volumes, in all containing some 3,000 pages, on *Roman Public Law*. To this, and to the volume on *Roman Criminal Law*, and to the preparation of correct texts of the great Roman codes of law, he devoted his last years. Only now and again he ventured on a political utterance ; one of the last was that severe condemnation of Great Britain for her conduct in the war in South Africa, which was published in the *North American Review*, and angered many of us at the time. His love of liberty was roused ; he thought that we, the former defenders of the cause of freedom, were grabbing at a valuable territory under the influence of capitalism. Whether he was right or wrong, it is certain that he wrote with very imperfect knowledge of the question, and that his indignation, as usual, made him imprudent in his language, and added something to the unfortunate national misunderstanding which we all regret. He felt, I think, that he had written too strongly ; for in the last year of his life he published a short paper which was meant to help the two nations to a better mutual understanding. ' No one knows ', said the great theological teacher who delivered the address to the mourners at his grave, ' how much pain these bitter and impulsive utterances cost him.' [1]

[1] Professor Harnack's remarks (p. 11 of his funeral oration) on Mommsen's political views are admirable. His chief failing was, he says, that he understood things better than men, and thus demanded in politics what was not always practicable. His three political convictions were : (1) that monarchy is the best form of government ; (2) that freedom is a necessary condition for the health and progress of a state ; (3) that the people must educate themselves for liberty. *He looked forward to a peace among all nations*

His was not the calm equable vision of the true statesman ; he gave way to his feeling, and that feeling was not always founded upon knowledge or judgement. The perfectly clear insight, the unerring judgement, which he possessed to an extraordinary degree in the world of learning, were never at his command in the world of practical politics. But his passionate feeling, however unfortunately expressed, was always honourable to himself, for it was based, like that of Gladstone—another great man who occasionally let his feeling outrun his judgement—on a deep and intense conviction of right and wrong.

In this sketch of his life, I hope I may have justified what I said at the beginning, that it was one of the most wonderful lives lived in the nineteenth century, perhaps one of the most wonderful on record. I have mentioned only his greatest works. I have said nothing of the innumerable lesser ones in which he dealt with details, clearing up doubtful points, solving old riddles ; nor even of whole volumes which he devoted to the elucidation of the languages of ancient Italy, to the history of Roman coinage, to the study of Roman chronology, and other subjects, the successful handling of any one of which would have made a single scholar's reputation. It is now impossible to touch any department of Roman life without finding that he has been at work upon it, clearing the way for others, just as his own Romans drove their great roads through all parts of their empire, making the work of organization comparatively easy for their successors, and civilization practicable for the peoples that were to come. To give you a single instance : it happened to me recently to study a single long and most interesting inscription, containing a touching record of domestic life just before the Christian era. Of course Mommsen's unerring skill had dealt with it years before, had for the first time made it intelligible as a whole, and almost all I had to do was to send to Berlin for his illuminating discussion of it.

on a basis of morality and culture. (I leave this, and all this lecture, which was written in 1909, without the comment that suggests itself in 1919.)

Let me try to sum up the quality in the man which thus placed him so high above the crowd of workers, basing all I say not on what others have said of him, but solely on what I myself know of his works and his utterances.

First, I note in him an absolute devotion to the cause of real knowledge, of *Wissenschaft* as the Germans call it, more especially in his own branch of learning, *but with full recognition of the value of the work of others in other departments* ; for in Germany, as he proudly says, it is rare indeed to undervalue a science of which you are not yourself master. ' The desire for truth ', he says in another passage, ' is the very fibre of our being, on which depends the well-being and the self-respect of the German people.' The ' performance ' of the *individual*, whether of himself or others, he only valued so far as it really contributed to the whole scientific end in view. The measure of the work before us, he insists more than once, is always increasing, and the individual workman grows of less and less account. Co-operation in science—I use the word in the widest sense—was an idea that gained on him in later life, and he pleaded for it again and again, not without fruitful result.

Secondly, I would mark that indomitable will of his, which brushed aside all petty obstacles of health or circumstances, and carried him safely through sixty years of continuous labour. It is seen best, I think, in the determined way in which he laid the solid foundations of his knowledge. If the chronology of Roman history seemed to him to need testing and re-casting, he left his other work and probed this new subject to the root, mastering ancient astronomy by the way, because it was essential to his purpose. If he found that the Roman history to be learnt from coins needed special attention, he wrapped himself in the study of ancient weights and measures, and, apart from his large volume on the *History of the Roman Coinage*, could deliver an admirable popular lecture on money as a medium of exchange. Let me quote a single sentence from it as an example of his way of putting life into every subject that he handled : ' A coin ', he says, ' is the product of four of the most wonderful things in the world : the State, commerce, science, and art '.

Thirdly, I know of no man except Darwin in our time who possessed in the same degree the power of minute attention to the smallest details, together with the rarer power of fitting them into their proper places as evidence for a conclusion, and of discerning among the thousands of these details where the true conclusion lay. The student of minutiae and the builder-up of great hypotheses are rarely united in the same man ; and the perfect union is perhaps only to be found, in the nineteenth century, in these two great workers.

Lastly, let me allude once more to what I may call his *humanity* as a historian. I mean that all history was to him charged with human life, like the history that is making now under our own eyes. For this reason all that he wrote is full of fervour ; sometimes even his Latin comments yield matter to think about, apart from the immediate subject in hand, though never foreign to it ; his mind was working at full force, never became deadened or dulled, and was ready to scintillate even in a dead language. He was never a machine, always a sensitive organism ; never an instrument, always an active agent. His individuality was always there, though his intellectual power was subordinated to the highest ends ; one cannot read many of his pages either in German or Latin without feeling oneself under the spell of a wonderful mind.

In the first sentence of this lecture I alluded to a common opinion that the classics are worked out. An eminent man of science, who has not that sense of the brotherhood of learning which Mommsen claimed for his fellow workers in Germany, lecturing once at Oxford on the future of physical science, spoke of ancient history as a collection of pretty stories, which can do no more than amuse an idle man, or pervert our growing youth from the acquisition of real and useful knowledge. Even my very imperfect sketch of Mommsen's life and work will have proved, I trust—if proof indeed were necessary—that such notions are at once baseless and childish. The study of humanity in all its ages and phases is surely the noblest of all noble employments ; and all honour is due to those who faithfully and unweariedly devote their lives to it.

THE TRAGIC ELEMENT IN SHAKE-SPEARE'S *JULIUS CAESAR*.

NORTH'S famous *Lives of the Noble Grecians and Romans*, translated from the French of Amyot, itself translated from the Greek of Plutarch, first appeared in the year 1579, when Shakespeare was fifteen years old ; other editions soon followed, for the book became popular at once. We cannot tell when he first made acquaintance with it,[1] or how far he may have been attracted to it by a knowledge of earlier English plays on Roman subjects. All we know is that when he did come to read it he left the Greek lives almost unheeded, and found his dramatic material in the careers of a few noble Romans. If he read the Lives in the order in which they stand in North, the first to attract him was that of the legendary hero Coriolanus, but he passed on, to return to it some years later, when his ideas of tragedy had undergone serious change. The story of the Gracchi, which has been used for tragedy in more recent times by the Italian Monti, made no impression on him that we know of ; it was probably too entirely Roman, too limited in interest. The Lives of Marius and Sulla had been used by Lodge for tragedy of a sort, and printed in 1594 ; possibly it was for this reason that Shakespeare let them alone. Next he would come to that group of lives concerned with a period of which he doubtless knew something beforehand, where the central and commanding figure is that of Caesar ; the Lives of Pompey, Cicero, Caesar himself, Cato, Crassus, Brutus, and Antony. Here, indeed, was a tragical age ;

---

[1] Professor Raleigh, in his volume on Shakespeare in the English Men of Letters series, pp. 72 ff., thinks that Shakespeare had been reading Plutarch ome time before he wrote *Julius Caesar*, searching for tragic subjects.

every one of these men came to a violent end. The atmosphere in which they lived was lurid and stormy, and some mysterious power might seem to be leading each one of them on to his destruction, his own will and character contributing ; and these are just the conditions which the tragic poet needs.

What choice among these noble and tragic personages should we have expected him to make ? Not Cicero, for this Life as Plutarch tells it is a comparatively dull one, and the man is difficult to understand and appreciate ; Shakespeare has in fact given us some slight reason to conjecture that the Cicero of Plutarch's Life did not attract him.[1] What of Cato ? Cato was reserved for Addison, whose idea of tragedy was very different from that of Shakespeare ; and he who reads that Life will hardly be astonished that Shakespeare should have passed it by. Interesting as it is—for a historian perhaps more so than any of them—it shows Cato as too eccentric and angular a character to be made into a tragic hero. Pompey's life, again, is long and apt to be dull ; great figure as he was in history, his soul did not burn with inward fire, and his death took place far away from home, without that detail of circumstance that is needed for dramatic presentation. Crassus we may put aside as even less suited for the playwright's purpose than the others. There remain three Lives— those of Caesar, Brutus, and Antony. It is most interesting to see how these three Lives worked upon Shakespeare, and how he finally worked upon them. Reading them through now, I think we should say with little hesitation that the least attractive of them is that of Caesar. The whole career of Caesar was so continuously military and political, his private character so hidden away, at any rate for a Greek like Plutarch, his personality so much bound up with his public work, that, but for his own writings and a few letters of Cicero, we should

---

[1] Professor MacCallum, *Shakespeare's Roman Plays and their Background*, p. 288, has some interesting remarks on the ' vignette ' of Cicero in this play. I have no doubt that Shakespeare had read Plutarch's *Cicero* ; but the references to Cicero in Act I. ii, and Act I. iii, are too slight to base any certain inference on as to the impression made on him.

know very little about it.[1] And clearly Plutarch is not in sympathy with Caesar. He perceives his greatness and his many fine qualities, but he is not the least enthusiastic about him. After describing his murder he wrote the following sentence, which shows that he did not understand his real claim to greatness :

So he reaped no other fruit of all his reign and dominion, which he had vehemently desired all his life and pursued with such extreme danger, but a vain name only and a superficial glory, that procured him the hate and envy of his country.[2]

And yet, in spite of Plutarch, Shakespeare proceeded to make his first experiment in Roman plays with Julius Caesar. At any rate, in or about the year 1601,[3] when he had come to the end of his English historical plays, and had been writing in his gayest and happiest mood his three best comedies, he produced a tragedy, or a tragic history, to which he gave Caesar's name. For its construction, however, he used not only the Life of Caesar, but that of Brutus, and to some extent that of Antony—a course, perhaps, suggested by the sentence which immediately follows the one I quoted a minute ago from the Life of Caesar :

But his great prosperity and good fortune that favoured him during his lifetime did continue afterwards in the revenge of his death, pursuing the murtherers both by sea and land, till they had not a man more left to be executed, of all them that were actors or counsellors in the conspiracy of his death.

Brutus was the most famous of the murderers, and here was a Life of Brutus, and a most fascinating one. And thus it came about that the hero of the play, as we ordinarily use the word in speaking of tragedies—the man to whom the final catastrophe happens, is not Caesar but Brutus, with Cassius as a fellow, though not as hero in quite the same sense ; and

[1] Plutarch's one idea about Caesar is that he was ambitious, which is an easy but often fallacious way of explaining a great man's character. There is an obvious echo of it in Antony's great speech in Act iii.

[2] chap. lxix.

[3] On the date all critics seem at present agreed ; the circumstantial evidence is convincing. It is recently examined and set forth by Professor MacCallum, op. cit., pp. 168 ff.

thus the play stands alone among Shakespeare's tragedies in bearing the name of a man who was not the hero. It is peculiar, too, in some other ways ; but this is the peculiarity which has caused so much trouble to critics, and the one on which I wish chiefly to dwell. The great man whose name it bears only appears in four scenes out of eighteen, and is killed at the beginning of the third act.

There have been in the main two opinions about this curious fact, which I will at once briefly state, and then return to Shakespeare and Plutarch. As long ago as the eighteenth century Malone gave his sanction to the view, expressed also, I believe, by Voltaire,[1] that the play ought to have been called ' Marcus Brutus ', ' Caesar being a very inconsiderable person in the scene, and being killed in the third act ' ; the idea being, I think, that Caesar was so much more famous a man than Brutus that it was impossible to put him and his death into a play without giving it his name also. Since then many critics have maintained this view. On the other hand it has been held that Caesar, if not strictly speaking the hero, is at least the protagonist of the play, not, indeed, in bodily presence, but in *spirit*. To quote Professor Dowden,[2] who first put this view forward in England : ' It is the *spirit of Caesar* which is the dominant power of the tragedy ; against this, the spirit of Caesar, Brutus fought ; for Brutus, who for ever errs in practical politics, succeeded only in striking down Caesar's body ; he who had been weak now rises as pure spirit, strong and terrible, and avenges himself on the conspirators.'

There is truth, I think, in both these views. No one can deny that the human interest of the play centres in Brutus ;

---

[1] MacCallum, p. 212.

[2] *Shakspere's Mind and Art*, pp. 287 ff. MacCallum seems to me to give a new and perhaps an unauthorized meaning to Professor Dowden's ' spirit of Caesar ' (p. 230). He thinks of it as representing the Roman imperial idea, and of Caesar as a kind of incarnate *imperium*. I think this is putting into Shakespeare's mind more Roman history than was really there. Doubtless he recognized Caesar's greatness in respect of the work he had done in the world, but at that point it is better to stop.

in his character, to borrow a phrase from Mr. Bradley,[1] as issuing in action which leads him to a tragic end. Yet, on the other hand, I believe that even if the play had been called by the name of 'Brutus' we should still feel that Caesar is the pivot on which it all turns ; that alive or dead he pervades it throughout ; and that his murder is not only a crisis in the story, like that of Duncan in *Macbeth*, but in some sense also a catastrophe, and that the third act, in which it happens, is the one which would most enthral the spectators, never losing its hold upon them to the last scene in the play.[2] But let us now return to look at the mind of Shakespeare working upon Plutarch, and so approach the question, so far as we can, independently.

As Shakespeare read through these Lives, looking out for tragic material, he must have entered on that of Caesar with peculiar interest. He must already have known something of the most famous of all Romans, who twice invaded Britain, and has, therefore, always been a figure of special interest in our history.[3] He may well have construed some fragments of the Dictator's own writings ; Roger Ascham,[4] in his *Scholemaster*, had advised that Caesar be learnt with 'all curiositie', and this book was published just six years after the poet's birth. The idea that Caesar was 'the noblest man that ever lived in the tide of times' must have been part of Shakespeare's education, and apart from Marc Antony's rhetoric, there is evidence that he really believed this. He had already put into the mouth of a precocious little boy, Prince Edward in *Richard III*, the often quoted lines :

> This Julius Caesar was a famous man :
> With what his valour did enrich his wit,
> His wit set down to make his valour live ;

---

[1] *Shakespearean Tragedy*, pp. 11 ff.   How much I owe to this book the reader who knows it will soon discover.

[2] This was the impression I derived from seeing the play acted.

[3] Caesar, *B. G.*, bk. vi, is alluded to in *Henry VI*, pt. ii, Act. IV. vii. 65.
> Kent, in the Commentaries Caesar writ,
> Is termed the civil'st place of all this isle.

[4] p. 92, ed. J. E. B. Mayor.

> Death makes no conquest of this conqueror,
> For now he lives in fame, though not in life.

And this idea he retained to the last, as more than one passage in *Cymbeline* shows.[1]

Now, if we ask how Shakespeare came by this idea of Caesar, I believe the answer to be that it was simply an inheritance from the education of the Middle Ages. So long as education remained in the hands of the monks the text-book for Roman history was the history of Orosius, the pupil and friend of St. Augustine. Orosius gave a whole chapter, we may note, to the conquest of Britain,[2] and in telling the story of Caesar's death, Christian though he was, he brings out in remarkable language the greatness and moderation of Caesar, and the cruel injustice of his murder. In this chapter, though the origin of the civil war is ascribed to *superbia*—apparently the *superbia* of Caesar—yet his murder is described as a *scelus*; he was *indigne peremptus*, and his murderers were but sowing dragons' teeth which were to spring up as armed men and destroy them. I may here just note, what may be useful in estimating the traditional view of Caesar that came down to Shakespeare, that in his translation of this passage into Anglo-Saxon Alfred left his original for a moment to express his admiration for Caesar.[3]

If, then, Shakespeare was dominated to begin with by this traditional view—in the main a just one—he must have entered on the Life of Caesar in Plutarch with special eagerness. Yet I think he must have read it with disappointment. As I have already said, it is not one of Plutarch's best; that mild and philosophic spirit could hardly appreciate the intensely active, practical, scientific mind of Caesar. Assuredly the playwright would not find there what he wanted; the catastrophe of a tragedy was there but not the character, or the action issuing from character, which could be so woven into a drama as to lead directly or with sufficient rapidity to

---

[1] *Cymbeline*, II. iv. 20; III. i. passim. Mr. Gollancz has collected the passages in other plays in which Caesar is alluded to in the Temple edition of *Julius Caesar*, Preface, p. xi.

[2] Orosius, vi. 17.   [3] *Plummer's Life and Times of Alfred*, p. 164.

that conclusion. Even if he could make *superbia* the moral cause of the murder, if he could impress his audience with the idea that Caesar's death was the punishment for such a weakness (a view which he would hardly find in Plutarch, unless very faintly at the end of chapter 45), still, the events in which this weakness would be shown him by Plutarch would not readily adapt themselves to the stage; and Shakespeare, who adhered steadily to Plutarch in all three Roman plays, assuredly never dreamt of altering him, except in small details, to suit his purpose.[1] It is useful in thinking over this point to compare the life of Coriolanus, which he used with wonderful effect some years later, with the material for tragedy offered him in the life of Caesar. The story of Coriolanus is concentrated within a comparatively short space of time, and explains itself without difficulty. The story of Caesar, to be made tragic even in the sense in which such a play as Marlowe's *Tamburlaine* is tragic, would have to be condensed from the events of some twenty years, and even then would hardly explain itself. Again, Coriolanus's pride, the leading and fatal feature of his character, is seen at once in his contact with those immediately about him; the quality that ruins him is visible in the concrete throughout Plutarch's Life, while the fatal quality in Caesar, even as seen in Plutarch, is so much less obvious and definable that we may read the Life and doubt whether it is there at all. Caesar's life and character touch the whole world, like the life and character of Alexander, with whom he is coupled in Plutarch's work; his real nature is but little known to us, and was almost entirely hidden from Shakespeare; it is the *facts of his life*, the range of his boundless activity, that recoil upon him and bring him to his end, rather than any personal traits that are obvious to us; and such bare facts cannot be used as tragic material in the true Shakespearean sense. Thus the Life of Caesar, as I said, must have disappointed Shakespeare, for its range was too large for the stage, and the striking incidents in it, up to the intensely dramatic ending, were

---

[1] Perhaps this is put too strongly; e. g. see MacCallum, pp. 257 ff.

very few and far between. Turn back to Coriolanus, or on to Antony, in Sir Thomas North's folio, and you will see the difference at once ; the interests in both these lives are not world-wide, but chiefly personal, and the relations are between man and man, or man and woman. In these lives it is the character as well as the catastrophe that interests us, while in the life of Caesar it is the achievements, the fortune, the intellectual skill. In other words, the personality of Caesar is lost in the world of politics and conquests, while in Coriolanus and Antony these are only the background against which the character stands out in Plutarch's picture.

Caesar, then, as seen in Plutarch, or, indeed, as known to us from any source, would not do for the hero of a tragedy ; he towered above the world so far that he left no dramatic incidents for the world to contemplate. But the one thing which every reader would at once recognize as tragic was exactly that which is so strongly brought out by Orosius, and must have been a leading feature in mediaeval tradition, for it appears both in Dante and Chaucer—*the cruelty, injustice, and folly of the murder*, and the retribution in store for the murderers, which is alluded to in a passage I have already quoted from the last chapter of the Life. Let us note that in these Lives of Cicero, Caesar, Brutus, and Antony, the same tragic story is repeated four times, in each case with reference to a different type of personal character. Thus the reader, disappointed in the treatment of Caesar's person and character, would have his imagination all the more strongly drawn to the murder itself, as not only the most striking but the most fateful event of the time ; an event which suddenly and violently disturbed the natural course of things, and threw the world back into confusion and civil war. To Shakespeare it must have seemed tragic, not so much in the light of Caesar's personal ambition and vast power, as in the light of what came immediately afterwards— the utter uselessness of it, the waste of energy ; but for these, and for the confusion of thought and paralysis of action which followed it, he had to read the sequel in the Life of Brutus.

It was a tremendous downfall ; it was tragic in the current sense of tragedy at the time ; it had been made the conclusion of at least one play called by Caesar's name : but it would not satisfy Shakespeare. It was so terrible and tremendous an event that if brought into the play at all it must dominate the whole action ; but to put it in a fifth act was for Shakespeare simply impossible, because there was no tragic material, in his sense of what was tragic, to lead up to it in four other acts. I imagine that he left it and read on into the Life of the most human of the murderers, with results of perennial value for English poetical drama.

We may assume, I think, that Shakespeare read the Life of Brutus immediately after that of Caesar, following the order in North's folio. Any one who will do this himself, even with a much greater knowledge of history than Shakespeare could have had, will be at once struck with the difference between the two lives, and will probably guess that Plutarch was much more interested in Brutus than in Caesar. Among the forty-eight Lives there were a few in which Plutarch had to do with a nature to which his own disposition could respond lovingly. Such Lives are those of Timoleon, Eumenes, Sertorius, and this one of Brutus. He tells us himself (ch. 6 *ad fin.*) that he had written the Life of Caesar when he came to that of Brutus ; and we cannot but feel that he must have been well pleased to find himself dealing with a character more after his own heart and more on the ordinary plane of human life, with whose very faults and failings he could sympathize. I am not here concerned with the interesting question how far he has given us a just idea of the historical Brutus, or what material he used ; [1] all I want to point out is that he found, or imagined, a character of singular human interest, as contrasted with Caesar, or Pompey, or Crassus, whose personalities, so far as he could discern them, worked entirely in the region of wars and politics. In his study of Brutus, too, he had two great opportunities which, con-

[1] See the introduction to vol. iii of Professor Tyrrell's edition of *Cicero's Letters.*

sciously or unconsciously, he used with something like
dramatic effect. First, he had the chance of contrasting his
hero with another character, Cassius, and of presenting two
intimate friends as acting together from different motives ;
secondly, he could give the life a unity of interest wanting
in so many of Plutarch's biographies, because it must be, so
to speak, pivoted upon the one most terrible and exciting
event of the age—the murder of the great Dictator.

The keynote of this character of Brutus is sounded with
clear emphasis at the very beginning of the Life, and rings
consistently throughout it. Shakespeare would only need
to read three sentences to hear it. ' Having framed his
manners of life by the rules of virtue and the study of philosophy, and having employed his wit, which was gentle and
constant, in attempting of great things, methinks he was
rightly made and framed unto virtue ',[1] and the contrast
with Cassius follows in the next words. A little farther on,
after quoting Caesar's famous saying about him (' Id quod
vult, valde vult '), he goes on, ' For as Brutus's gravity and
constant mind would not grant all men their requests that sued
unto him, but being moved with reason and discretion, did
always incline to that which was good and honest ; even so,
when it was moved to follow any matter, he used a kind of
forcible and vehement persuasion, that calmed not till he had
obtained his desire '. Plutarch saw in him a gentle and
thoughtful student—a Platonist, as we learn later on [2]—after
his own heart, but one who, when his mind was made up to
a course of action by conviction that it was right, would stick
to it with extraordinary tenacity. There is no direct condemnation of his part in the murder to be found in the Life ; and
the reason is, no doubt, that Brutus made up his mind to it,

[1] *Life of Brutus*, chap. i.   The word ' wit ' is in the Greek φύσις.   I do
not quite endorse MacCallum's comparison of Brutus to Philip Sidney,
p. 234.

[2] chap. ii, *init.*   Brutus was not a Stoic, though he is often so represented,
e. g. by Dowden, p. 292.   It is true, however, that a Roman Stoic might
well be an admirer of Plato : Panaetius, the founder of Roman Stoicism,
had been such.

after a brief but severe struggle, on moral as well as political grounds, and that Plutarch, whose verdict on the death of Caesar I quoted just now, was disposed to agree with Brutus.

But in place of moral iniquity we have that kind of blundering that is liable to be caused by imperfect knowledge of ordinary human nature.[1] I doubt if any one can read through the Life without feeling that the murder itself was a blunder, and that the retribution which fell on the conspirators, whether their motives were good, like those of Brutus, or personal, as Plutarch inclines to think of the rest, was in some sense deserved. And Brutus was plainly not the man to carry out his own project ; he made two serious practical blunders, as Plutarch is careful to point out ;[2] he persuaded the conspirators to spare Antony, and then gave that able man, in whose hands he was himself as a child, the chance to undo all their work by letting him speak at Caesar's funeral. Later on, after reading philosophy all night, he blundered on the field of battle.[3]

Let us try and imagine the effect of the reading of this Life on the mind of Shakespeare. He had found, if I am right, that to make a tragedy out of the life and death of Caesar was impossible. He might have made a ' history ' out of it, as Ben Jonson did shortly afterwards out of the story of Sejanus ; but even that would have been extremely difficult, and if he was ever tempted to try it, the experience of that intolerably dull play, in which he himself acted,[4] must have made him congratulate himself on his escape. But the reading of the Life of Brutus, I make bold to conjecture, gave him an entirely new interest in the story of Caesar's murder, and showed him a way in which after all it might be used as the central fact in a tragedy.

[1] I should hesitate to call Brutus an idealist, as does Dowden, op. cit., pp. 290, 293, &c. The word hardly seems to suit a Roman, or an Englishman of Shakespeare's day. It does not follow that because a man is given to philosophy he is therefore unpractical or idealist. Brutus was mentally short-sighted, and his obstinacy and his ' much reading ' had a tendency to increase this failing.

[2] Life of Brutus, chap. 15.   [3] Ibid., chap. 42.

[4] So I learn from Cunningham's edition of Ben Jonson, i. 271.

The idea that a good man could do incalculable harm from the best possible motives was, as far as I know, a new one in tragedy. True, that incalculable harm would not be found by Shakespeare in Plutarch ; but he would come to the contemplation of the murder with other ideas than those of Plutarch—with the inherited tradition of the overwhelming greatness of Caesar, and the appalling horror of the deed. Thus the contrast between the goodness of Brutus and the awful crime into which he was drawn would be far more vivid in his reading of the Life than in Plutarch's telling of it ; and for the moment that contrast was a godsend—a delivery from all doubt as to the tragic possibilities of the story. And here at the same time was a new path opened out for the development of the tragic art. The crash of fate falling on a good man, brought on himself by his own blunders or self-deception or noble pride—by character issuing in action—this was an idea of human life and fortune suggesting most fascinating possibilities, such as neither Marlowe nor Shakespeare himself had ever yet thought of dealing with. I am strongly inclined to think that this Life of Brutus was in some degree a turning-point in Shakespeare's artistic life ; it may be that some personal experience of his own was in his mind as he read it, and gave it special meaning for him ; it may be that it attracted him to the character of Hamlet, which he used in his next tragedy, and which has so often been compared, rightly or wrongly, with that of Brutus.[1]

Yet none the less, in constructing the play, it was impossible for him to escape the necessity of making the murder of Caesar its central and dominating fact : Caesar bestrode the world like a Colossus, and the others are in comparison but ordinary men. And the play must bear his name not only because the common Englishman knew something of him and little or nothing of Brutus, but because his greatness was such that if his death were introduced into the play

[1] Mr. Gollancz has an interesting suggestion by way of connecting the two plays in his *Julius Caesar* (Temple edition, Preface, p. x). See also MacCallum, p. 173.

at all it must inevitably control the whole action. Caesar was not a king like Duncan—a king and little more ; in Macbeth it is the murder of his king that dominates the action, but in our play it is the murder of *Caesar*. Duncan's death was not of vital importance to the world : Caesar's was the great fact of his time, and a man like Shakespeare reading these Lives could not possibly escape the conviction that it was so. The result of this conviction was that this tragedy stands apart from all the others in point of construction ; the crisis, the turning-point of the hero's fortunes, is a deed of such magnitude, and the murdered man is so great in his fall as in his life, that this crisis becomes itself a catastrophe, and the victim must give his name to the play. We have in fact in Julius Caesar the meeting-point of the old and the new ideas of tragedy. We have the sudden fall of a man of overwhelming greatness—this was the old idea, of which Marlowe's *Tamburlaine* may be cited as the type ; and at the same time we have retribution falling upon a good man whose very goodness has made him wrong-headed in action— this is the new idea, which could be used in various ways in the tragedies that were to follow. The result on the play of this compromise between the old and the new is not wholly to its advantage. It falls too clearly into two parts, and neither part is perfect. A play with a double plan of construction, in which the crisis overbears the catastrophe in interest, must have given its author unusual trouble. In spite of the remarkable clearness both of language and design, I think he was conscious of having to meet certain difficulties ; and I propose to conclude this paper by a few words about the way in which he met the two most formidable of them.

First, how was a colossus like Caesar to be put on the stage in the form of an ordinary human being and without any knowledge of his real character, which, as I said, is not to be found in Plutarch ? The design was full of danger, but it was carried out with wonderful skill, and is on the whole successful. Shakespeare found in his Plutarch that Caesar was physically weak towards the end of his life, and from

Plutarch he might also draw the conclusion that his powers of mind and will were not all that they had been ; for example, he was ' superstitious grown of late '.[1] His plan was to introduce Caesar in this aspect, but to introduce him as little as possible. The danger was, of course, that the colossal idea of Caesar might suffer, and if that were so, the whole structure of the play would suffer too. It was necessary that the man should be overwhelmingly great, in order that his murder might be overwhelmingly terrible ; and further, it was his abnormal greatness (surely not his apparent weakness as Gervinus fancied) that suggested the murder, and that instantly brought paralysis and eventually retribution on the conspirators. Caesar is, in fact, the rock on which the hero is wrecked, and the more formidable the rock the more hopeless the shipwreck. Now let us allow that the colossal idea of Caesar does actually suffer to some extent from the application of this plan—that there is a compromise involved in this method of treatment, unavoidable owing to the nature of the material, and not without a slightly depressing effect upon the spectators ; for if the part of Caesar be in the least over-acted, some of his utterances in the first two acts are liable to seem almost ludicrous. Nevertheless, the majesty of the master of the world seems to me to be on the whole sufficiently maintained,[2] and it is interesting to observe the devices by which this is effected. First, he is held back as far as possible, hardly does more than pass across the stage with a few words until the beginning of the third act, while at that point, in the last hour or two of his life, he seems to recover all his greatness of soul. It is a greatness such as we see nowhere else in Shakespeare—a greatness of self-conscious

---

[1] Professor MacCallum minimizes this weakness of Caesar, pp. 224 ff. ' Only minute analysis discovers Caesar's defects ', p. 226. Here I cannot agree with him.

[2] See MacCallum, p. 227. The shortening of Acts IV and V, and their embodiment in a third act, at His Majesty's Theatre, seemed to me to have the effect of making Caesar more prominent in the play than Shakespeare intended, as I understand him. At the same time it diminished relatively the importance of Brutus.

power, born of the feeling that there is no one else who can do what he has done, no one whose will is like the northern star—

> Of whose true-fixed and resting quality
> There is no fellow in the firmament.

And even a bad actor might find it difficult to make this last speech of his seem absurd. It is worth noting that Caesar here abandons the foible of speaking of himself in the third person (which may, indeed, be a reminiscence, conscious or unconscious, of his habit in the commentaries), and speaks quite naturally in the first.

> I could be well mov'd if I were as you :
> If I could pray to move prayers would move me.
> But I am constant as the northern star, &c.

Again, let us notice that all detraction of Caesar is put into the mouths of snarling men like Cassius and Casca, who represent the Roman satirical vein, which we have later in a somewhat different form in Menenius Agrippa ; [1] Brutus not only never says a word against him as a human being, but acknowledges that there was a feeling of affection between them. Thus Shakespeare has contrived, even from the beginning of the play, to suggest that it is only the men of small minds and motives who find Caesar intolerable, and that the gentle and generous Brutus can only be brought to such a feeling with difficulty and by cajoling. Once more, Shakespeare has turned to account with great effect the record of supernatural phenomena which he found in Plutarch, preceding and foreboding the death of Caesar—that ' strange impatience of the heavens ' which puts almost the whole of the first act, and much of the second, in a lurid light contrasted somewhat strangely, it is true, with the weakness of the bodily presence of the mighty victim. That there may be no mistake on the part of the audience about the meaning of these phenomena he puts some lines into the mouth of Cassius which connect them directly with Caesar :

[1] Professor MacCallum seems to miss this point in his treatment of Menenius, pp. 559 ff.

> Now could I, Casca, name to thee a man
> Most like this dreadful night,
> That thunders, lightens, opens graves, and roars
> As doth the lion in the Capitol,
> A man no mightier than thyself or me
> In personal action, yet prodigious grown,
> And fearful as these strange eruptions are.

Lastly, no sooner has the murder been committed, and even before Antony's wonderful funeral oration, Shakespeare introduces a servant sent by Antony (in Plutarch it is Antony's young son) with a message which is obviously meant to make us realize the kingly quality of the slain man :

> Brutus is noble, wise, valiant, and honest ;
> *Caesar was mighty, bold, royal, and loving* :
> Say I love Brutus and I honour him :
> *Say I fear'd Caesar, honour'd him, and lov'd him.*

This last wonderful line, extended beyond the normal length, beginning with fear and ending with love, needs no comment. As the act goes on we become inevitably convinced that Caesar was indeed ' the noblest man that ever lived in the tide of times '. The little that we have seen of him on the stage passes out of our minds ; Antony's superb rhetoric masters us as it mastered the people of Rome ; and Shakespeare, beyond doubt, meant that this should be so.

Now let us turn to the second chief difficulty in the construction of the play. How was it possible to preserve a unity of interest throughout it ? Though careless of other unities Shakespeare is always careful to keep the interest of a play the same in all essential parts of it. Here I may perhaps be allowed to distinguish for a moment the interest of the spectators and that of the playwright himself. To maintain the interest of the audience after the murder in the second act, and the excitement and the brilliant rhetoric of the third, might seem an almost hopeless task, and I think we must allow that in spite of alarums and excursions, in these last two acts, with the deaths of Cassius and Brutus following each other in the fifth, the attempt has not been entirely successful. Still, whatever could be done has here been done with skill. Let us remember that the murder is the central fact of the drama ; that has been driven home to the minds of spectators by Antony's superb rhetoric in the third act, on which the poet lavished all his resources with little or no help from Plutarch ; and with it the idea which had been emphasized in the story since the days of Orosius—nay, even of Plutarch himself—that Nemesis must inevitably fall on those who, from whatever motive, shed the blood of a great ruler of men without understanding what they do. I need not quote the familiar lines in which this fatefulness is emphasized. The murder and the fatefulness of it reaching far into the future—this is what holds the play together to the end. We are never allowed to lose sight of either the deed or the idea ; again and again, even in the famous quarrel scene between Brutus and Cassius, the speakers recur to the deed :

> Remember March, the Ides of March remember :
> Did not great Julius bleed for justice' sake ?
> What villain touched his body that did stab
> And not for justice ?

So Brutus. Cassius's mind is equally full of it :

> Strike as thou didst at Caesar ; for I know
> When thou didst hate him worst, thou lovedst him better
> Than ever thou lovedst Cassius.

Both Brutus and Cassius have it brought home to them by the bitter taunts of Antony and Octavius when they meet on the field of battle : not a chance is lost by Shakespeare of emphasizing this central fact of the play :

> In your bad strokes, Brutus, you give good words :
> Witness the hole you made in Caesar's heart,
> Crying, ' Long live ! hail Caesar.'

And again :

> Villains, you did not so when your vile daggers
> Hacked one another in the sides of Caesar, &c.

And once more Octavius :

> Come, come, the cause : if arguing make us sweat,
> The proof of it will turn to redder drops.

Look :
I draw a sword against conspirators :
When do you think that sword goes up again ?
Never, till Caesar's three and thirty wounds
Be well avenged.

The murder is continually haunting the mind of Brutus, in spite of his ' constant ' conviction of his own righteousness ; his last words to Cassius are :

This same day,
Must end the work the Ides of March began.

And his own last words are :

Caesar now be still,
I killed thee not with half so good a will.

That is, in slaying myself I am making a propitiatory sacrifice to the Manes of the man who is mighty yet, whose spirit ' ranging for revenge ' has twice appeared to his murderer ; but now Caesar may rest in peace ; he is no longer the ' evil spirit ' of Brutus ; his wrath is appeased. The fact that Shakespeare converted the nameless apparition of Plutarch's story into the ghost of Caesar is to my mind an additional proof that he thought of Brutus as being haunted by the bloody deed—a thought which could be more effectually emphasized afterwards in *Macbeth*. I seem to see this same thought even in single words and phrases of Brutus. Why, in the beautiful and tender scene with his boy Lucius, who is Shakespeare's own invention, does he make Brutus say :

O *murderous* slumber !
Lay'st thou thy leaden mace upon my boy,
That plays thee music ?

And at the beginning of the last scene of the play—

Sit thee down, Clitus, slaying is the word :
It is a deed in fashion.

He had already exclaimed, on hearing of the death of Cassius :

O, Julius Caesar, thou art mighty yet :
Thy spirit walks abroad, and turns our swords
In our own proper entrails.

For the audience, then, the interest of the play was to be maintained in the last two acts mainly by the haunting recollection of the murder, and of its fatefulness ; the dragon's teeth had been sown, to use the simile of Orosius, and the revengeful crop springs up. The play might thus be called, in the manner of the older historical drama, *The Death of Julius Caesar* ; [1] but the personality and fame of the victim were so great that it bore his name and no more.

But lastly, for Shakespeare as a poet and observer of human nature, there need be no doubt that the interest from first to last lay in the character of Brutus. How carefully and lovingly he has dealt with this man, whose nobility and honesty led him to waste his own good quality, and bring incalculable harm on his fellow men ! His love for Caesar himself makes him, after the period of doubt, most weakly excuse his own fatal resolve in that strange soliloquy at the beginning of Act II ; [2] but once resolved, he is tenacious of his own righteousness, never for a moment doubting, constant in his determination to throw himself away. When the murder is done he glories in it, and becomes not only unpractical but brutal :

> Let us bathe our hands in Caesar's blood,
> Up to the elbows, and besmear our swords :
> Then walk we forth even to the market-place :
> And waving our red weapons o'er our heads
> Let's all cry ' Peace, freedom, and liberty ! '

In such folly he throws away his best chances : time is lost ; Antony appears on the scene, and Brutus's incapacity is manifest. And yet he is all along not only the constant but the gentle Brutus—a man whom the gentle Shakespeare could love. His love for Caesar and for Cassius, his devotion

---

[1] *Caesar's Fall* was the name of a play which was being prepared by several authors in 1602 (Gollancz, Preface, p. xiii). Ben Jonson alludes to his play as *The Fall of Sejanus* in the letter prefixed to the first edition.

[2] This speech puzzled Coleridge (MacCallum, p. 201). I think Shakespeare is only following Plutarch's suggestion that Brutus would stick to a conclusion when once he was convinced ; he is here convincing himself, and the process, difficult to manage on the stage and by soliloquy, seems a little lame.

to his noble wife (of whom I have had no opportunity to speak), his sympathetic tenderness for his boy Lucius—all these traits, so exquisitely touched into the story, show what care the poet lavished on him, and if they be compared with the character in Plutarch, prove beyond all doubt that the Life of Brutus inspired him, as no material for a play had ever yet inspired him, with a sympathetic insight into human nature, and a sense of the sadness of human life. *Sunt lacrimae rerum, et mentem mortalia tangunt.* Of this experience the natural sequel was the new type of tragedy, the tragedy which, in Mr. Bradley's words, ' would not be tragedy if it were not a painful mystery '. The mystery is hardly so painful in this tragedy as in those that followed it ; but it is unmistakably there. The story of Brutus confronts us with the inexplicable problem—Why should a good man be suffered to waste himself by the committal of one evil deed ?

To sum up, I think those are wrong who say that the play should have been called ' Marcus Brutus ', for the murder which wrecks Brutus is that of a man infinitely greater than he—a man whose greatness pervades the whole play, and gives it at least half its tragic element. Nor can I altogether agree with those, among whom we must now reckon Professor MacCallum, who hold that the protagonist of the play is the *spirit* of Caesar, whether we take that word spirit as meaning Caesar's ghost ranging for revenge, or as MacCallum seems to take it, the Spirit of Caesarean imperialism. Brutus is unquestionably the hero, but as unquestionably Brutus is overshadowed ; his heroic part in the play is overshadowed by the greatness of the man he murders. The death of that man is the one overpowering feature of the tragedy, and no character, not even Brutus, can contend against it. In *Hamlet* and *Macbeth* the overpowering interest is in these two heroic characters ; in the earlier play the overpowering interest cannot centre in Brutus, because he is Caesar's murderer. The play thus stands alone as a tragedy, and stands imperfect, because the crisis, the murder of Caesar, overshadows the catastrophe, the fateful death of his murderers.

INDEX OF LATIN WORDS AND PHRASES

Printed in England at the Oxford University Press